ST CYPRIAN OF CARTHAGE

On the Church: Select Letters

ST VLADIMIR'S SEMINARY PRESS
Popular Patristics Series
Number 33

The Popular Patristics Series published by St Vladimir's Seminary Press provides readable and accurate translations of a wide range of early Christian literature to a wide audience—students of Christian history to lay Christians reading for spiritual benefit. Recognized scholars in their fields provide short but comprehensive and clear introductions to the material. The texts include classics of Christian literature, thematic volumes, collections of homilies, letters on spiritual counsel, and poetical works from a variety of geographical contexts and historical backgrounds. The mission of the series is to mine the riches of the early Church and to make these treasures available to all.

Series Editor
BOGDAN BUCUR

Associate Editor
IGNATIUS GREEN

* * *

Series Editor
1999–2020
JOHN BEHR

ST CYPRIAN OF CARTHAGE

On the Church
Select Letters

Translation with Introduction and
Commentary by

ALLEN BRENT

ST VLADIMIR'S SEMINARY PRESS
CRESTWOOD, NEW YORK
2006

Library of Congress Cataloging-in-Publication Data

Cyprian, Saint, Bishop of Carthage.
 [Selections. English. 2006]
 On the church : select letters / St. Cyprian of Carthage ; commentary by
Allen Brent.
       p. cm. — (Popular patristics series ; no. 33)
    Includes bibliographical references and index.
    ISBN–13: 978–0–88141–313–7 (alk. paper)
    ISBN–10: 0–88141–313–5 (alk. paper)
    1. Church discipline—History—Early church, ca. 30–600. 2. Church—
Unity. 3. Christianity and other religions. I. Brent, Allen. II. Title. III. Series:
St. Vladimir's Seminary Press "popular patristics" series ; no. 33.

    BR65.C82E5 2006
    270.1—dc22

                                                            2006017890

COPYRIGHT © 2006
ST VLADIMIR'S SEMINARY PRESS
575 Scarsdale Rd, Crestwood, NY 10707
1-800-204-2665
www.svspress.com

ISBN 0–88141–313–5
ISBN 978–088141–313–7
ISSN 1555-5755

PRINTED IN THE UNITED STATES OF AMERICA

Caroline Penrose Hammond Bammel, F.B.A.
In piam memoriam

Contents

References are in accordance with the abbreviations in
The SBL Handbook of Style (Peabody, MA: Hendrickson, 1999).

*Means that the work is not included in this present translation.

Psalms are cited according to the Vulgate/LXX numeration.

Preface

These translations with their introductions and notes are the product of a continuing research project begun at the British School at Rome in 1999, supported then by a Grant in Aid of Research by the Leverhulme Trust. My work has been concerned with the interface between the development of church order and Christian theology and Graeco Roman culture and history.

Cyprian was the great publicist who argued his theory of church unity with such success that it achieved almost universal acceptance before the European Reformation. To be a member of the Church that is the body of Christ you needed to be in communion with a priest who was in communion with a bishop who in turn was in communion with all other bishops in the world. But how could you tell or decide? And on what kind of issue would it be right for dioceses to break off communion with each other, or to threaten to do so?

Were there not other kinds of self-authenticating ministries, like those of martyrs and confessors who had suffered for the Faith? And did the Church not need, and in what form, a universal bishop who could guarantee the integrity of the network of bishops? These were the questions with which Cyprian wrestled and to which he sought to give answers in his selected works translated in this book, and in its companion volume, *On the Church: Select Treatises,* SVS Popular Patristics Series, Number 32. They are questions that continue to be asked in the contemporary Church.

The appearance of a new work of this nature is timely given the stalling of the process of ecumenical reconciliation, for which there seemed so great hopes in the 60s and 70s of the last century.

In Cyprian's work we have the classical statement of church order, based upon the theology of a bishop presiding over a diocese but needing to remain in communion with the episcopal college throughout the world. It is a work that continues to raise issues that are pertinent to the modern church.

These two volumes are presented in the hope that they will assist our understanding of the historical and cultural development of this historical order of Christendom and the form in which it may be continued in those churches that claim to continue the historic episcopate (Orthodox, Roman and Anglican), and in others who seek mutual understanding and reconciliation with it.

ALLEN BRENT
St Edmund's College, Cambridge

Introduction

§1 THE LIFE OF CYPRIAN

Little is known of the early life of Cyprian. We possess a *Life of Cyprian* by the deacon Pontius, which is in reality rather an apologetic defense of his subject against critics within the Church. These critics distrusted his meteoric rise from converted layman to bishop, and would not accept Cyprian's flight into hiding during persecution as anything but cowardice.[1] Pontius ignores his pagan life prior to his conversion, but focuses upon his actions as a bishop and the details of his martyrdom. Subsequent to his death in AD 258, such an apology would have had a point in view of his controversy with Pope Stephen over the issue of rebaptizing schismatics and heretics.[2] We have in addition the *Consular Acts (Acta Proconsularia) of Carthage,* also with an account of his martyrdom, which Pontius appears to have utilized.[3] We also possess some statements by Jerome and Augustine.[4]

Thacius Caecilius Cyprianus may have been born around AD 202, and became a teacher of rhetoric following the relevant course of pagan, classical education. His ancestral country estate (*horti*) was in his birthplace, Carthage. Thus he owed both wealth and education to his family and not to a patron. Shadows of his pagan career seem to have left their traces on his treatises *Ad Donatum* and *Ad*

---

[1]See *Ep.* 81.

[2]See *Ep.*73 and 75, and **Ep.* 74.

[3]For a discussion of the problems of the biography, see M. Sage, *Cyprian*, Patristics Monographs Series 1 (Philadelphia, PA: Philadelphia Patristic Foundation, 1975), 385–94.

[4]Jerome *Vir. ill.* 53; *Ep.* 84.2; Augustine *Serm.* 312.4.

Demetrianum, for which see the notes and commentary accompanying the translations of these works in the companion volume to this book, *On the Church: Select Treatises,* by St Cyprian.

Following his conversion, Cyprian was baptised into the Catholic Church at the time of the Easter Vigil, around AD 246. He took the name of his Christian teacher, the presbyter Caecilian.[5] Along with that experience went a commitment to celibacy that also characterized membership of many pagan philosophical schools.[6] In *Donatus* we read his own description of his divine illumination in his "Second Birth." He turned from what he characterizes as a corrupt and hypocritical society of Roman, North Africa, on its way to cosmic ruin in the collapsing world society of the mid-third century.[7] His reflections there on the law courts in the Forum seem supportive of Jerome's description of his fame as a *rhetor,* who practiced and taught oratory generally, and perhaps even specifically as an *aduocatus* practicing law.[8] Around 248, following the death of another Donatus, bishop of Carthage, Cyprian was apparently with some reluctance elected bishop of Carthage by the clergy and people.

Cyprian was a neophyte, or newly baptised. As such he was bypassing the minor orders such as reader, acolyte, and doorkeeper, and even the diaconate itself, and succeeding with unseemly haste to the episcopate. He showed the generosity with his wealth to the Church that was characteristic of those of curial or magisterial rank towards their clients and supporters.[9] It may well have been that the "old guard" of five presbyters who led the opposition resented the way in which a man of wealth, influence, and education came to the episcopate. To them Cyprian might have seemed too much like a secular, Roman *patronus* whose links of charity with his subservient

---

[5]Pontius *Vita* 4.

[6]Pontius *Vita* 2.4–5.

[7]Cyprian *Don.* 4.

[8]Jerome *Vir. ill.* 67.53. See also G. W. Clarke, "The Secular Profession of St Cyprian of Carthage," *Latomus* 24 (1965): 633–638.

[9]Pontius *Vita* 2.7.

clients lead to influence and votes for the magistracies that he chose to pursue.[10]

In AD 249 Decius Trajan became emperor of an empire that had been almost permanently in a state of revolt for thirteen years, with the frontiers threatened externally by the Goths in the West and Persia to the East, while rival claimants for the empire clashed with each other in civil war. Famine and pestilence were adding to a political crisis reflected in a widespread feeling of hopelessness in the face of decline. Decius gave himself the name of Trajan when he made his entrance into Rome in triumph in the last months of 249. As such he associated himself with the image of Trajan in contemporary historiography as the most enlightened of Emperors, having been commemorated as such in Pliny's *Panegyricus,* who had reigned over an empire in victorious peace. His edict, that all imperial subjects should sacrifice to the gods of the Roman state, was promulgated in late 249–250. Cyprian went into hiding, citing in justification Mt 10.33, from which place he administered his Church.[11] Later, we shall consider the divisions caused by the question of how to deal with those Christians who sacrificed (§2.1). Fabian, bishop of Rome was martyred, and Dionysius, bishop of Alexandria, went, like Cyprian, into hiding. Cornelius was to succeed Fabian in an election that was disputed after an interregnum in which Novatian appeared as a rival bishop.

In June 251, following the death both of the emperor Decius and his son, Trebonius Gallus became emperor and the policy of general

---

[10]Pontius *Vita* 5.6; cf. Cyprian *Ep.* 59.9. Bobertz has argued convincingly that it was the social discourse of the client-patron relationship with his original electors that enabled Cyprian to rebuild his authority in the chaotic situation that he found within the Carthaginian Church on his return from hiding; see C. A. Bobertz, *Cyprian of Carthage as Patron: A Social and Historical Study of the Role of Bishop in the Ancient Christian Community of North Africa* (Ann Arbor, MI: UMI, 1993); idem, "Patronage Networks and the Study of Ancient Christianity," in StPatr 24 (1991): 20–27; idem, "Patronal Letters of Commendation: Cyprian's *Epistulae* 38–40," StPatr 31 (1995): 252–59.

[11]Cyprian *Ep.* 5.2 and 7.2; cf. *Laps.* 10. For criticisms of Cyprian see *Ep.* 8.

persecution appears to have ceased. Councils could now take place in Carthage (23 March 251) and in Rome (251) on the divisive question over the appropriate treatment of the lapsed or fallen. It was in connection with these divisions that, at this time, Cyprian wrote both his work *On the Fallen (De lapsis)*, and *The Unity of the Catholic Church (De catholicae ecclesiae unitate)*.

A plague followed, the experiences of which occasioned the writing of his treatise *On Mortality*. It also appears to have been the reason for his writing an apologetic work to the pagan Demetrian since an event like a plague would tend to lead to suspicions of witchcraft by such groups as Christians and thus inspire a local persecution.[12] Under such a threat, a council that took place in Carthage in May 253 affirmed, notwithstanding the decisions of previous councils, that a general peace should be granted to all the penitent fallen, in view of the new persecution that threatened, in order to strengthen the faithful with the means of grace for the oncoming trial.[13]

Gallus appears to have confirmed expectations of renewing the persecution, at least in the case of Rome itself, where Cornelius was condemned to exile as a first stage in his trial of endurance.[14] Though Cyprian expected him to progress to a further examination and martyrdom in blood, his expectation was to remain unfulfilled. In June 253 he died of natural causes at Centumcellae on his way to face the magistrate, and was succeeded by Lucius.[15]

The controversial issue over baptism was to erupt when Lucius died after a short episcopate of eight months, and was, by early March 254, succeeded by Stephen. There ensued the famous dispute

---

[12]A. Brent, *The Imperial Cult and the Development of Church Order: Concepts and Images of Authority in Paganism and Early Christianity before the Age of Cyprian*, Supplements to Vigiliae Christianae 45 (Leiden: Brill, 1999), 104–105; 110–112. See also L. F. Janssen, "'Superstitio' and the Persecution of the Christians," *VC* 33.2 (1979): 131–59.

[13]Cyprian *Ep.*57.1.1–2.

[14]Sage, *Cyprian,* 284–86; G. Clarke, *The Letters of St Cyprian*, 4 vols., ACW 43, 44, 46 and 47 (New York: Newman Press, 1984, 1986, 1989), 3.4–17.

[15]Cyprian *Ep.* 60 and 61.

between the Pope of Africa and the Pope of Rome over the issue of whether someone baptised in schism or heresy needed to be re-baptised on the grounds of the invalidity of sacraments celebrated outside the Church. Cyprian's *Letters* 67–75 are taken up with this controversy, of which *Letters* 72, 73 and (by Firmilian) 75 are included in this edition. In consequence, Stephen began to excommunicate Cyprian's Eastern allies.[16] The annual Carthaginian council of 256 was to support Cyprian's position against that of Stephen, as had the smaller council in the previous year.[17] We shall sketch in detail the basic issues of this controversy when we consider briefly Cyprian's doctrine of the Church (in §3 below).

In 253 Gallus was killed at Interama, in consequence of the Gothic campaign, by the rebel forces of Aemilianus. But by August or September 253 Valerian had ended this short reign. Valerian raised his son Gallienus, destined to succeed him, to the rank of Augustus. The following three years were years of disasters, and involved the difficult defense of both eastern and western frontiers.[18] But in August 257 they were to issue a joint edict that "those who do not follow the Roman religion ought to recognize Roman ceremonies."[19] The edict seemed to be directed against the clergy (presbyters and bishops) and church property, indeed against the very episcopal structure that Cyprian had strengthened and further defined.[20]

Thus Cyprian was summoned to appear before the governor (proconsul) of Africa, Aspasius Paternus, in Carthage on 30 August 257.[21] When demanded the names of the presbyters, Cyprian refused to give them. The proconsul then read the edict, which forbade Christians meeting or using their cemeteries. He then exiled Cyprian to Curubis. Significantly, pagan friends of both senatorial

[16]Eusebius *Hist. eccl.* 7.5.4.

[17]Cyprian *Ep.* 70 and 74.

[18]Sage, *Cyprian*, 293–94, 337–41.

[19]H. Musurillo, *Acts of the Christian Martyrs. Introduction. Texts and Translations* (Oxford: Clarendon Press, 1972), 172 (=*Acta Procons.* 3.4).

[20]*Acta Procons.* 1.5.

[21]For a more detailed, secondary account see Sage, *Cyprian*, chap. 7.

and of equestrian rank were to come to visit him, and to try to per-
suade him to go into hiding. Clearly he had maintained contacts
with both the political and business leaders of Carthage, who no
doubt had also been influential in securing the safety of his Decian
exile. But this time the bishop of Carthage was not to flee. It would
indeed have been difficult for him to argue on this occasion that he
needed to flee in order to preserve the constancy of faith of the laity
when initially it was only the clergy who were under direct attack.

In September 257 the exiled Cyprian had a vision in his sleep.
A youth of more than human stature led Cyprian to the proconsul,
who began immediately to write his verdict on a tablet that he be put
to death. The youth indicated that in answer to Cyprian's request, a
short stay of execution would be allowed. It was during this period
that he wrote *Fortunatus* on the subject of martyrdom, assembling
consolatory proof texts from Scripture. In 258 Valerian strengthened
his policy with a decree, with immediate punishment for clergy, and
a policy of initial exile and confiscation for highborn Christians, with
degradation from their rank followed finally by the Decian test.[22]

Thus Cyprian was recalled to Carthage in early September 258
for a new trial. Cyprian returned to his country estate (*horti*) when
orders reached him that he was to be conducted by the military
police (*commentarii*) to appear before the proconsul at Utica. He
then went into hiding for a short time, so that he could make his
confession in Carthage as bishop amongst the people in his own
diocese. Thus only when the proconsul had arrived back in Carthage
would Cyprian give himself up.[23]

On 14 September Galerius Maximus, now proconsul, heard
his case in his palace or *praetorium*. Cyprian refused to perform
the required sacrifice to the gods, and, as a Roman citizen, was
sentenced to death by beheading.[24] He was now taken to the Ager

[22]Cyprian *Ep.* 80.1.2–3.

[23]Cyprian *Ep.* 81.1.1–4.

[24]*Acta Procons.* 4 and Pontius *Vita* 17.1–3. For the former, see Musurillo, *Acts*,
168–75.

Sexti, a large valley surrounded by a circle of trees.[25] Behaving like a
Roman patrician to the last, he gave twenty-five gold coins (*aurei*) to
his executioner. Behaving like a bishop, he handed his dalmatic to a
presbyter and to a subdeacon. He tried to tie a blindfold to his eyes
but could not, so a presbyter and a subdeacon came to his assistance.
He placed his head upon the block, and the executioner wielded his
sword with the required effect.[26]

Thus, to use the ancient title of a Metropolitan Bishop, Cyprian,
Pope of Carthage, confounded his earlier critics and made his confession.

§2 Cyprian's Controversies

There were two principal controversies with which Cyprian was
to deal. The first was over the conditions on which those who had
lapsed or fallen[27] in the persecution could be re-admitted to the
Eucharist. The second, which arose from principles that Cyprian had
developed in connection with the first, was the question of whether
there could be a valid sacrament of baptism in heretical and schismatic communities so that reconciliation with the Catholic Church
would not require rebaptism. We will now consider a brief sketch of
both controversies.

§2.1 *Absolution of the Fallen in Persecution*

In 249 the Emperor Philip had died in battle at Verona in Northern
Italy and was succeeded by his opponent, Decius. The later adopted
his own version of a typically third-century policy of proclaiming
a new, returning golden age, in which ancient discipline would be

[25]*Acta Procons.* 5.2; Pontius *Vita* 18.2.
[26]*Acta Procons.* 5.5; Pontius *Vita* 18.3–4.
[27]*Lapsi* means "fallen" and I have translated it as such.

revived, and the unity of a disintegrating empire restored. Decius, as accordingly Trebonius and Valerian after him, was to continue the ideology of the *saeculum novum*.[28] We find on his coins, as of Trebonius Gallus and Volusian, the legend SAECVLVM NOVVM ("new age").[29] It was a tradition followed by Valerian, as evidenced by a coins from the mint of Rome with the inscription RESTITVTOR ORBIS ("restorer of the world"),[30] who also has a coin commemorating his *consecratio* (or "divination"), dedicated to *divo Valeriano* ("divine Valerian").[31]

Conformity was to be given religious impetus and sanction in the form of every Roman citizen sacrificing to the gods of the Roman state, principally the Capitoline Triad (Jupiter, Juno and Minerva), with whom the Decian coinage suggests that the dead and deified imperial families were conjoined. The peculiar character of a mint of coins celebrating the *divi,* or previous divinized emperors and their consorts, indicated the revival of the cult of collective worship of past emperors. Those emperors and empresses had been also associated with Jupiter and Juno on their coinage, in a religion in which the essences of individual divinities flowed into one another.[32]

Decius' edict to sacrifice was universal and worldwide. It was systematic in that it required clear evidence of sacrifice in the form of a *libellus* or certificate to say that one had conformed. Cyprian believed, and through his letter writing attempted to ensure, that the Christian response was worldwide. Christian bishops throughout the world were linked together in a web of intercommunion and mutual recognition. To be a member of the body of Christ you had to be in communion with a presbyter who was in communion with a bishop. To take part in the act of sacrifice, you sundered your union

[28]For Valerian as *restitutor* see H. Mattingly and E. A. Sydenham, *The Roman Imperial Coinage* (London: Spink, 1936), cited as *RIC* V.1: 42, n. 50; 47, nn. 116–119; 50, n. 149; 51, n. 171.

[29]*RIC* IV.3: 169, nn. 90–91, cf. n. 89; and 166, n. 71; 184, n. 222; 186, nn. 235–236.

[30]E.g. *RIC* V.1: 42, n. 50; 47, nn. 116–119; 51, n. 171.

[31]*RIC* V.1: 116, n. 7; 118, n. 24.

[32]Brent, *Imperial Cult,* 64–67.

with the body of Christ. The effect of these events on Cyprian's theology of the Church will be considered further below (in §3).

From his hiding place, Cyprian administered his Church through letters written to his presbyters and deacons, who were to remain at their posts. From such a vantage point he issued his instructions not to seek martyrdom, but if apprehended and challenged to refuse to sacrifice. This policy could not be as straightforwardly administered as he thought, with infringements punished by using the weapon of excommunication. There were degrees of conformity with many special cases, ranging from those who had sacrificed eagerly and without reservation; to those who had done so after imprisonment and torture; to those who had bribed a magistrate for a *libellus* (certificate) without actually sacrificing themselves; and finally, to those who were exempt because their husbands or fathers had sacrificed for the whole family in order to preserve them.[33]

The arrangement for ensuring the act of worship for obtaining the *pax deorum* was original and recent. According to Frend, it was the *Constitutio Antoniana* of the Severan Emperor that had made possible the order of a universal act of propitiation of the gods throughout the Roman Empire.[34] The existence of census and tax registers would make it possible to check names against official lists. Clarke is skeptical about the existence of such comprehensive documents. In the account of Dionysius of Alexandria, when the crowd gathered in conformity with the decrees and were called by name to sacrifice, was there in the magistrate's hand an official citizen list, or did they simply register their names themselves for the occasion, to be called out in order?[35] But however haphazard or thorough the means, the intention was to enforce a universal act that expressed the reassertion of the unity and order of all nations and peoples within

[33]Cyprian *Ep.* 55.17; *Laps.* 7–8, 13, 27–28.
[34]W. C. H. Frend, *Martyrdom and Persecution in the Early Church* (Oxford: Blackwell, 1965), 338.
[35]Clarke, *Letters of St Cyprian*, 1.33–34.

the one Empire. It was to be a sacrament of imperial unity that symbolized what it effected and effected what it symbolized.

The means for enforcing conformity were systematically worked
out and systematically applied. Each citizen or even perhaps household slave[36] was to obtain a *libellus* or certificate of sacrifice, and
we have 44 such *libelli* from Egypt, dated between 12 June and 14
July 250. From these we can gather that the local authorities had to
appoint a given date for the sacrifices to the gods.[37] An examining
board, consisting of local magistrates joined by five prominent local
citizens would then be set up to place the orders into effect. First of
all the subject mounted the hill to the temple of the Capitoline Triad
and there he gave sacrificial meat to the pagan priest to be placed
upon the altar, and poured a libation of wine. Instead he might prefer
an offering of incense such as Pliny permitted to the emperor's image
in order to give a minimal indication of submission to Rome's gods.[38]
Secondly the petitioner now read out his declaration to the commissioners that he had sacrificed, and one or more of them signed the
document as witnesses.[39]

In consequence we have two categories of apostates mentioned
by Cyprian, namely the *sacrificati* ("those who had sacrificed") and
thurificati ("those who had offered incense").[40] A third category
consisted of those who never went up to the Capitoline Temple on
the summit of the Byrsa, but bribed the magistrate instead to issue a
certificate saying that they had. These were known as the *libellatici*.[41]
For Cyprian all three groups had apostatised. Because the *sacrificati*
had eaten idol meats, they could no longer be in communion with

[36]Cyprian *Ep.* 15.4 implies that more than Roman citizens were involved since
the martyr's *libellus pacis* (certificate of peace) named *liberti* (freedmen) and *domestici*
(domestic slaves).

[37]J. R. Knipfing, "The Libelli of the Decian Persecution," *HTR* 16 (1923): 345–90.

[38]G. E. M. De Ste. Croix, "Why were the Early Christians Persecuted?—A Rejoinder," *Past and Present* 27 (1964): 28–33; cf. R. L. Wilken, *The Christians as the Romans
Saw Them* (New Haven, CT and London: Yale University Press, 1984), 41–44.

[39]Clarke, *The Letters of St Cyprian*, 1.30–32.

[40]Cyprian *Ep.* 55.2.1, 12.1; *Laps.* 22–26.

[41]Cyprian *Ep.* 55.14.1–2; *Laps.* 27–30.

the Church that received the body and blood of Christ. Because the *thurificati* had offered incense to propitiate the gods, Christ's propitiation no longer availed. Though the *libellatici* had done neither of these things, nevertheless they had solemnly professed that they had done them before the commissioners signed their *libellus*. Accordingly they had fallen because they had denied their baptism, which involved their profession of the name of Christ. Behind such a view, as we shall later see (in §3), was Cyprian's corporate view of the Church. Baptism and Eucharist were the means for incorporation into the Church as the body of Christ. To receive pagan sacraments or to affirm falsely that one had received them was to sunder one's union in the body of Christ.

But Cyprian's position was further complicated by the existence of a group of confessors, or those who had confessed their faith unwaveringly and yet managed to survive without actually dying as martyrs. There were a large number of these in the Decian persecution, the aim of which was to secure apostates rather than martyrs in a process of savage re-education in ancient Roman discipline. These claimed the right to absolve the fallen and issued a *libellus pacis*, a certificate which declared them reconciled and at peace with the Church. Cyprian considered this a challenge to his authority, and his reasons against the practice he sets out in his treatise *On the Fallen* as well as in several of his *Letters*.[42] The practice of absolving by issuing a *libellus pacis* was indeed new, and clearly the counterpart to Decius' *libellus* of sacrifice. But the prerogatives of the martyrs to absolve by offering the Eucharistic sacrifice and communicating the penitent as the act of reconciliation per se, with the claim that they were ordained to the presbyterate by virtue of their confession without imposition of hands, may well have been of great antiquity.[43]

Whether separate from this group or as part of it, there arose a group of presbyters who themselves claimed the prerogative to

[42]*Ep.* 16 and 27, see also **Ep.* 17–20; 25–26.

[43]A. Brent, "Cyprian and the question of *ordinatio per confessionem*," StPatr 36 (2001): 323–37.

reconcile those who had fallen from their faith in persecution. Their action, like that of the martyrs with whom perhaps they were associated, was to cause controversy. Novatus in Africa and Novatian in Rome were to end up consecrated as rival bishops to Cyprian and Cornelius because they supported a rigorist position that would not re-admit anyone who had fallen to full communion, but insisted on a lifelong penitence. Cyprian took a mediating position between these groups, which he was in time to develop, and over which, to some extent, to vacillate. His position was that any decision on the reconciliation of the fallen must await a council to be summoned after the persecution was over. Meanwhile the fallen were to remain in a state of repentance, desirous of receiving the Eucharist but cut off from actually receiving it. If they wished to wash away the sin of apostasy, they could do so with their own blood whilst the persecution still raged.[44]

As his *Letters* progress, he changes his position. At first he is prepared only to re-admit a fallen person to communion on their deathbed and then only if they received a *libellus pacis* from a confessor.[45] Then he is prepared to admit a *libellaticus* after penance but only a *sacrificatus* on his deathbed. Finally, in 253, as I have already mentioned, Fortunatus and Felicissimus were deprived of any *raison d'être* by the decision of the Council of Carthage of that year to admit all penitent fallen, on the grounds that their period of penance had been long enough and that a new persecution required their strengthening with the grace of the sacraments in order to prevail.[46]

Novatian, at least, when writing in the name of the Roman presbyterate deprived of bishop Fabian following his martyrdom, initially supported Cyprian's position, without even mentioning the need for a confessor's *libellus*.[47] But in 251 the five presbyters who

[44]Cyprian *Ep*. 19.2.3; cf. *Ep*. 55.4.1–3.
[45]Cyprian *Ep*. 20.3.1–2.
[46]Cyprian *Ep*. 57.1.2.
[47]Cyprian (Novatian) *Ep*. 30.8; Sage, *Cyprian*, 250–52; Clarke, *Letters of St Cyprian*, 2.116–19; J. Patout Burns, Jr., *Cyprian the Bishop* (London-New York: Routledge, 2002), 34–41.

had opposed Cyprian, under the leadership of Privatus, bishop of Lambaesis and a deacon, Felicissimus, insisted that the fallen be re-admitted, and proceeded to excommunicate all those who remained in communion with Cyprian who at that time would refuse such reconciliation except on deathbeds. They were destined to set up a rival bishop when one of the five, Fortunatus, was consecrated bishop. Cyprian retorted in turn by excommunicating him and his group.[48]

Novatus had been the presbyter who appointed Fortunatus as his deacon.[49] It was subsequent to the council that finally met in 251, and its decisions on the fallen, that led to Novatian at Rome breaking with Cyprian on the grounds that the latter was too lax. Church politics were also involved, in that Cornelius had also been elected and consecrated bishop, and he had accepted the position of Cyprian's Carthaginian council. Novatus, the laxist Carthaginian presbyter, was now to join the newly consecrated, rigorist bishop Novatian in a marriage of convenience against Cyprian at Carthage and Cornelius at Rome.[50] Cornelius called a council at Rome in AD 253, perhaps contemporaneous with that at Carthage, and in both *fora* Novatian was condemned and excommunicated. The council decided that those who had bribed magistrates and not sacrificed (the *libellatici*) could be received back after examination of individual cases but not those who had actually sacrificed.[51] Cornelius gave the consent of his council. In consequence, the permanence of Novatian's schism was sealed, and his rival Church in his eyes legitimated. It was as a background to the controversies surrounding these councils that Cyprian composed *On the Fallen* and *The Unity of the Catholic Church*.

But following the council of 253, another dispute was to break out on the issue of the baptism or rebaptism of heretics and schismatics.

---

[48]Cyprian *Ep.* 41.2.1; see also *Ep.* 59.9.1.
[49]Cyprian *Ep.* 52.2.3.
[50]Sage, *Cyprian*, 229–30, 249–54.
[51]Cyprian *Ep.* 55.17.1–2; cf. 23.4. See also *Ep.* 28.1–3.

§2.2 *Baptism in Heresy or Schism*

The grounds on which Cyprian argues that schism is a denial of what the Eucharist effects are corporate and organic. It is not that schismatics fail to understand Eucharistic doctrine, but they are not part of the reality of what the Eucharist affirms about the corporate character of the Church:

> Our Lord's own sacrifices proclaim the truth of our common agreement in Christ, bound together by the unshakable bond of filial love that cannot be broken. The Lord points to this truth that our people whom he bore are joined as one by calling the bread, kneaded and pressed together out of many grains, his very body. In like manner, he calls the wine, pressed out from so many clusters of individual grapes crushed together into one, his very own blood. Thus in the same way he points to the truth that we are one flock joined from being mixed together from a collection of individuals into a unity.[52]

Thus far Stephen will agree. There is nothing to suggest that his predecessor, Cornelius, was not in complete agreement with the Council of Carthage of May 252,[53] when it rebuffed Novatian's overtures to reestablish communion between himself as bishop and the community over which he presided. The council would only allow him to return as an individual layperson and not as a bishop.[54] For Stephen, as for Cyprian, Novatian could not preside as High Priest and bishop at the Eucharist, nor would grace be obtained at his altar. But regarding the validity of baptism outside the Church Stephen and Cyprian were to profoundly disagree.

[52]Cyprian *Ep. 69.5.2; see also Ep. 63.13.1–2.
[53]For a discussion of this date and council, see Clarke, *Letters of St Cyprian*, 4.165–66, n. 9.
[54]Cyprian Ep. 72.2.1.

According to Cyprian, precisely because Novatian and his followers cannot validly celebrate the Eucharist, they cannot baptise. If therefore someone whom they have baptised wishes to be reconciled to a Catholic bishop, that is to say a bishop with whose network Cyprian is in communion, he must be baptised again. Indeed it is from Cyprian's point of view mistaken to speak of the "re-baptism" of heretics and schismatics since they were never truly baptised in the first place. Novatian's baptism is no true baptism but "a defiling deluge of pagan water."[55] Cyprian's views on baptism are expressed thus:

> The Lord declares and vindicates the principle in his gospel that only through those who possess the Holy Spirit can sins be absolved. But in baptism sins are absolved to everyone as an individual . . . Therefore, in this passage (Jn 20.21–23) he gives us the proof that only someone who possesses the Holy Spirit can grant baptism and the forgiveness of sins that accompanies it.[56]

How indeed was Stephen to reply to this carefully argued position, founded as it was on Cyprian's systematically worked out understanding of the Church as the body of Christ?[57]

Undoubtedly the tradition, as Stephen had received it, was that those baptised in heresy, and who were converted to Catholic Christianity, should be received through a rite of the imposition of hands by a bishop, with prayer, without repeating their baptism.[58] Cyprian's account of Stephen's position is:

> In addition to any arrogance that leads him to write inept and ill-judged claims that either are not relevant to the point

---

[55]Cyprian *Ep.* 72.1.1.

[56]Cyprian *Ep.* 69.11.1. See also *Ep.* 73.7.1 and *Ep.* 74.4.2.

[57]For an account of this controversy and the issues raised, see Sage, *Cyprian*, 299–335; Patout Burns, *Cyprian the Bishop*, 118–31.

[58]Eusebius *Hist. eccl.* 7.2.

that he is trying to make, or are mutually inconsistent with each other, he cannot resist this further statement: "If anyone therefore should approach you from some heresy or other, you should not introduce a novel practice but only what accords with tradition: you should lay hands on them in response to their expression of penitence. The heretics themselves, after all, do not administer their own idiosyncratic baptism to those who approach them, but simply admit them to communion."[59]

Stephen claimed that Cyprian was guilty of innovating in the light of his new theology and not giving heed to the tradition. As Eusebius says:

But Stephen was angry with him, because he considered that one ought not to add anything more recent in contravention of the tradition that had strongly prevailed from the beginning.[60]

Cyprian however could claim African tradition on his side, against that of Rome. An earlier council had met somewhere in the shadows of the early-third century under Agrippinus, bishop of Carthage, and had held rebaptism of heretics to be necessary. The clear need for such a judgment showed that the denial of that necessity was widespread even in North Africa. In the council of 255, Cyprian's North African episcopal colleagues re-affirmed Cyprian's position.[61] But his *Letters,* written subsequent to that council, revealed widespread unease.[62] Another, larger council assembled in spring 256.[63]

---

[59]Cyprian *Ep.* 74.1.2.
[60]Eusebius *Hist. eccl.* 7.3.
[61]Cyprian *Ep.* 70.
[62]Cyprian *Ep.* 72–73. See also Sage, *Cyprian,* 309–11.
[63]Cyprian *Ep.* 72.1.1.

By autumn he had summoned a further council, whose Acts reveal an identical outcome.[64]

Stephen was to attempt a theological justification of that tradition, and of his own claims that tradition must be accepted. We can glimpse his case in what Cyprian says in his *Letters* 72–73, and Firmilian, bishop of Caesarea in Cappadocia, in *Letter* 75.[65] We also have the anonymous treatise *On the Rebaptism of Heretics,* which argues Stephen's case.[66] Basically, that case is as follows:

Heretics and schismatics, whilst not possessing the Holy Spirit, have been baptised into the Name of Jesus. As a result, they are renewed and sanctified.[67] If the name of Jesus is not invoked, then Stephen will agree that it is not Christian baptism, but this would neither be usually nor generally the case with schismatics and heretics. But they have not received with the name the Holy Spirit, which can only be imparted through the imposition of episcopal hands. Here Stephen appears to be commenting upon traditional baptismal practice, as witnessed by the Hippolytan school in the *Apostolic Tradition*. On Easter Eve, immediately before the baptismal rite is performed, the bishop lays hands on the catechumens. Then, in order to exorcise them, he breathes upon them (insufflation), and anoints them with the sign of the cross.[68] Were heretics re-admitted by the imposition of hands as a rite of exorcism? If so, Stephen claims the rite to be one, not of negative daemonic expulsion, but of positive insufflation of the Spirit.[69] We have here the genesis of the practice of the Western Church in separating baptism in infancy from the imposition of hands and anointing in a separate rite of confirmation

---

[64]Cyprian *Sententiae Episcoporum Numero LXXXVII De Haereticis Baptizandis,* in CCSL III E. (Turnhout: Brepols 2004).

[65]See also Cyprian *Ep.* 69–71 and 74.

[66]For the Latin text of that treatise, see G. Hartel, ed., *S. Thasci Caecili Cypriani, Opera Omnia*, Part III, V (Vienna 1871).

[67]Cyprian **Ep.* 74.5.1.

[68]Pseudo-Hippolytus *Trad. ap.* 20.8. See also Tertullian *Bapt.* 7–8. For these and other early texts, see E. C. Whitaker, *Documents of the Baptismal Liturgy* (London: SPCK 1960), 1–32.

[69]Cyprian **Ep.* 69.15.2.

at a later stage. Stephen certainly distinguished between giving the name of Christ and receiving the Spirit through the imposition of hands. Thus Cyprian will respond:

> Furthermore, no one is born by receiving the Holy Spirit through the imposition of hands, but through baptism. As in the case of the first man, Adam, only by being already born does he receive spirit: it was after God had moulded him that he breathed into him through his face the breath that gave him life. Some one must already be in living existence to be able to receive the Spirit; otherwise he cannot receive it. Birth, in the case of Christians, is at their baptism so that the act of giving birth in baptism and sanctification exists with the bride of Christ alone. She alone can conceive and give birth to sons for God. From whom else can someone who is a son of the Church have been born to God? Any one who has God as his Father must have had previously the Church as his Mother.[70]

Firmilian also supports Cyprian in his claim that Stephen held that heretical baptism can produce remission of sins and the Second Birth, even though he himself admits that heretics do not have the Holy Spirit.[71] Cyprian's final response, shared by Firmilian, is that Stephen is finally inconsistent: on the one hand Stephen will agree with his predecessors but one, Cornelius, that Novatian has founded an imitation Church with pseudo bishops who cannot therefore by their acts convey grace; on the other hand he will accept the validity of baptisms even though they have been performed in a sham Church. Firmilian thinks that he has found the *reductio ad absurdum* of Stephen's argument when he points to an example of baptism not simply performed by heretical men but by an heretical woman.

---

[70]Cyprian *Ep.* 74.7.1.
[71]Cyprian (Firmilian) *Ep.* 75.8.1.

Put in an anachronistic way that Cyprian's contemporaries might not have recognized, if the sacrament of baptism is valid amongst schismatics and heretics, then so is the sacrament of ordination to the ministry, or the sacrament of Holy Orders. Firmilian produces the example of a charismatic, woman presbyter who, at the end of the reign of Severus Alexander, under the proconsul Serenianus (AD 235), carried out baptisms.[72] His *reductio ad absurdum* would not convince everyone today: a schismatical Church is not held necessarily thereby to be a sham Church. Furthermore, in accepting the validity of baptism given in schism or heresy, the problem is raised as to why, therefore, the ordinations of those Churches cannot also be held to be valid.

Cyprian, it must be acknowledged, for all his stringency, held a more coherent theology of the Church and sacraments than did Stephen. It was the role of his successors to try to prove the consistency and quality of his arguments in defense of the tradition, in terms of which, despite their radical brilliance, Cyprian's were clearly theological innovations.

§3 CYPRIAN ON THE CHURCH

Cyprian's understanding of the Church as the body of Christ is thus fundamentally Pauline. The Church is organic and collective, to which one's existence, as an individual, is subsidiary. There is one body and one Spirit, within which we have purpose and significance by being individual members who contribute to the life of the whole. One example of this is found when Cyprian writes (probably in AD 253) his letter to eight bishops who had sought financial assistance to pay ransom for Christian captives taken in barbarian raids. The grounds for Christian compassion are expressed in the following passage:

[72]Cyprian (Firmilian) *Ep.* 75.10.5.

For who would not grieve in calamities of this kind or who would not reckon his brother's grief as his very own? Paul himself is speaking when he says: "If one member suffers, the remaining members suffer together with him; and if one member rejoices, the remaining members rejoice together with him," and in another place, he says: "Who becomes weak, and I am not made weak?" Wherefore now we must reckon the captivity of our brothers to be our captivity, and the grief of those at risk we must account as our own grief, since in consequence of our union there is one Body, and not only love's yearning but also our religious obligation ought to spur us on and enable us to pay our brothers' ransom, who are members of ourselves.[73]

But Paul will speak of an individual believer as having an individual body which is a Temple, and which he must not defile with idolatry or fornication. The question of defilement is individual for Paul and not necessarily corporate. Thus in this letter also Cyprian will go on to speak of the captives as being, individually, "captive temples of God." But Cyprian generally speaks of the Church collectively also as a body that is in danger of contracting defilement. On such a view, the defilement of one member of the body can defile the whole body. For Cyprian, unlike for Paul, it is not simply a question of "if one member suffers all the members suffer," but also, we may say, "if one member is defiled then all the members are defiled." This principle was articulated clearly originally in connection with participation in pagan sacrifices. Those who had thus apostatized and eaten of the sacrifice are described thusly: "returning from the altars of the devil they approach the sacrament of the Lord with hands filthy and tainted with the roasting smell of the sacrifice . . . they are on the point of invading the body of the Lord."[74] It is the

---

[73]Cyprian *Ep.*, 62.1.1–2, quoting 1 Cor 12.26 and 2 Cor 11.29 respectively.
[74]Cyprian *Laps.* 15, quoting 1 Cor 10.20 and 1 Cor 11.27.

corporate Church as the body of Christ that they have thus contaminated and invaded.[75]

Such was the rigorist line taken also by Novatian and his followers that emphasized the permanent exclusion of those who would contaminate the body of Christ by their apostasy. Cyprian earlier supported such a rigorist line, which he considerably mitigated when he came to support Cornelius against Novatian.[76] But his theological assumption of the danger of corporate defilement from a defiled member nevertheless remains. The fallen are allowed absolution following confession after the persecution, and in consequence of Cyprian's promised episcopal council. They are to come in penitence and are likened to those receiving treatment from a doctor. As a result of his period of penitence, the diseased member receives healing so that he will no longer contaminate the ecclesial body corporate.[77]

Cyprian will however extend his concept of invading the corporate body from those who commit apostasy to schismatics such as Felicissimus or Novatian, whom he will not distinguish from heretics. It is not their teaching that corrupts, but their dividing the Church, which is Christ's seamless robe. Yet irresistibly here too Cyprian will introduced the concept of contamination of the corporate body through contamination by an individual member. Quoting Num 16.26, Cyprian concludes:

> The faithful are not to allow themselves to be seduced by the idea that they are immune to catching the disease from a bishop whilst having communion with him in his sin. They are acting in collusion with the exercise of an episcopal presidency that is illegal and contrary to justice.[78]

[75]Cyprian *Laps.* 10.
[76]Cyprian *Ep.* 55.4.2, quoting **Ep.* 19.2.3.
[77]Cyprian **Ep.*68.4.1.
[78]Cyprian **Ep.* 67.3.1.

It is for this reason that, in the case of a schismatical bishop: "every follower without exception is to be linked in their punishment with his leaders in that he has been defiled with their sin."[79]

Thus whether they are heretics or schismatics, the very damage that they do outside the Church is not principally the dissemination of false teaching, as if the episcopal succession was simply a succession of true teachers, as Irenaeus had suggested.[80] If so, it would not be difficult to lambaste Marcion and Valentinus, as Cyprian does. But it would be difficult to include Novatian and Felicissimus on such heretical grounds, since they had no doctrinal differences with Cyprian. Their inability to give salvation to their adherents was that they had no communion with the corporate body of Christ so that they could not transmit the grace that they pretended. In Jn 20.22–23 Christ breathed into the disciples the Holy Spirit and commissioned them to forgive sins. For Cyprian, what is corporately given can only be corporately transmitted, and through bishops in succession—with whom he identified the disciples in this passage. This is why, in his letter to Iubaianus, he must deny the validity of baptism by either schismatics or heretics.[81]

Novatian and his followers cannot claim to be organically united with the inbreathed body of Christ founded at the Johannine Pentecost. Because they are not, any act or affirmation, however orthodox it might appear, is a sham imitation devoid of power.[82] Thus we may say that from the Pauline image of the Church as the body of Christ, and the Johannine image of the Church as the community corporately inbreathed with the Holy Spirit by the risen Christ, Cyprian derives the theology of the Church that he expresses to Puppianus in such terms as:

[79]Cyprian *Ep. 69.9.1–2.
[80]Irenaeus Haer. 3.3.1–3.
[81]Cyprian Ep. 73.7.2.
[82]Cyprian Ep. 73.2.1.

The Peter who is speaking in this passage (Jn 6.68–70) is he upon whom the Church had been built. It is he who teaches in the name of the Church . . . that the Church herself does not depart from Christ. The Church is a people united with its sacred bishop and a flock that stands behind its own shepherd. The conclusion you should therefore draw is that the bishop is in the Church and the Church is in the bishop: if any one is not with the bishop he is not in the Church. It is vain for some to let themselves be seduced by the idea that they can lurk in corners and be in secret communion with certain persons without being reconciled with God's sacred bishops. The Catholic Church is one, and cannot be rent asunder nor divided. Rather it is everywhere interconnected and joined by the glue of sacred bishops mutually adhering together with one another.[83]

However, there is a problem with Cyprian's move to such a position on the basis of such Pauline and Johannine texts. Cyprian's theology may not be unfairly expressed as follows:

1. To be a Christian, you must be a member of the Church, and thus incorporated or made part of Christ's mystical body.
2. Without that incorporation, you cannot receive the Spirit.
3. In order to be so incorporated, you must be in communion with a priest who is in communion with a bishop.
4. In turn that bishop must be in communion with all other true bishops, whose mutual recognition is the glue that binds all in the "bond of charity."

However, according to many contemporary exegetes, points 3 and 4 do not necessarily follow from 1 and 2. Neither the Pauline nor

[83]Cyprian *Ep. 66.8.3.

Johannine communities knew of a threefold hierarchy of bishop, presbyters (priests), and deacons, nor of a network of bishops mutually accepting each other's authority on the basis of councils from time to time laying down certain basic ground rules.

Many scholars would argue that Paul's early communities were charismatic communities.[84] A community as the body of Christ was created by the contagion of the Spirit in life and doctrine from one believer to another, whose many members were united by the same Spirit in a self-authenticating society, which did not need the validation of an external apostolic succession.[85] Similarly Schweizer argued that the Johannine community was originally a charismatic community, in consequence of the fact, amongst other things, that the Twelve in the Upper Room are always disciples and never described as apostles. Why cannot therefore the Church as the body of Christ be understood as such a self-authenticating movement of the Spirit, creating new communities without hierarchy, in which every Spirit filled believer receives the power to absolve?

Cyprian has not the fruits, if such they be, of modern literary criticism of the Fourth Gospel, which would see the Petrine passages, principally John 21, as the later imposition of a hierarchical principal in which Peter as a named individual receives the ministry of teaching and preserving the flock.[86] Thus he would introduce, understandably, his first reply to our criticism in the form of the figure of Peter, entrusted by divine commandment with the care of the Church. From the unifying figure of Peter, who stands as the one

---

[84]E. Schweitzer, "Der johannneische Kirchenbegriff," TU 73 (1959): 363–81, with which cf. A. Brent, *Cultural Episcopacy, with Special Reference to Contemporary Ecumenism*, Studies in Christian Mission 6 (Leiden: E. J. Brill, 1992), 73–80.

[85]I have argued elsewhere that even Ignatius of Antioch did not validate his threefold hierarchy in terms of an external apostolic chain reaching through secular history to the time of the apostles, see A. Brent, "History and Eschatological Mysticism in Ignatius of Antioch," *ETL* 65.4 (1989): 309–29.

[86]R. Bultmann, *The Gospel of John: A Commentary*, trans. G. R. Beasley-Murray (Oxford: Blackwell, 1971), 711–17.

bishop in every diocese, he derives his hierarchical principle from Scripture. Characteristically, quoting Jn 20.21–23, he says:

> After the resurrection he also speaks to the apostles saying: "As the Father has sent me, even I send you." After he had said this, he breathed into them and said, "Receive the Holy Spirit. If you remit anyone's sins, they are remitted to him, and if you retain his sins, they will be retained."[87]

It is "from this that we know" all that he claims about the unity of the episcopal college as the "glue" of the "bond of charity." We might concede to Cyprian this hierarchical principal, and add that of the bishop as successor of the Apostle Peter and to each succeeding bishop from him as source.[88] But we can still ask why there can in fact not be a collection of teachers in a given place, with different congregations, each claiming a teaching succession from Peter, and each exhibiting what Tertullian called *consanguinitas*, or a family resemblance, in their doctrine that indicated that they all received the grace of the Spirit by their participation in the mystical body of Christ.[89] Indeed, as has been argued elsewhere, the Roman community before Pontian, and the revolution initiated by Victor and Callistus that anteceded him, was a fractionalised group of house churches, in a loose bond of intercommunion. Each presiding presbyter-bishop over each house church had received the Holy Spirit and was handing on the orthodox teaching: there was no claim before Callistus that only one figure had authority to do so within a defined geographical space.[90]

---

[87]Cyprian *Ep.* 69.11.1. See also *Unit. eccl.* 4; *Ep.* 73.7.2.

[88]Cyprian *Ep.* 33.1.1.

[89]Tertullian *Praescr.* 32; cf. Brent, *Cultural Episcopacy*, 153–60.

[90]P. Lampe, *From Paul to Valentinus: Christians at Rome in the First Two Centuries*, trans. M. Steinhauser (Minneapolis. MN: Fortress Press, 2003 [German, 1989]); A. Brent, *Hippolytus and the Roman Church in the Third Century: Communities in Tension before the Emergence of a Monarch-Bishop*, Supplements to Vigiliae Christianae 31 (Leiden: E. J. Brill, 1995), 453–457; see also A. Stewart Sykes, introduction to

There is, therefore, an unexplained spatial and geographical dimension to Cyprian's argument that cannot be derived from his New Testament texts. The real determinant of the shape of his argument is the cultural background of Roman Carthage and its principles of polity and governance. The reason, never to be found in Pauline or Johannine theology, but which, nevertheless, shapes his exegesis of Scripture is the location of episcopal jurisdiction within a spatially bounded *imperium*.[91] There can be only one episcopal chair within a given *prouincia*. There can be only one legal and constitutional space with the consequence that, if Cornelius occupies such a space, Novatian cannot:

> So if the Church is with Novatian, she could not have been with Cornelius. But if on the other hand she was with Cornelius (who succeeded Bishop Fabian as a result of a quite lawful ordination) . . . Novatian cannot be in the Church neither can he be numbered amongst its bishops. This is the person who he has trampled upon the tradition handed on by the gospels and by the apostles. He is not anyone's successor. He has produced himself by his own action.[92]

Thus the Church for Cyprian can neither be understood on the model of a self-authenticating, Spirit-filled community, nor can it be understood as lead by presidents of philosophical schools in succession to one another.[93] Cyprian the convert, having experienced the

---

Hippolytus: On the Apostolic Tradition, Popular Patristics Series No. 22 (Crestwood, NY: St Vladimir's Seminary Press, 2001).

[91] For an account of the secularization of concepts of ecclesial authority in Cyprian, see E. F. Osborn, "Cyprian's Imagery," in *Antichthon* 7 (1973): 65–79.

[92] Cyprian *Ep.* 69.3.2.

[93] The technical terms in Greek for teachers as successors are διαδοχή and διαδόχοι. Presidents of philosophical schools are called προεστῶτες, a term which in Latin is *praepositi* and therefore preserved by Cyprian but with a radically different, juridical meaning; see A. Brent, "Diogenes Laertius and the Apostolic Succession," *JEH* 44.3 (1993): 367–89 and Brent, *Hippolytus*, 475–502.

enlightenment of the laver of regeneration, was in denial about the continuing influence of Roman political theory upon his thought.

Thus Cyprian sought what Fahey has shown to be a contrived exegesis of Old Testament passages, in which what is shadowy and ill-formed in the New Testament is somehow better fulfilled in the Old, in reversal to what was usually the case.[94] He argues that the Old Testament type of schism is to be found in 2 Kgs 17.20, where the ten tribes split from Judah and Benjamin and set up an altar separate from that of Jerusalem. Likewise 1 Kgs 11.31–32, 36 is cited, in which the separation of the twelve tribes is symbolized by the act of the prophet Ahijah in dividing his robe.[95] Thus he is able to castigate Novatian as not only lacking an episcopal chair, but as offering sacrilegious sacrifices:

> He could not be admitted into our communion by any one of us. Novatian had attempted the erection of an altar outside the true sanctuary, and the establishment of a counterfeit Chair (*cathedra adultera*), in opposition to Cornelius whose ordination as bishop in the Catholic Church followed God's judgment and his election by the clergy and people. He was thus trying to offer up sacrilegious sacrifices (*sacrilegia*) in opposition to the priestly office of the true bishop . . .[96]

But subsequent to the reforms of Deuteronomy, the location of sacred, high priestly and political authority was, in the Old Testament, centered on one altar located in one place, Jerusalem. Cyprian envisages the bishops as high priests presiding over many altars in different, geographically determined places. Thus it is the imperial

---

[94]A. Brent, "Cyprian's Exegesis and Roman Political Rhetoric," in *L'Esegesi dei Padri Latini dale origini a Gregorio Magno*, in SE Aug 68 (2000): 145–58; cf. M. A. Fahey, *Cyprian and the Bible: A Study in Third-Century Exegesis*, Beiträge zur Geschichte der Biblischen Hermeneutik 9 (Tübingen: Mohr-Siebeck, 1971), 46.

[95]Cyprian *Unit. eccl. 7.*

[96]Cyprian **Ep.* 68.2.1.

ideal that leaves its final impress upon his theology, to which his scriptural exegesis is subservient.

For Cyprian there can be no salvation outside the Church as he has theologically defined it. For him Novatian can be no valid bishop because, cut off from the network of bishops in mutual recognition and intercommunion, he has no organic link either with the forgiveness or with the grace given to the Church in Mt 16.18 and Jn 20.22–23. Novatian and his presbyters cannot celebrate a valid Eucharist because their altar is both "outside the sanctuary (*profanus*)" and their chair is "counterfeit (*cathedra adultera*)." As a bishop already occupies the chair, with presbyters, deacons, and laity in communion with him, there is no sacred space within which the Eucharistic sacrifice can be validly offered.

We must now examine how such a theology of the Church is reflected in the debate both about the primacy of the bishop of Rome, and the controversy with Stephen on the issue of the rebaptism of schismatics and heretics that we have previously discussed (§2.2).

§4 Cyprian and Papal Primacy

Clearly Cyprian's theology of the Church seems to render unnecessary a pope of Rome as the guarantor of the unity of the Church. Cyprian views church unity as arising from a consensus on doctrine and discipline among each of the geographically located bishops throughout the Roman world. Episcopal councils expressed that consensus in concrete when they met from time to time to resolve controversies and affirm new decisions of individual bishops. It was also expressed in the way in which the new occupant of a vacant see was received into the college of bishops by an exchange of letters with bishops who may not have participated in their consecration.

Certainly Cyprian was actively involved in letter writing in order to determine whether Cornelius was the lawful bishop of Rome, namely whether he was the prior and therefore valid occupant of the bishop's chair, whether in other words he had been elected by the clergy and people, and whether others already ordained bishops had laid hands on him in consecration, and so forth. Furthermore Peter's Chair is the chair of any bishop in any diocese and not exclusively at Rome.

However, Cyprian is conscious of the tradition of Tertullian and Irenaeus that made the See of Rome analogous to that of the emperor as *princeps,* or first citizen and leader of the Senate.[97] He will therefore speak of Novatian and his followers as beginning with Rome and going out to form their pseudo Church on the basis of pseudo bishops.[98] The Christian bishop of Rome finally was seen analogously with the pagan emperor of Rome as a result of Cyprian's abiding formation in the constitutional principles and laws governing the unity of civil society in the Roman Empire, despite the apparent ability of his theology of episcopacy to dispense with such a concept. Decius had, after all, expressed the strong ideology of the emperor and his family, through the imperial cult, constituting the divine principle of light and order and creating imperial unity and a new age (see above §2.1). But Cyprian was, as we shall shortly see, to modify his view of Roman primacy in the light of his dispute with Pope Stephen over rebaptising heretics.

Yet Cyprian, far from giving special deference to Cornelius after deciding the disputed election and consecration in his favour, criticises him as his equal. He writes to him a very critical letter about the way in which he allowed himself to be intimidated by the followers of the laxist Felicissimus, who had forced Cornelius to accept their letters requesting they be allowed into communion.[99] Certainly Benson, Archbishop of Canterbury at the close of the nineteenth century, used his account of Cyprian as a veiled criticism of Roman Catholicism in favor of what he regarded as the true Catholic order

---

[97]Irenaeus *Haer.* 3.2.2 and Tertullian *Praescr.* 44.14.
[98]Cyprian *Ep.* 59.14.1.
[99]Cyprian *Ep.* 59.2.1.

of his Anglican Church, before Roman encroachments upon his and his fellow bishops' proper, geographical spheres.[100]

The problem is that an ambiguity arises in the text of *Unit. eccl.* 4–5 because we have two versions, from two different sets of manuscripts, regarding Cyprian's exegesis of Mt 16.18 and Jn 20.21 in those chapters. One version claims that individual bishops are successors of other apostles, who nevertheless have "equal power (*parem . . . potestatem*)," but the bishop of the Roman Church is the successor of Peter who has the ministry of holding the unity of the whole college together as the "source of unity (*originem unitatis*)." The other, as we shall see, implies that each bishop, in his individual diocese, occupies the Chair of Peter, with whom, including the bishop of Rome, they were endowed with an equal fellowship of honour and power (*pari consortio praediti et honoris et potestatis*).[101] We shall shortly discuss further whether the pro-Roman passage represents a later, papalist rewriting of Cyprian's original text, or whether it was the first of two, original versions from his own hand (see below §6.3).[102]

Benson interpreted the more papal of the two manuscript traditions as a later, papalist forgery. More recently, Bévenot has argued with considerable conviction that both passages come from Cyprian's hand, but that the lukewarm version was written subsequent to Cyprian's dispute with Stephen, who was to succeed Cornelius after Lucius.[103]

[100]E.W. Benson, *Cyprian: His Life, His Times, His Work* (London: Macmillan, 1897), 186–221; 432–36.

[101]Cyprian *Unit. eccl.* 4.

[102]Recently Adolph has attempted to resolve Cyprian's ambiguity in favor of the view that he acknowledged Cornelius' primacy despite his hard words, in a way that I find unconvincing; see A. Adolph, *Die Theologie der Einheit der Kirche bei Cyprian,* Europäische Hochschulstudien 33.460 (Frankfurt am Main: Peter Lang, 1993).

[103]M. Bévenot, *St Cyprian's De Unitate Chap. 4 in the Light of the MSS,* Analecta Gregoriana 11 (Rome, 1937); idem, " 'Primatus Petro datur': St Cyprian on the Papacy," *JTS* 5 (1954): 19–35.

§5 Issues of Text and Translation

§5.1 *The Latin Edition*

The Latin edition used for these translations is from *Sancti Cypriani Episcopi Opera* in the *Series Latina* 3, 3 A, B, and C of *Corpus Christianorum* (Turnholt: Brepols) and are as follows:

1. *De lapsis* and *De catholicae ecclesiae unitate* (*On the Fallen* and *On Unity*), M. Bévenot, ed., Part 1 (1957).
2. *Ad Donatum* and *Ad Demetrianum* (*To Donatus* and *To Demetrian*), M. Simonetti, ed., Part 2 (1976).
3. *Epistulae* (*Letters*), G. F. Diercks, ed., Parts 3.1 and 2 (1994 and 1996).

§5.2 *English Translations*

I draw attention here to some previous English Translations, which will be particularly relevant for those without Latin who may wish to refer to individual works not translated in this selection:

1. M. Bévenot, *St Cyprian: The Lapsed; The Unity of the Catholic Church,* ACW 25 (Westminster, MD/London: Newman Press/Longmans Green, 1957).
2. G. Clarke, *The Letters of St Cyprian,* 4 Vols., ACW 43, 44, 46 and 47 (Washington, D.C.: Newman Press, 1984, 1986 and 1989).
3. R. J. Deferrari et al., eds., *Saint Cyprian: Treatises,* FC 36 (New York: Catholic University of America Press, 1958).
4. R. B. Donna, ed., *Saint Cyprian: Letters (1–81),* FC 51 (Washington, D.C.: Catholic University of America Press, 1958).

5. R. E. Wallis, *The Writings of Cyprian, Bishop of Carthage*,
    ANF 5.

§5.3 *The Textual Tradition*

Two essential families of manuscripts are identified through their
relations to an established two versions thesis of the *De catholicae
ecclesiae unitate* (*On the Unity of the Catholic Church*), chapters 4–5.

Bévenot focused on a manuscript that contained only the *Primacy Text* (*PT*) without any trace of the *Textus Receptus* (*TR*) that,
as the name suggests, has very many witnesses. Clearly this was an
essential move against a thesis like that of Benson who claimed that
the *PT* was a later reworking of the received text and thus never
existed in any pure form. It had no separate existence.[104] Benson's
fallacy lay partly in the textual critics quest for a stemma at the root
of which would be an archetypal *ms* of which other *mss* had been
copies and the transcribing errors of their scribes the source of later
corruptions.

But such a model rests upon the false assumption that scribes
will continue within a single tradition of manuscripts, and that two
or more traditions will continue their degenerating corruption in
isolation from one another. Yet what happens in reality is that later
scribes might actually refer to another tradition of manuscripts less
contaminated, and seek to make some corrections from their knowledge of such manuscripts. At that point two consequences emerge:

(i) it becomes impossible to construct neatly two stemmas
     and to show that the source of one is derivative from
     the other because one cannot be sure that the scribe
     is incorporating another tradition or whether he is a
     witness to some third tradition with its own stemma,
     and,

[104]Benson, *Cyprian.*

(ii) there might be two stemmas heavily obscured by the coalescing of traditions in this way that lead back to a first and second edition of a work.

Both points were ignored by the approach of Benson that presupposed that there was only one true archetypal text of which later readings had to be construed as corruptions, accidental or intentional.

To simplify Bévenot's complex textual analysis in a form that, I appreciate, does it scant justice, we have several families of manuscripts that relate to *PT* and *TR* respectively.[105] The ultimate independence of the texts found opposite each other set out in two columns (Cyprian, *Unit. eccl.*, 4–5) is indicated by the existence of *PT* approximately as it stands in a single *ms.*, H or Paris *lat.* 15282. We therefore have four groups:

1. H alone with no trace of the version *TR*.
2. Two *mss* that contain both texts in immediate succession, first *PT* and then *TR*, but without any attempt by the scribe to amalgamate them into a single text. These are M (Munich *lat.* 208) and Q (*Troyes* 581).
3. Two *mss* that have *PT* followed by *TR* but whose last two sentences of the former replace those that they parallel in the middle of the latter, namely T (Vatican *Reg. Lat.* 116) and U (Oxford, Bodleian *Laud Misc.* 105).[106]
4. Finally we have *PT* but with insertions of two passages from *TR* and a word or two more in h (Leyden, Univ. *Voss lat. oct.* 7) and a whole series of *mss* in the same tradition.

---

[105]M. Bévenot, *The Tradition of Manuscripts: A Study in the Transmission of Cyprian's Treatises* (Oxford: Clarendon Press 1961), 56–57. For a full bibliography, see n. 3 to the commentary on *Unit. eccl.*, 4–5, below.

[106]Benson, *Cyprian*, 207 confidently claimed that the *mss* listed in 2 and 3 (except T) were "all copied from one lost ms which we may call the Archetype."

For an interpolationist thesis such as Benson's to succeed, it must, after all, have been *TR* that originally stood alone with evidence of a planned alteration of that text.[107] The evidence to the contrary however is of two distinct texts combined into one *ms*, and it is on this that the generally agreed modern position relies, following Bévenot.

[107]Benson, *Cyprian*, 200–209.

Select Letters

§1 The Crisis from the Decian Persecution

LETTER 8
Roman Presbyters Criticise Cyprian on His Flight

This Letter was written shortly after the martyrdom of Pope Fabian on 20 January 250. It bears no title and clearly addresses Cyprian with his title as primatial bishop (pope) in a highly sarcastic fashion (1.1), with the charges in defence against which Cyprian wrote *Ep. 20. Apparently its bearer, the subdeacon Crementius, also carried another letter addressed directly to Cyprian himself, recounting the martyrdom of Pope Fabian. Unfortunately, this letter has been lost. Cyprian's reply is his eulogy of Fabian in *Ep. 9. Crementius could hardly have represented a group very supportive of Cyprian's position. Certainly their language (1.1: "for a particular purpose," *certa ex causa*) is very noncommittal on the specific character of what Crementius was doing in Rome, and the issues that he was no doubt raising. The letter is therefore a general address to the Carthaginian presbyterate, whom they consider capable of presiding (*praepositi*) in the absence of their bishop.

The Roman presbytery, of which Novatian was secretary, always adopted a more rigorist line, with the support of their martyrs (See *Ep. 27, 33* and 55). It may therefore have been Cyprian's position on the fallen lapsed, over which he clashed with the Carthaginian martyrs, that finally won him the support of a significant part of the Church of Rome, which he was able to use in favour of Cornelius in the disputed papal succession with Novatian, who was to be consecrated as a rival bishop. It would be Cyprian's contention that, as Cornelius already occupied the magisterial chair as bishop, any rival claimant was involved in insurrection against a lawful magistrate. On the other hand, it may be that the remaining correspondence with Rome was from groups that supported Cyprian, with others, such as the Novatianists, simply ignoring him.

1.1 We have learned from Crementius the subdeacon,[1] who came from you to us for a particular purpose, that the blessed Pope Cyprian[2] has withdrawn from public life. Of course he had to do this not unreasonably on account of the fact that he is a person of distinction! And all this, when the contest is at hand which God has allowed in this present age by reason of the struggle between his servants and their Adversary.

God wishes to make this battle visible to angels and to men in order that the overcomer may receive the victor's crown, but that the person overcome should carry off as his prize the sentence that has been laid down in God's declaration to us.[3]

It has been impressed upon us that we are seen to be presiding presbyters, and to have guardianship of the flock, as is the fate of shepherds.[4] If we should be found to be negligent, it would be said

[1] This is the first example of this minor order that was perhaps required because the deacons were to be kept to the scriptural seven in number, see G. Clarke, *The Letters of St Cyprian*, 4 vols. ACW 43, 44, 46, 47 (New York: Newman Press 1984, 1986, 1989), 1.205, n.1.

[2] "Blessed (*benedictum*)" is used sarcastically here as in Tertullian *Pud.* 13.7. *Benedictus* was normally used of a martyr or confessor. Cyprian in his defense wished to extend the concept of martyrdom beyond physical suffering to include confiscation of property and exile; see e.g. *Laps.* 3.

[3] "Laid down" = *manifestare,* used of what is decreed in an imperial rescript; see *Cod. Justin.* (Ulpian) 1.6.2: "It is laid down in certain rescripts (*rescriptis quibusdam manifestatur*) that neither the goods in totality nor in part should be sequestered."

[4] Clarke, *Letters of St Cyprian*, 1.68 insists on translating this phrase "acting in the place of our shepherds" on the grounds that they were acknowledging that they could only have this role whilst awaiting the successor of Fabian as bishop. But this letter does not reveal any admission about the "high" role of the bishop. If *vice* did mean "in place of," it was here used in place of a plurality of shepherds and not of one single bishop, and who could these be? It would appear that, although by AD 231 there was a single monarch bishop in Rome, the development of such a monarchical episcopal role had been recent. The Rome of the early third century had been a loose confederation of house churches with minimal conditions for intercommunion between them. This may account for the strength and influence of the Roman presbyterate, and the confidence with which they assume the office of *praepositus* here, and indeed

to us what was said to our predecessors who had been so negligent in exercising their presiding office. We would not have sought that which was lost and we would not have set the wanderer on a straight path. The lame would have gone unbandaged. We would have consumed their milk and clothed ourselves with their wool.

2 Finally the Lord himself, in fulfillment of what had been written in the law and in the prophets, teaches this with the words: "I am the Good Shepherd, who lays down my life for my sheep. A hireling, however, and one whose sheep are not his own property, when he sees the wolf coming, abandons them and flees, and the wolf scatters them" (Jn 10.11–12). And also to Simon he speaks thus: "'Do you love me?' He replied: 'I love you.' He says to him: 'Feed my sheep'" (Jn 21.15–17). We recognize that this word was fulfilled in the very act by which he himself departed this life, and the rest of the disciples behaved similarly.

2.1 We do not want you to be found to be hirelings, most beloved brothers, but good shepherds. You have grasped that no small danger will be your burden if you have failed to exhort our brothers to stand unshakably in their faith. They must not be allowed to rush headlong into idolatry so that the brotherhood is utterly wiped out. **2** Our exhortation is not purely verbal. You can learn instead from many who come from us to you that we have done those things by God's help, and are so doing.

We have before our eyes, in the face of every anxiety and danger of the world, the fear of God and his everlasting punishments rather than the fear of men and the short time of injury here. We exhort

the expectations of their secretary, Novatian, who was to become in Cyprian's sense a schismatical bishop. See A. Brent, *Hippolytus and the Roman Church in the Third Century: Communities in Tension before the Emergence of a Monarch-Bishop*, Supplements to *Vigiliae Christianae* 31 (Leiden: E. J. Brill, 1995), 398–457; A. Stewart-Sykes, *Hippolytus: On the Apostolic Tradition: An English Version with Introduction and Commentary*, Popular Patristics Series 22 (Crestwood, NY: St Vladimir's Seminary Press, 2001), 12–16.

them to stand fast in the faith, not forsaking the brotherhood, but standing prepared with their obligation to walk with the Lord. **3** We even managed to call back those in process of ascending to the place where they were being compelled to sacrifice.[5]

The Church stands bravely in the faith, even though some have fallen to their ruin overwhelmed by the terror of it, either because they were so entitled since they were eminent persons,[6] or because they were simply overcome by human fear. We have not abandoned them, even though they have become separate from us, but we encourage and exhort them to the path of penance, if there is any way they are able to obtain pardon from him who is able to provide it. We should not make them worse Christians as a result of our abandoning of them.

3.1 You see, therefore, brothers that this should be your practice too. As a result, through your exhortation you will cause the souls of those who have fallen to stand again upright. If they should be arrested, should on a second occasion become confessors, they should be able to put straight their previous error.

We mention here also those other pressures upon you. If those who have fallen in this time of trial show signs of being overcome by illness, and would do penance for what they have done, and should earnestly seek communion, then you must come to their aid. This is the case whether they are widows, or other downtrodden people who are unable to maintain themselves. Those who are in prison or ejected from their own homes generally ought to have those who will minister to them.

Catechumens especially, when overcome with illness, ought not to be cheated but rather they should be afforded aid.

[5] A reference here to the Capitoline hill on one side of the Roman Forum where there was a Temple to the three principle deities of the Roman State, before whose altar they were to sacrifice under the terms of Decius' decree. Such a temple was replicated in the *Fora* of Roman colonies such as Carthage. See also Cyprian, *Laps.*, 24, n. 45; 25, n. 49.

[6] Clearly they include Cyprian in his flight as having fallen.

2 Another important point! A great danger hangs over those whose duty it is if the bodies of the martyrs and of the rest remain unburied. We are certain that by whomever and on what occasion this duty of yours is fulfilled,[7] the person in question will be considered a good servant. He will be like him who has been faithful in least and should be placed over ten cities (Lk 19.17). May the God who provides all things to those who hope in him grant that we may be found occupied in these works.

3 The brothers greet you who are in chains, and the presbyters and the whole Church, who also herself watches over with the greatest care for all who call upon the name of the Lord. But we also ask in turn that you be mindful of us. **4** For your information, Bassianus has arrived with us. We beseech you who have zeal for God that you send at your convenience a copy of this letter, by the hand of as many as you have available. Otherwise compose your own, or send a messenger. The object is that the addressees stand steadfast and unmovable in faith. We pray you, dearest brothers, that you may ever fare well.

[7]It would be carried out by "diggers (*fossores*)," such as those depicted in the Roman catacomb of St Peter and St Marcellinus; see Clarke, *Letters of St Cyprian*, 1.217, n. 29.

Questionable Practices of Some Confessors

Cyprian writes from hiding to the confessors at Carthage in mid-April AD 250. He addresses various disputes that have broken out amongst this group now released from prison, some of whom had been sent into exile. Not much is known about Rogatian apart from his status as presbyter, and one of three presbyters who were also confessors. The ranks of the higher clergy did not furnish too many examples of confessorship or martyrdom.

This letter presents an interesting picture of how the confessors were becoming organized into a distinctive group. Mainly of lower social status, they were clearly given the "special name" of confessor and their group started to take on certain characteristics, by no means all of which Cyprian found savory. They became proud and aggressive about their status. According to some traditions, their confessorship, involving painful sufferings by being tortured, meant that they could assume the presbyterate without the imposition of Cyprian' hands in ordination.[1] That being the case, they could as presbyters offer the Eucharistic sacrifice. They were quickly becoming a distinctive ecclesial community, a kind of Church of the Martyrs. Cyprian never mentions such a claim, preferring to leave it suppressed. But according to the *Apostolic Constitutions* 8.23.4 the very behavior against which he protests when he calls for *tranquillitas* or nonaggressiveness is described explicitly as a claim to exercise the office of presbyter.[2]

Cyprian prefers to focus upon the drunkenness and self-indulgence of the group, the airs that they assume in swollen pride, and particularly (5) the practice of sleeping in the same bed as women without indulging in sexual intercourse as an example of their charism of self-denial. He finally ends with reference to the material basis in his patronal role for his episcopal authority: large numbers of his flock were dependent on him financially like sections of the Roman populace were to their wealthy patrons.

---

[1]A. Brent, "Cyprian and the question of *ordinatio per confessionem*," StPatr 36 (2001): 323–37.

[2]Ibid., 331–32.

To Rogatianus Presbyter, and His Fellow Confessors

1.1 Some time ago, my dearest and bravest brothers, I dispatched a letter to you in which I expressed my thanks for your faith and moral courage in words of unrestrained joy. There is now no other subject with which our words should be concerned in the beginning of our letter than that we should proclaim the glory of your name often and always with a joyful spirit. What can be a greater subject in my prayers, or worthy of better attention, than when I see Christ's flock illumined by the mark of esteem that is your confession?

For although all the brothers ought to rejoice in this, nevertheless the share of the bishop in the joy felt by all is greater. For the glory of the Church is the glory of the one who presides over it. We grieve for those whom the threatening storm of persecution laid low as much as we rejoice on your account that the Devil was not able to overcome you.

2.1 Nevertheless we must exhort you through the faith that we share, by the true and sincere heavenly love surrounding you within our breast, that you who overcame the adversary at your first confrontation with him might preserve your renown by remaining strong and continuing resolutely in your moral courage. Each day we contend for our lives all the while we are in this present age, all the while drawn up in battle line. Effort must be made that progress from these first beginnings might increase. What you began with as the blessed fruits of early lessons can be brought to further completion in you.

It is too easy an achievement simply to be able to acquire something. It is a greater achievement to be able to preserve that which you have acquired. In the same way, the faith itself and the saving birth also continue giving life, not because they have been once received, but because they have been preserved by protecting them. For it is not a process concluded once for all that preserves a human being safe for God but a process of gradual completion.

2 The Lord taught this by his own authority when he said: "Behold, you have been made whole, do not now sin lest something worse befall you" (Jn 5.14).[3] Think of Christ saying to his confessor: "Behold, you have become a confessor, do not now sin lest something worse befall you." Solomon finally and Saul and many of the others, were able to retain the grace given to them as long as they walked in the ways of the Lord. As the discipline learnt from the Lord departed from them, the grace also departed.

3.1 We must continue resolutely in the strict and narrow path to his praise and glory. Nonaggressiveness and humility, and the calm that comes from good standards, befits all Christians according to God's spoken word. Since God respects no one unless he is humble and nonaggressive, and trembles at his oracles, the confessors ought to observe and perfect this behavior the more. They have been made an example to the rest of the brothers, towards whose moral standards the life and action of everyone ought to be attracted.

2 Just as the Jews are made aliens to God, on whose account the name of God is blasphemed among the pagans, so, on the contrary, they are beloved of God through whose discipline the name of the Lord is proclaimed with a witness of praise. It is written as much, with the Lord admonishing and stating: "Let your light shine in the presence of men, that they may see you good works and glorify your Father who is in heaven." (Mt 5.16). And Paul the Apostle says: "So shine as lights in the world" (Phil 2.15). And Peter likewise exhorts: "'Just as guests,'" he says, "and resident aliens, abstain from carnal desires, which make war against the soul, practicing good conduct among the pagans, in order that though they withdraw from you as if from the spiteful, seeing your good works they may magnify the Lord" (1 Pet 2.11–12).

The greater group of you, to my joy, show improvement as a result of the honor paid to them for their confession. They guard

---

[3]Note that Cyprian's manuscript clearly contained the passage in John regarding the woman in adultery, omitted by the most ancient tradition of Greek manuscripts.

and preserve their reputation by the practice of gentleness and of high moral standards.

4.1 But notwithstanding, I hear that some are tainting your number with their moral corruption, and are destroying the esteem merited from the award of your special name[4] by their misguided conduct. You yourselves also ought to reprove and get these people under control, and correct them, as, naturally, you have respect for your own reputation and need to preserve it.

How great is the lack of respect owed to your name? One or other of these people spends time drunk and frolicking, someone else returns to his own country from where he has been exiled with the result that he, under arrest, perishes, not on grounds that he is a Christian, but on the grounds that he is guilty of a crime.[5]

2 I hear that some are filled with conceit and swollen with pride, though it is written: "Do not be high minded, but fear. For if the Lord spared not the natural branches, perhaps neither will he spare you" (Rom 11.20–21). Our Lord "has been led as a sheep to the slaughter and just as a lamb in the presence of his shearer is voiceless so he did not open his mouth" (Is 53.7 [= Acts 8:32]). "I am not," he says, "stubborn, nor do I talk back. I gave my back to their whips and my cheeks to their blows. My face I did not turn away from the foulness of their spitting" (Is 50.5–6).

3 Who would dare now, while living for him and in him, to exalt himself and be arrogant, unmindful both of the deeds which he accomplished, and of the commandments which he delivered to

[4]"Esteem merited by the award of your special name," = *laudem praecipui nominis*, which I construe as a reference to the name of "confessor," a term awarded to someone who undergoes martyrdom with considerable physical suffering but manages or happens to survive. Such survival was characteristic of the Decian persecution, whose object was the harsh education of wayward wills to conform to Roman imperial *disciplina,* and not punishment by execution, though that may nevertheless also take place.

[5]This may constitute evidence that Decius' persecution was directed against Christianity itself and not simply incidentally as against any cult that did not so conform; see also Introduction, §2.1.

us through himself or through the apostles? For, if "the servant is not greater than the master" (Jn 13.16 and 15.20), let those who are following the Lord imitate these features of his by being humble, noncombative, and maintaining silence. For every one who will be more lowly will become more exalted, as the Lord says: "He who is least among you, he will be great" (Lk 9.48).

5.1 Next, another matter! We learned of something to the deepest distress and sorrow of our heart that we must think to be appalling to you as well. You have those who are even defiling the members of their bodies that are the temples of God, made holy after their confession and further enlightened.[6] They are doing this by their shameful and scandalous sleeping together. Sharing together jointly their beds indiscriminately with women, they are giving grounds for accusations to be made even when there is no unchastity on their conscience. Their acts give birth to offensive examples that result in others calamitously falling.

2 There ought to be no arguments and rivalries amongst you, since the Lord committed his peace to you as it is written: " 'You shall love your neighbor as yourself.' If, however, you bite and condemn each other, take care lest you shall be consumed with each other" (Gal 5.14–15). Abstain from abuse and insults, I beg you, in view of the fact that those who insult will not find their way to the kingdom of God. It is the tongue that has confessed Christ that must be preserved with its honor intact, unharmed and pure. For he who speaks good and righteous words that make for peace according to the commandment of Christ confesses Christ daily.

3 We renounced the present age when we were baptised. But now we are really renouncing the present age when, tested and

---

[6]The reference here is to the confession of faith before the magistrate that, like martyrdom, was a baptism in blood, such that if the person was not already baptised, his confession removed the need for baptism in water. Thus confession, like baptism, becomes a source of divine illumination; see Cyprian *Don.* 4–5.

examined by God, we leave all our possessions and follow the Lord, and we stand fast and live by his faith and fear.

6.1 Let us strengthen ourselves by exhorting one another, and let us progress more and more in the Lord. When in his mercy he has provided the peace that he promised that he would provide, let us return to the Church renewed and almost changed. Our brothers and the pagans alike will welcome us, corrected and reformed for the better in all respects. Those who had previously admired our reputation for glorious acts of courage should now admire our training in moral standards.

7.1 Lately, when you were still holed up in prison, I wrote to our clergy what now I write again more fully, that if you have any need for your clothing or for food, it should be supplied. Nevertheless, I have sent you 250 sesterces from my own expense, money that I am carrying with me.[7] But also I will soon send another additional 250. Victor the deacon, formerly a reader, who is with me, sent you 175. I rejoice furthermore, when I discover that many of our brothers are rushing in competition for the same object of expressing their love and to alleviate your own needs by their contributions.

I pray you, dearest brother that you always fare well.

---

[7]Cyprian here is acting as a *patronus* or patron to his flock, just like a secular patrician giving support from his own wealth to his clients and retainers. See C. A. Bobertz, "Patronage Networks and the Study of Ancient Christianity," StPatr 24 (1991): 20–27, who argues that Cyprian supported and interpreted his ecclesiastical and episcopal authority by means of such a model. See also A. Stewart–Sykes, "Ordination Rites and Patronage Systems in Third-Century North Africa," *VC* 56.2 (2002): 115–30.

Presbyters and Deacons Who Fail the Martyrs

In early June AD 250, Cyprian addressed this letter to the martyrs and confessors[1] with the aim of dissuading them from issuing certificates of reconciliation (*libelli pacis*), and thus reconciling the fallen without a due period of penance, the conditions for which could only be established after the persecution and the calling of a council of bishops.[2]

Cyprian begins (1.1) circumspectly without criticising the martyrs directly but blaming rather certain presbyters and deacons who ministered to them in prison. Thus he indirectly testifies to the respect in which they and their acts are held, as well as to the requirement that a deacon as well as a presbyter were necessary in order to offer the Eucharistic sacrifice in prison (1.2). His concept of discipline is again a military one, with Christ's commandments those of a general in the field (1.1). He accuses the presbyters of breaking the Church's discipline by following the instructions of the martyrs in a *libellus pacis* without seeking the approval of Cyprian and his council, which has yet to meet due to the persecution. He describes the functions of that council by means of juridical analogies, which is thus understood as a court considering the *libellus* as evidence in a plea, rather than itself a sacramental act of absolution.

Cyprian tries to distance the confessors from the act on their behalf of the presbyters and deacons that he is criticising. His case is that the latter were going beyond the brief that Cyprian claims to have agreed with them (3). Here at many points he seems to concede to them authority that he pleads with them not to exercise (3.1). He invites the support of that authority to the case that he is making (3.2). Finally he objects to certificates that

---

[1]Cyprian uses the term "martyr" generally of anyone about to die for the faith, with whom Christ is specially present. The "confessors" are those released after suffering physical torture even though they have not yielded and denied their faith. The latter considered themselves as acting in fellowship with the former and carrying out their last requests.

[2]Cf. Introduction, §2.1.

have no specified name, and thus seemingly implies that those with names do possess authority that he would like nevertheless to limit (4).

To the Martyrs and Confessors

1.1 Anxiety for our position and God's fear compel us, bravest and most blessed martyrs, to give you firm advice in our letter. Our purpose is that the very people who should keep as their aim the law and also the discipline of the Lord preserve with devotion and with courage the faith of the Lord. All Christ's soldiers ought to keep the orders of their general. But it is fitting that especially you ought to obey his orders, for you have become an example to all others of moral courage and of the reverential fear that comes from God.

2 I had trusted of course that the presbyters and deacons who were present there in prison[3] would advise you and fully instruct you concerning the law of the gospel. Previously that had always happened in the time of our ancestors. Deacons going to and fro from the prison would guide the petitions of the martyrs by their counsels and by the precepts of the Scriptures.[4] But now it has come to my knowledge, accompanied by the greatest distress of spirit, that

[3] I take *illuc* in both places here to mean from the context "there in prison" rather than "there in Carthage" with Clarke, *Letters of St Cyprian*, 1.90.

[4] Cyprian, in the style of Roman political rhetoric, is claiming the antiquity of hallowed custom for what is at best ambiguously so. Eusebius (*Hist. eccl.* 5.1.5), when describing the martyrs of Lyons and Vienne, bears witness to a long tradition in which the martyrs were accorded the power of absolution; see further A. Brent, "Cyprian and the question of *ordinatio per confessionem*," 334–36. What was new was a "certificate of reconciliation (*libellus pacis*)" from the martyr pronouncing forgiveness paralleling the *libellus* signed by the Roman magistrates to say that one had sacrificed, and had thus renounced one's faith. Cyprian insists that the *lex euangelii* granted to Peter the power of absolution and of reconciliation (Mt 16.18–19; Jn 20.21–23). That power, he continues, is committed to each individual bishop in his diocese in union with the college of bishops throughout the world. Thus according to Cyprian the law of Christ commanded the martyrs to conform to the discipline of an ecclesiastical hierarchy through which alone absolution could be granted. But this was Cyprian's own new formulation pushing the tradition in a new direction; see also notes and commentary in Cyprian *Unit. eccl.* 4–5.

not only there in prison the consideration of the divine precepts has not been advanced, but also has been rather up to this moment in time impeded.

As a result, those things that you are doing yourselves circumspectly with regard to God and respectfully with regard to God's priest[5] are being undone by the conduct of certain presbyters. These presbyters have no thought about reverence for God, nor for honoring their bishop. You addressed a letter to me accordingly in which you made application to me that I examine your petitions that reconciliation be granted to certain fallen persons, when, once the persecution has ended, we can meet in one place and assemble together with the clergy.[6]

Those presbyters instead, contrary to the law of the gospel, contrary even to your own honorable petition to the court,[7] are offering the Eucharist for them and administering communion. They are

[5]"Priest" = *sacerdos* refers here to the bishop, the only office to bear this title at this time, although presbyters in the African Church offered the Eucharistic sacrifice, as he now makes clear.

[6]"With the persecution ended ... clergy": It is doubtful whether the martyrs were aware that they had signed up to this last clause. "Have made application to me" = *rogare*, which can be used generally for "to request" but is used in this more restricted sense of to formally petition for the decision of an assembly or court; see Livy 30.40.14: "in order that the consul should petition whom they were resolved should be named dictator (*ut consul rogaret quem dictatorem dici placeret*)." Likewise in the phrase "examine (*examinari*) your petitions (*desideria vostra*)," *desideria* indicates that Cyprian regards the bishops as Roman magistrates hearing petitions to be granted or refused, following a due process of law. *Desiderium* is used specifically of such a petition granted by the Emperor Trajan in Pliny *Ep.* 10.24 (35): "We are able to grant their petition (*possumus desiderio eorum indulgere*)." As a skilful bureaucrat, Cyprian is able to change the general sense of what the martyrs were claiming, namely immediate absolution, into agreement with him that a council was needed before these requests could be granted. You needed a formally gathered assembly in order to grant a petition, and for this to be possible, the persecution must end. Only then could petitions be duly considered and granted or otherwise. Cyprian is assimilating ecclesiastical authority to Roman imperial provincial administrative structures, and thus putting his own spin on the martyrs' claims.

[7]The martyrs presented their petition, which Cyprian understands as a *petitio* in the sense of "law suit," which his future ecclesiastical council over which he is to preside will adjudicate; see also below section 3.1.

doing this before performance of penitence, before confession has been made for the most serious and desperate sin, before imposition of hands by the bishop and clergy in recognition of penitence. In other words they are daring to profane the holy Body of the Lord, since it is written: "He who will eat the bread or drink the chalice of the Lord in an unworthy fashion will be guilty of the body and blood of the Lord" (1 Cor 11.27).

2.1 It may of course be possible for pardon in this matter to be granted to the fallen. What dead person would not hasten to be brought to life? Who would not move quickly to arrive at his own salvation?

It is the task of those who preside to keep to a rule and to instruct those who are in careless haste or who are ignorant, lest those who ought to be the shepherds of the flocks become their butchers. It is an act of deceit to make concessions for sins that lead to self-destruction. Someone who has fallen is not raised upright by such an act, but rather, by giving offence to God, he is being driven all the way towards a more catastrophic collapse.

2 So let them accordingly learn from you what they ought to teach. Let them reserve the cases that are the subject of your plea for the bishop. Let them await the appropriate time when there is peace from persecution for reconciliation to be granted in accordance with your requests. The mother first wins peace from her Lord, and then discussion can take place in accordance with your petitions concerning the reconciling peace for her sons.

3.1 I also hear, bravest and dearest brothers, that you are under pressure from certain people who have no shame, who disregard, and with violence, the respect owed to you. I implore you with all the entreaties that I am able that you would weigh with care and caution the petitions of those who seek them.[8] Be mindful and considerate

[8]Despite his insistence that the right to decide the case of the fallen and their reconciliation lies only with the discretion of the bishop, Cyprian here shows

of the kinds of concessions made by your martyr predecessors in the past, and how careful they were in everything. As friends of the Lord, and destined afterwards to sit in the Judgment with him, you should examine the activity and work and merits of each individual case. You should reflect on the categories and kinds of their offences.

In such an instance, if you should promise anything rash and unworthy and we should execute it, our Church may cause to blush with shame in the presence of the very pagans. **2** For we receive divine visitations,[9] and we are constantly reprimanded and admonished that the commandments of the Lord might be allowed to remain incorrupt and inviolate.

I recognize that this continues to be the case with you even when in prison,[10] where God's examination of your right to Christian citizenship[11] is proving instructive in the Church's required discipline for very many even of you. I know that this could be achieved with total success if you were to limit by careful consideration those requests made of you. You should catch on to and restrain those who make distinctions between persons in granting your benefits. They are either seeking to gain thanks for themselves from these or are on the look out for questionable markets in an illicit trade.[12]

grudging acknowledgement of a Church of the Martyrs, with predecessors like the bishops, with their own right to hear petitions (*desideria*) that are subjects of formal pronouncements. He even concedes that there was a due process of consideration and examination by the martyrs. Clearly those about to reign with Christ share his juridical functions. Nevertheless Cyprian insists that, though the martyrs may promise, the bishop alone can perform.

[9]*Uisitamur* means literally "we are visited," but I have adopted here the translation and justification offered in Clarke, *Letters of St Cyprian*, 1.92 and 280, n. 27, where he refers to Cyprian *Ep.* 16.4.1.

[10]"In prison" = again *illuc* and not "Carthage"; see also n. 2 above. Though some may be out of prison, "very many of you (*plurimos quoque ex vobis*)" are still in prison, and Cyprian is addressing the martyrs as a corporate body.

[11]"God's examination" = *diuina censura*, the latter term refers to the office of a censor who organizes the citizen roles, identifies taxation categories, and so forth. God as censor is through the persecution drawing up the citizen role of true Christians.

[12]These words imply that *libelli pacis* are being sold for money with blank spaces in which to write a recipient's name. A clearer reference to this abuse can be found below in the immediately following, section 4.

4.1 On this subject I have composed letters both to the clergy and to the people, both of which I have instructed to be read to you. But there is also a further matter you ought to recall to your attention and seek to remedy. I mean that you should specify those to whom you desire reconciliation to be granted by name.[13] For I hear from some that certificates are composed so that they read: "Let so and so be admitted to communion along with his household."

Such was never at all a custom with the martyrs. The effect of our doubting an originally blank claim form will increase the overwhelming ill will that will subsequently be directed against us. There are wide implications in the statement: "So and so with his household." There can be twenty and thirty and more at a time presenting themselves to us who claim that they are relations, in laws, freedmen or household slaves of him who received a certificate.

On these grounds I request that you specify by name on the certificate those whom you yourselves see, with whom you are personally acquainted, whose acts of penitence you observe to be near the point of gaining forgiveness. Thus you will be able to direct letters to us fully consistent with faith and discipline.

I pray that you, bravest and most beloved brothers, will always fare well in the Lord and keep us in mind. Farewell.

---

[13]Clearly, though reluctantly, Cyprian is acknowledging the authority of the corporate body of the martyrs, whilst allocating it surreptitiously to an advisory status.

Martyrs and Confessors Who Fail the Church

Cyprian writes, at the same time as *Ep.* 15, this letter to the confessors and martyrs. He pretends once again that it is not the martyrs that he considers to be at fault, but presbyters pretending to act in their name in order to oppose episcopal authority (1.1–2). Here Cyprian claims that the martyrs themselves accept his due place and observe, or ought to observe, God's law, found in Mt 16.16–18 and Jn 20.21–23, giving the power of absolution to the bishop (3.1).[1]

He claims that the martyrs fully agreed with his position. Furthermore, whilst proclaiming his respect for the martyrs, and claiming that those who act for them are provoking the conflict rather than they themselves, he finally admits that some if not most of them were claiming an authority that he would deny them. The presbyters should have corrected them (3.2). He concludes with a threat to suspend them, for which he claims divine authority as a bishop (4.2). He implies however that this punitive authority comes from visions rather than the law of Scripture (4.1).

To the Holy Brothers, the Presbyters and Deacons

1.1 For a long time I have kept my temper, most beloved brothers, on the grounds that our restrained silence might contribute to an absence of controversy. But when certain persons, in an unrestrained and uncompromising spirit of presumption, strive to make us confused, by their own reckless behavior, about the nature of the honor given to the martyrs and the respect owed towards the confessors, I cannot further keep silence. My problem is that too much of saying nothing will result in danger both for the laity as well as for ourselves also.

[1]See also *Unit. eccl.* 4–5.

65

2 Ought we not to fear the danger from an affronted Lord when certain of the presbyters are claiming for themselves the total authority that never ever was claimed by their predecessors? They are acting with insults and contempt for the presiding bishop, neither mindful of the gospel nor their own rank. They are not considering the judgment of the Lord that is destined to come, nor the bishop who for the moment presides over them.

2.1 I wish they would not keep making these claims for self- justification over the wrecked downfall of the salvation of our brothers! I would then have been able to leave threats to our episcopate unnoticed and to tolerate them, just as I have always left them unnoticed and entirely tolerated them. But this is not the moment to leave them unnoticed, when our brotherhood is being led astray by certain of your own company.

While these desire to be able to win applause without any explanation of how salvation can be restored, they are instead acting prejudicially to the interests of the fallen. **2** For theirs is the supreme offence that the persecution forced them to commit. These very people who committed it know this when our Lord and Judge said: "He who shall confess me before men, even I will confess him before my Father who is in heaven; he who however shall deny me, even I will deny him" (Mt 10.32–33).[2]

Again he said: "All sins and blasphemies shall be forgiven to the sons of men. He who however will blaspheme against the Holy Spirit, he will not have forgiveness, but is guilty of an eternal sin" (Mk 3.28–29). The same point the blessed Apostle made: "You are not able to drink the chalice of the Lord and the chalice of daemons. You are not able to have communion at the table of the Lord and the table of daemons" (1 Cor 10.12). **3** He who deprives our brothers of these truths is deceiving men of the mercy of which they stand in need.

My reason is that those who are able to perform acts of true penitence for God as Father of mercy, and to make amends with

[2]See also Cyprian *Laps.* 20–26.

prayers and good works, are being lead softly astray. In consequence, they may rather perish and may fall the more, even though they might have been able to set themselves upright. For sinners, in the case of minor sins, practice penance for a reasonable period of time, and come to public confession in accordance with a program of discipline. They then regain the right of receiving communion through the imposition of hands of the bishop and clergy. But at the present time, because the persecution continues persistently, this is not possible. They are being admitted to receiving communion, and the offering is made in their name, though peace has not yet been restored to the Church.

They have not yet done penance, they have not yet made their public confession, and the bishop and the clergy have not yet laid hands on them. Yet the Eucharist is granted to them even though it is written: "He who eats the bread or drinks the chalice of the Lord unworthily will be guilty of the body and blood of the Lord" (1 Cor 11.27).[3]

3.1 But in this instance those who have failed to keep the law of Scripture are not the guilty ones.[4] It is those who preside but who do not put these things forward for the brothers' consideration. The latter should be able to be so instructed by those who preside, they may do everything accompanied by God's fear, and following closely the practice given and laid down by him. **2** Furthermore, they are exposing the blessed martyrs to ill will, and are setting the glorious servants of God against God's sacred bishop. Consequently, these martyrs, precisely because they were mindful of our position, directed letters to me. These letters sought that their own petitions be examined and reconciliation to be granted only after our Mother Church experienced the resumption of peace as a result of the Lord's mercy, and when God's protecting power had allowed us to return to his Church.

---

[3]See also Cyprian *Laps.* 15.

[4]"Guilty ones" and the "law of Scripture" refer to the fallen who have not confessed Christ before men in accordance with Mt 10.32–33; see also chapter 2.3.

Despite and in the face of this provision, these people are taking for themselves[5] the place of honor that the blessed martyrs along with the confessors reserve for us [who are bishops]. They are receiving the fallen back into communion, and making the offering and administering the Eucharist to them,[6] with scant regard both for the law of the Lord and its due observance the adoption of which the selfsame martyrs command.[7] They do this before the terror of the persecution has been assuaged, before we have returned, almost before the very final decease of the martyrs themselves.[8] Even if the martyrs should desire anything more contrary to the law of the Lord, in a fevered enthusiasm for their esteemed place and considering Scripture less, they ought to be admonished by the presbyters and deacons who are ministering to their needs, just as was always done in the past.

4.1 Accordingly God's examination of us does not cease its rebuking of us neither by night nor by day. Besides visions of the night, throughout the day also boys of an innocent time of life here with us are filled with the Holy Spirit, who see in ecstasy with their eyes, and hear and speak those things by means of which the Lord deigns to warn and instruct us. You will hear everything when the Lord who ordered my withdrawal causes my return to you.

2 Meanwhile, certain among you who are thoughtless and unwary, and inflamed with zeal, who have no consideration for mankind or rather no consideration about their fearing God, should

---

[5]"Taking upon themselves the . . . honor" = *sublato honore*. Clarke's "sweeping aside the honour" comes from his adopting the variant reading *ablato honore*; see Clarke, *Letters of St Cyprian*, 1.95 from the Münich *ms*; see G. F. Diercks, ed., *Sancti Cypriani Episcopi Epistulae* (Turnhout: Brepols. 1994), Part 3.1, 95.

[6]Note that the presbyters were thus following traditional practice witnessed in Eusebius; see n. 3 to Cyprian *Ep.* 15.1.2

[7]No doubt the martyrs do hold to "the law of the Lord and its due observance" but whether they were prepared to follow Cyprian in interpreting Mt 16:18 in Cyprian's precise sense is a mute question.

[8]This raises the question whether the martyr need actually to die rather than suffer physically in order to absolve.

know that if they will persist in this behavior, I may use that cautionary reminder that the Lord is ordering me to use. I will in other words temporarily prohibit them from offering the sacrifice. Then in the future they will have to plead their case before our good selves, before the confessors themselves, and before a general gathering of the laity. But that will only be when we are, with the Lord's permission, in a position to be gathered again into the bosom of Mother Church.

I have composed a letter on this subject to the martyrs and confessors[9] and to the laity,[10] and both of these I have instructed to be read to you. I entreat you, dearest and most beloved brothers, to fare well always in the Lord and to be mindful of us. Farewell.

[9]Cyprian *Ep.* 15.
[10]Cyprian *Ep.* 17.

Celerinus Seeks Absolution for His Sisters

This is one of several letters preserved in Cyprian's *corpus* not written by him. It provides us with a fascinating example of the case employed by members of the laxist group and their theological grounds for martyr absolution. Why did Cyprian preserve this letter of an opponent? Undoubtedly because, from his point of view, its author, the young Celerinus, did return to the Church over which Cyprian presided, and as a confessor was ordained reader with the hope of his progressing when old enough to the presbyterate, see *Ep.* 39. Thus Celerinus became a model of submission by a confessor to episcopal authority after past waywardness.

Written from Rome by Celerinus, himself a confessor, around April AD 250, he writes to Lucianus at Carthage, *antistes et minister* of the Church of the Martyrs (3.1), asking for absolution for his sisters Numeria and Candida, each of whom provide examples of different ways of falling in persecution. The picture that Celerinus presents is of a corporate group dispensing absolution on their collective authority, and not as the individual act of any one of them (3.2). Celerinus sends his request to Lucianus who is "bishop" or "high priest (*antistes*)" of the group, but the decision for which he may wish has to be put to all the "most holy martyrs (*martyres sanctissimos*)" who are called "Lords (*Domini*)."

Celerinus to Lucianus

1.1 I am happy and sad, my Lord and brother, that I should write to you this letter. I am happy for the reason that you are being held for the sake of the name of our Lord and Savior Jesus Christ, in other words that you have confessed his name before the magistrates of this world.[1] I am sad however because, from the time in which I

---

[1] "Before the magistrates of this world" = *Penes magistratos huius mundi* = the five commissioners who supervised the local sacrifices at Carthage and who examined and issued certificates of sacrifice (*libelli*).

escorted you to the harbor,[2] I have never been able to receive your letters.

In other words, I am now in a way weighed down by two kinds of sorrow, because I gained the knowledge[3] that Montanus, the brother whom we share, is to come from the prison to me from you, and still you gave me no indication concerning your safety, or what was the state of affairs with you. But this is how it usually turns out for the servants of God, most of all those who stand fast in their confession of Jesus Christ.

2 Of course I know that each and every such person does not give his attention to the affairs of this present age such as they are, since he is hoping for a heavenly crown. Thus I have said that possibly you have forgotten to write to me. If I would be worthy to hear you call "Celerinus" from the lowest depths of your prison, I would speak to you as your brother. But since I am also in the full flower my confession, I will mention also my brother martyrs[4] far more ancient than me, as I mentioned in my letter that their ancient bond of Christian love remains now with me so that they are my own family.

3 I seek however from the Lord, dearest, that before you shall be washed in your sacred blood for the name of our Lord Jesus Christ, my letter will catch up with you in this world. I mean, if it will catch you, you will write in reply. So may he crown you whose name you have confessed. I believe, though, even if we will not see each other in this world, we will nevertheless embrace in the future world in the presence of Christ. Pray that I should be worthy and be crowned with your number.

---

[2]"I escorted you to the harbor" = *te deduxi*. I follow Clarke, *The Letters of St Cyprian*, 1.319, n. 5 who points out: "It was a standard courtesy to escort travellers down to the harbour and there to wait with them until favourable winds blew."

[3]Clarke, *Letters of St Cyprian*, 1.103 translates "you were aware" reading *sciebas* for *sciebam*, which I follow here from the Dierck's edition. Celerinus' rough and ungrammatical Latin at this point has been generally subjected to tidying up by more linguistically adept scribes.

[4]See also below, section 4.1.

2.1 You should know that we are found in the Great Tribulation.[5] If you were now present with me, I would keep calling to mind your acts of love from of old by day and by night. God alone knows it. For this reason I am making my request that you might make a sign of approval to my petition and grieve with me in the death of my sister who had fallen in this devastation against Christ.

For she offered her sacrifice and provoked our Lord to anger, as it seems quite evident to us. Weeping by day and by night for what she did, on the joyful day of Easter, I spent days abounding in tears in sackcloth and ashes. I continue to do so right up until today, while there is still the aid of our Lord Jesus Christ and consanguinity with him[6] through you and through my Lords,[7] who are destined to be crowned. By these acts of contrition, you are asked, along with your fellow martyrs, to provide a means of rescue for such persons shipwrecked by such an act of sacrilege. **2** I remember from your Christian affection of old that you would grieve with all the others for my sisters whom you know well: I mean Numeria and Candida.

[5]Clarke, *Letters of St Cyprian*, 1.104 translates *in magna tribulatione constitutum scias* as: "I must tell you that I am in the greatest distress." *Tribulatio* is unusual in classical Latin and not listed in the New Oxford Latin Dictionary. It is used in Tertullian *Adv. Jud.* 11; Augustine *Enarrat. Ps.* 125.2; Jerome *Ep.* 108.18. I have translated *tribulatio* therefore as a reference to the persecution as an apocalyptic event (the Great Tribulation), in which the Church of the Martyrs believed that they were participating, see Lucianus *Ep.* 22.1.1. Thus the persecution is in fact the Tribulation during which Antichrist will come and attempt to destroy the saints.

[6]*Pietas* can mean "filial duty" or "respect" or "dutifulness," but is also used of "consanguinity" in family or religious ties; see Justinian (Ulpian) *Dig.* 37.15.1.2: "If a son abuses the mother or father (*si filius matrem aut patrem contumeliis adficit*) or lays hands in sacrilege upon them (*uel impias manus eis infert*) . . . the prefect of the city (*praefectus urbis*) should punish (. . . *uindicat*) this crime that relates to the obligation of their public family tie (*delictum ad publicam pietatem pertinens*)." The point here is to stress the ecclesial character of the martyrs as a group mediating the grace of absolution.

[7]It seems clear from this passage that the martyrs are called *domini* (Lords), as is Lucianus in chapter 1.1 (*domine frater*), because they will reign with the Lord Christ and receive their crowns from him. Thus they can judge and absolve the fallen without reference to the bishop. For a discussion of this title, see Clarke, *Letters of St Cyprian*, 1.317, n. 2.

We ought to watch over their sin, for they are part of our brother-hood.

For I believe that Christ, yes Christ, will grant their pardon through you his martyrs who make the request, because they are penitent, and because of the good works which they perform towards our fellow members who are exiles. Those exiles have come from you, from whom you would have heard of their good works.

3.1 I have heard that you have assumed ministerial functions over those who wear the flowers of martyrdom.[8] You bring them the favor of your blessing![9] Resume the prayers that were always your petitions for them, even if you repose in the earth.[10] You have prayed "for his name sake" to be sent to prison, which has now happened to you, just as it is written: "May the Lord grant you according to your heart's desire" (Gen 28.13). And now, I have recognized, you have been made God's high priest over them, in other words their sacred minister.[11] **2** I request accordingly, my Lord, and I seek through our Lord Jesus Christ that you would refer my plea to the rest of your brothers and colleagues and my Lords, and that you would petition whoever of your company will be first crowned. I ask them that they

---

[8]"Flowers of martyrdom" = *floridii* which is a word (*floridius*) from *floridus/flo-ridi*, and coined as a club name for the congregation of the martyrs and confessors over which Lucianus presided; see Clarke, *Letters of St Cyprian*, 1.324, n. 21.

[9]"You bring them the blessing of your favour" = *O te felicem. Felix* = "fruit bear-ing," and then "auspicious," "favorable," or "propitious"; see Virgil *Aen.* 1.330: "May you be auspicious (*sis felix*), and, whoever you may be, may you relieve our toil (*nostrum leves, quaecumque, laborem*)."

[10]Celerinus has already ascribed a ministry to Lucianus that is awesome and brings blessing (*felix*). Here he is asked to resume the solemn prayers of his petition for the fallen lapsed when in heaven.

[11]"God's high priest" or even "bishop" = *antistes*, used in a pagan sense for a high priest who oversees a temple; see Cicero *Dom.* 39.104: *antistes caerimoniarum et sacrorum*. It translates literally Justin Martyr's προεστώς, meaning bishop as in *1 Apol.* 67, as also in Cyprian *Ep.* 59.18.3: "May they seek for themselves from their presiding priest the outpouring of prayers and petitions (*petant fundi pro se preces atque ora-tiones antistitis*), choosing this to the pouring out of the blood of their sacred bishop (*quam ipsi fundant sanguinem sacerdotis*)."

will forgive the sin, such as it is, of our sisters Numeria and Candida.[12] I have always given to the former sister the name of Etecusa, as God is our witness, because she counted out bribes on her own behalf so that she should not sacrifice.[13]

But she was only seen to have ascended as far as the Three Fates[14] and she came down again from that point. I know therefore that she has not sacrificed. Their case has now been heard, and those who preside have ordered them to continue as they are until a bishop is appointed. But forgive as far as you do through your prayers and petitions, since you are friends but also witnesses of Christ, you who can grant forgiveness to all.

4.1 I ask, therefore, my Lord, dearest Lucianus, that you remember me, and that you grant me my petition. So Christ is handing on to you that holy wreath of victory which is yours not only for your confession, but also for your holiness, for which you have always run the race and have been an example and witness for the saints. Please make your representations concerning this matter to all those who are my Lords your brothers, that my sisters may receive your aid.

For you ought to know this, my Lord and brother, that I am not the only one to make this request, but also Statius and Severianus, and all the confessors who have come here to Rome from Carthage. My sisters went down to the harbour to meet them, and conducted them into the city, where they have ministered to the sixty-five confessors, and they have cared for them in every way. For they are in their company.

---

[12]Here we have quite clearly absolution as the corporate act of the whole body of confessors, albeit by the grace of the one of their number who has actually laid down his life.

[13]Her real name, Numeria, was too reminiscent of her sin because she had "paid out bribes (*numerauit*)" for a *libellus* from the magistrate to say that she had sacrificed. Etecusa was, therefore, her new name given in order not to remind her of her sin.

[14]These were Clotho, Lachesis, and Nemesis, who stood on the north side of the Rostra near to the Curia or Senate House in the Forum at Rome. See Pliny *Nat.* 34.11.22 and Clarke, *Letters of St Cyprian*, 1.327, n. 26.

2 I ought not to burden your sacred heart any more, when I know that you are ready and willing to perform this act. Macarius greets you with his sisters Cornelia and Emerita, who are joyful for the abundant flowers of your confession, but also for those of all the brothers. Saturninus also greets you, who also is one who has wrestled with the Devil, and who has bravely confessed the name of Christ. He was also in prison when he bravely confessed though tortured with the claw.[15] Here with me, he also petitions and entreats to an extent too great to describe.

Your brothers greet you, Calpurnius and Maria and all the holy brothers. Would you also be obliged in this connection to understand that I have written this also to my Lords and your brothers.

I therefore request that, if you consider it fit, to read this letter to them.

---

[15]Saturninus is a confessor, like Celerinus and Aurelius, all of whom were released after torture. Cyprian will write in justification of their ordinations as readers in *Ep.* 38–39. Such examples show that the Decian legislation was designed not to punish with execution, but to discipline and reform so as to produce conformity.

Lucianus Replies for the Corporate Body

It is to be emphasized that in this letter, as well as 21, the Latin is very ungrammatical and rough, which has made it impossible in a translation of necessity in grammatical English to do justice to the rustic character of the style. Lucianus greets Celerinus as a confessor ("Lord"), who will reign with Christ. He also identifies Decius as forerunner of Antichrist (1.1). Lucianus records the martyr Paulus' commission to him to absolve. The persecution is considered the Great Tribulation of apocalyptic writings that prepares for Christ's Second Advent (2.1).

The martyrs as a corporate group issue a decree of absolution in the name of Paulus for all dear sisters including those of Celerinus. According to Paulus' command, Cyprian's council is to proceed to reconcile them (2.2).

Lucianus to Lord Celerinus,
(if I have been found worthy to be called his holy colleague in
Christ)

1.1 I have received your letter, my Lord brother most beloved, in which you grieved me so much that as a result of your grief I almost lost the sense of joy. Here was a letter for which I had yearned for so long a time to read, in which I was found worthy to receive my mention. Thank you for the favor of your great humility of one of whom I was delighted to read of him writing to me that you should say: "If I have been found worthy to be named as your brother"—of a man like me who with reverential fear confessed the name of God in the presence of the petty officials.[1]

---

[1] The committee of assessors; see Introduction, §2.1.

But you, by God's will, have not only made your confession but also you have terrified the great serpent himself, the military organizer for the Antichrist.[2] By those words and inspired utterances with which you did this, I know that you have lived as a lover of faith and jealous for Christ's discipline. You have the vitality, the joy, of someone who has recently turned the tables on him.

2 Now, my dearest friend, you are to be assigned to the ranks of the martyrs. You clearly have wished for us to bear the burden of your letter, in which you make a serious suggestion regarding your sisters. Would to God it were possible for it to happen for their sakes that we could make mention of them without the great sin they have committed! How quickly would we commit ourselves to tears for them as we do now!

2.1 You are to be informed what we have resolved on this matter. While the blessed martyr Paulus was still "in the body," he summoned me and said to me: "Lucianus, I tell you before Christ that if anyone will petition you for reconciliation after I am called to heaven, grant it in my name." But all of us also, whom the Lord has deigned to summon to him in this Great Tribulation, have all addressed a letter by common agreement for reconciliation for everyone universally.[3]

You will see, brother, how we have decided, in part on what Paulus commanded me, and in part all of us together in our own right, in those circumstances that existed even before this Tribulation intensified. When we were ordered by the command of the Emperor to

---

[2]"Camp organizer for the Antichrist" = *metatorem Antichristi*. I find it difficult to translate with Clarke "forerunner," however felicitous this may sound. *Metator* means someone who measures or marks out a military camp in preparation for war; see Cicero *Phil.* 11.12 and 14.10. There may be a reference here to Rev 20.7–8, where Satan is released from his prison, marshals Gog and Magog for war, and surrounds the camp of the saints. Lucianus refers to the commissioners as "minor officials," like Clerinus' "magistrates of this present age (*magistratus huius mundi*)" in *Ep.* 21.1.1. It seems that by this term Lucianus is identifying the figure behind them as Decius, serpent and forerunner of the Antichrist. See also Clarke, *Letters of St Cyprian*, 1.331, n. 5.

[3]Lucianus is clear referring here to Cyprian (Lucianus) *Ep.* 23.

be killed by means of hunger and thirst, and we were then confined in two cells, of course he achieved nothing by making us hunger and thirst. Then there was the heat from being packed tightly together that was so unbearable, which no one could stand. But now we have been transferred into the light of day.

2 And so, dearest brother, greet Numeria and Candida, to whom according to the commandment of Paulus and of the other martyrs, we grant reconciliation. Their names I now append: In the name of Bassus martyred in a debtor's prison, of Mappalicus under interrogation, of Fortunio in prison. Paulus under interrogation, Fortunata, Victorinus, Victor, Herennius, Credula, Hereda, Donatus, Firmus, Venustus, Fructus, Iulia, Martialis and Ariston, who, when God willed, were killed by starvation in prison. You will hear that we are destined to share their destiny within days.

Now we are confined for a second time for eight days, on the eighth day of which I have written this letter to you. For also before the eight days, for five days we received severally a measure of modest quantity, of bread and water. For this reason, brother, I make my petition just as I am doing so here. It will be effective when the Lord gives peace to the Church. They should have the peace of reconciliation according to the commandment of Paul and our own resolution, when the case has been set out before the bishop and public confession has been made.[4] Not only these sisters should have the peace of reconciliation, but also those whom you know are near to our heart.

3.1 All my colleagues together greet you. You greet the confessors of the Lord who are there with you, whose names you have specified amongst whom is Saturninus and his companions, but also my colleague, and Maris, Collecta and Emerita, Calpurnius and Maria,

---

[4]It remains a moot point as to what extent Lucianus envisages the episcopal right to re-examine the case, as opposed to simply hearing the explanation of the martyrs' decision on the case. He insists that Paulus gave a "praeceptum," which, presumably, was to the bishop; see also *Ep.* 23 that follows.

Sabina, Spesina, and the sisters Januaria, Dativa, Donata. **2** We greet Satyrus with his family, Bassianus and all the clergy, Uranius, Alexius, Quintianus, Colonica. I make my petition for everyone else whose names I have not in my great exhaustion been able to write. Therefore they ought to pardon me. I pray that Alexius and Getulicus and the brothers Argentarius and their sisters will fare well. My sisters Januaria and Sophia greet you, whom I commit to your care.

Lucianus Grants General Absolution by the Martyrs

This Letter was the response of the confessors to Cyprian's respectful attempt (*Ep.* 15) to control the issue of *libelli pacis*, and to modify through diplomacy their claim to an autonomous ministry, see *Ep.* 27.2.1.[1] The Letter claims this authority for the confessors and martyrs as a corporate group, according to whom the faithful should have peace with the martyrs, and not, as Cyprian would have it, the martyrs' peace with their bishop. The style adopted is that of a formal council deciding its *forma,* or procedure.

The Confessors in General to Cyprian, Holy Pope[2]

Be it known to you that we all together have granted reconciliation to those for whom the balance of the account has been drawn up on your behalf,[3] following what has been brought to us for a verdict,[4]

---

[1] See Perpetua's dream in *Acta Perpetua* 13.

[2] "Holy pope"= an ancient title for a metropolitan bishop = *papas*, originally a child's term for "father." See also J. Moorhead, "Papa as 'Bishop of Rome,'" *JEH* 36.3 (1985): 337–38.

[3] "An account balance has been drawn up for you" = *in te ratio constiterit.* For *ratio* in this sense, see Justinian (Ulpian) Dig. 37.15.1: "An account balance for the performance of family duty should be drawn up even in the case of soldiers (*etiam militibus pietatis ratio ad parentes constare debet*)"; Pliny *Ep.* 2.4.4: "In your case (*in te*) . . . an account balance will easily be drawn up because of my kindness (*facile ei [sc. meae liberalitati] ratio constabit*), even though it is excessive (*etiamsi modum excesserit*)."

[4] "Following what has been brought to us for a verdict" = *post commissum*; cf. Cicero *Verr.* 3.61.142: . . . that he had decreed (*istum statuisse*) in his province (*in prouincia sua*) that a legal proceeding of which his reputation was the subject *(existimationis suae iudicium)* was not to be brought before anyone outside his staff (*extra cohortem suam committendum fuisse nemini*)."

and we wish that this formal procedure[5] be brought by you to the notice of other bishops. We pray you to be reconciled with the holy martyrs. Lucian has signed in the presence of an exorcist and a reader from the clergy.

---

[5]"This formal procedure" = *hanc formam*. I do not follow here Clarke's translation as "decree" but prefer "procedure," as in Quintillian *Inst.* 5.13.5: ". . . judges who are not bound by a fixed procedure for delivering their verdict (*iudices qui nulla certa pronuntiandi forma tenentur*)." I take the sense to be that the confessors are laying down a procedure, namely that they examine and produce their verdict with a balance of account (*ratio constat*) of the sins and their absolution, and the bishops are to take note and receive those thus absolved into communion. Cyprian, as a good bureaucrat, will read into this statement an interpretation most favorable to his own case (*Ep.* 27.2.2).

Caldonius Consults Cyprian on Difficult Cases

Clarke argues convincingly that Caldonius' Letter and Cyprian's reply were exchanged before he had received *Letter* 23 from the Confessors.[1] The letter therefore is to be dated midsummer AD 250. Thus Caldonius, who is also a bishop, states his grounds for absolution before he and his fellow confessors have made it clear that they require their *libelli* to be followed by readmission to communion or reconciliation (*pax*). Indeed, he is, by the example that he cites, showing cracks in any uniform policy towards the fallen given that there were so many honorable exceptions.

We have here the example of those who were challenged to sacrifice a second time, even though they had done so once. Perhaps this was because their spectacular and quite public penitence attracted the attention of the civil authorities, who did not take kindly to the disciplinary purpose of the Edict being thus thwarted. But under second examination, they stood firm but were punished with exile rather than torture. Then there was the lady Bona whose hands were physically pressed to make the sacrifice against her will (1.1). Could Cyprian continue to insist that such as these must await the pleasure of his future episcopal council? Caldonius emerges as a highly moderate confessor wishing to submit to Cyprian and his presbyteral council that he assumes can simply resolve the issue in his favor (1.2). The authors of *Ep.* 23 were to make larger claims, and Cyprian must have cherished this moderate letter justifying, for the most part, his own position from one confessor in his dossier.

Cyprian replies (*Ep.* 25) commending Caldonius and asking him to send the enclosed copies of five letters (*Ep.* 15–19) asking him to circulate these generally. *Letter* 26 is then addressed to his presbyters and deacons enclosing the Caldonius correspondence as his answer to Lucianus in *Letter* 23.

---

[1]Clarke, *Letters of St Cyprian*, 1.340.

Blessed Caldonius to Cyprian and His Fellow Presbyters Assembled at Carthage

1.1 The compelling circumstance of the present time means that we should not grant reconciliation without good cause. In consequence I am under obligation to write to you because there are those who, when examined a second time after they had already offered sacrifice, were forced into exile. Accordingly, they seem to me to have washed out their previous offence because they yielded up estates and houses and, performing penance, they follow Christ.

It is also true of the Felix who acted as assistant to the presbyterate in the time of Decimus.[2] He lay next to me in chains (I know that Felix well!). He, and Victoria his wife, and Lucius, forced into exile, have abandoned their estates that now the treasury holds in possession.

Moreover, in the same persecution a woman by name Bona was dragged by her husband and forced to sacrifice. She therefore did not betray her conscience immorally. It was others who were clasping her hands so that it was they and not her who performed the sacrifice. She herself was speaking against their act: "I have not done it, you have done it," in consequence of which she has been forced into exile. **2** All of these have petitioned for reconciliation from me with the words: "We have recovered the faith which we lost, we have now made public confession of Christ by the performance of an act of penitence."

Although I think that they ought to receive reconciliation, nevertheless I have let the issue rest on your decision so that I might not seem to have made an assumption without good cause. If you have resolved anything by the decision of your joint council, communicate it to me in writing.[3] Greetings to our brothers. We also to yours. I pray that you blessed ones will fare well.

[2]Decimus could have been Caldonius' ecclesiastical predecessor and Felix a layman or deacon standing in for the presbyterate; cf. Clarke, *Letters of St Cyprian*, 1.347, n. 4.

[3]Clearly, Caldonius knows nothing of Cyprian's own situation in flight; nor does he know that a council is not planned until after the persecution has ended.

Cyprian Replies to the Claims of Lucianus

In August or September AD 250 Cyprian wrote this letter to a Rome without a bishop following the death of Fabian. He had subsequent to writing his conciliatory letter to the martyrs,[1] received *Ep.* 23 from Lucianus. He regards this as a new development, and as a "mutiny (*seditio*)," within "our province (*nostra prouincia*)" (3.1).

He enclosed the correspondence with Caldonius as well as the letter of Lucianus, with the intention of gaining support from the Roman community. With bureaucratic cunning and skill he studiously avoids the theological claims of the Church of the Martyrs to be an ecclesial and corporate body in which one member can act for all. In consequence, he can accuse Lucianus of duplicity in writing letters in the names of Paulus, Saturninus, or of Mappalicus after their deaths.[2]

Cyprian continues this bureaucratic stratagem in 2.2 where he interprets Lucianus' edict as allowing nevertheless for episcopal consideration of cases that the former clearly believes that he has already decided.[3]

Cyprian to the Presbyters and Deacons,
His Brothers Dwelling in Rome

1.1 Further to my previous letter to you,[4] dearest brothers, something else took place that must not be concealed from you. That letter contained a description of our conduct, and the declaration of an account of our policy and its management, however inadequate.

I refer to the fact that our brother Lucianus, himself one of the confessors, has inadvisably embarked upon a certain course

---

[1]Cyprian *Ep.* 15.
[2]Cyprian **Ep.* 25.
[3]See also Cyprian *Ep.* 15, n. 3.
[4]Cyprian **Ep.* 20.

of action. He is no doubt fervid in faith and strong in courage, but without strong claims to literacy regarding the Lord's commands. For some time previously he had set himself up as a figure of authority, in consequence of which certificates, written under his hand, were granted *en bloc* to large numbers under the name of Paulus. This was despite the fact that the martyr Mappalicus, a cautious and respectful man, mindful of the law and discipline, composed no letters contrary to the gospel. He was merely moved by his family duty for his mother and sister who had fallen in ordering the granting of reconciliation.

Also Saturninus, until now locked in prison after torture, issued no letters of this kind. **2** In truth Lucianus continued granting general certificates written in his own handwriting in his name, not only for as long as Paulus was in prison, but even after his decease he kept on with the same practice under the latter's name. His assertion was that this had been commanded him by the latter, also being ignorant that one should obey one's master rather than a fellow servant. Many certificates have been granted in the handwriting of this same Lucianus in the name of Aurelius who, on the verge of manhood, suffered torture. His justification was Aurelius' illiteracy.

2.1 In order to place some block on this proceeding, I composed a letter to them that I sent to you under cover of a previous mailing, in which I did not shrink from demanding and urging that they might hold to the ruling principle of the law and of the gospel.[5] After that letter—such was his moderation and restraint!—the same Lucianus wrote a letter in the name of the confessors in general, through which he became responsible for the disintegration of almost every bond of faith and fear of God and commandment of the Lord, as well as the sanctity and firm foundation of the gospel.

For he has written in the name of all that they all have granted reconciliation, and that they wish this "formal procedure" be brought to the notice of other bishops by me. I have sent you a copy of this

[5]Mt 16.16–18; Jn 20.21–22; see also Cyprian *Unit. eccl.* 4–5.

letter.[6] **2** It is clearly added: "to those for whom the balance of the account has been drawn up on your behalf, following what has been brought to us for a verdict." This process fans the flames of ill will even greater against us so that when we begin to hear and to scrutinize individual cases, we are seen to deny to many what they are all now boasting that they have received from the martyrs and confessors.[7]

3.1 In direct consequence the beginning of this mutiny came to birth. For in several cities throughout our province[8] the mob has assaulted presiding bishops. The bishops have been compelled to make immediately available the reconciliation that the mob kept bleating had been granted to all at the same time by the martyrs and confessors.[9] They have terrorized their bishops and forced them into submission. Those bishops, admittedly, hardly showed great strength of mind in resisting them, or the courage of an unshakable faith. **2** With us here also unruly elements, which in the past were only with difficulty under our control and kept waiting for our judgment, have been enflamed by this letter and have blazed up as if ignited by some burning firebrands. They have begun to demand that a reconciliation be granted under extortion.

I have sent to you a copy of the letter that I have composed to the clergy. But also I have sent to you for you to read both letters, one of which Caldonius my colleague has written to me indicative of his integrity and good faith, and the second as my reply. I have sent you furthermore copies of the letter of Celerinus, a good and

[6]Cyprian (Lucianus) *Ep.* 23.

[7]Note that Cyprian is clearly admitting here the interpretation of Lucianus' words that he is seeking here to deny. See the introduction to this letter and Cyprian (Lucianus) *Ep.* 23.

[8]Note here that Cyprian claims that his diocese is his "province (*prouincia*)" and thus assimilates episcopal to proconsular authority, against which any resistance is "rebellion" or "mutiny (=*seditio*)"; see also Cyprian *Ep.* 48.3.2

[9]Cyprian continues to imply that this was merely an accidental consequence of Lucianus' intention rather than its proper fulfillment, so that he can attempt to make of the former's bare words some provision for the role of the bishop as final judge.

unshakeable confessor, which he wrote to the same Lucianus, also what Lucianus replied to him.[10] As a result, you will find out that we have striven to be watchful concerning everything, and you will become aware from the truth itself how temperate and careful the confessor Celerinus is, and restrained by his subservience and respect for our religion.

Lucianus, on the other hand, is quite illiterate, as I have said, in his understanding of the sacred text, and unrestrained in his readiness to leave a legacy of hatred directed against our moderate policy. **3** The Lord has said that the nations are washed in baptism in the name of the Father, and Son, and Holy Spirit, and in baptism past sins are forgiven (Mt 28.19). But Lucianus, ignorant of the precept and the law, commands that reconciliation be granted and sins forgiven in the name of Paul. He also says that this command comes to him from someone else, just as you will notice in the letter of the same Lucianus addressed to Celerinus, in which no reflection is given on the fact that martyrs do not make the gospel, but that martyrs are made through the gospel.

Thus Paul the apostle, whom the Lord has called the vessel of his election, (Acts 9.15) explains in his letter with the words: "I marvel that thus so quickly you have changed from him who has called you in grace to another gospel, which is not another: unless it is because there are some who would disturb you and wish to overturn the gospel of Christ. But even though an angel should proclaim from heaven otherwise contrary to what we have proclaimed to you, let him be accursed. Just us we have said before, even now a second time I say: 'if anyone proclaim to you contrary to what you have received, let him be accursed'" (Gal 1.6–9).

4.1 Indeed the arrival of your letter was timely, which I received addressed to the clergy, the same which the blessed confessors Moyses, Maximus, Nicostratus and the rest sent to Saturninus and Aurelius and all their group, in which the full vigour of the gospel

[10]Cyprian *Ep.* 21 and **Ep.* 22.

and the unshaken discipline of the Lord's law is included.[11] What you say comes much to our aid as we struggle also against the assault of those who bear us ill, resting on the support of the total strength of our faith.

In consequence, providentially, we have had a short solution to the problem. You have already resolutely declared to us that your opinion supports ours and is in total agreement with the law of the gospel, and that before you were in receipt of the letter that I most recently sent you.[12] I pray that you, dearest and most cherished brothers, will always fare well.

[11]Clarke, *Letters of St Cyprian*, 1.361, n. 27: "The purport of this letter (now lost) can be discerned in *Letter* 30.3.1 ff."

[12]See Cyprian *Ep.* 20.

Cyprian, in Response to an Anonymous Document

In this letter we become aware of how loaded the Cyprianic *corpus* is with correspondents who at least eventually will agree with his position. Here we have expressed Cyprian's reply to his critics, who were a formidable movement and difficult for him to crush. There is no introductory salutation since he does not know to whom or where to address this reply.

He mentions two letters, the first of which comes from a group of the fallen lapsed who demand immediate reentry to the Church (1). The second is from another such group who wish to submit to doing penance (2). Cyprian does not make it clear whether the first lapsed group claimed the support of the martyrs and their certificates of reconciliation, and whether it was as part of their ecclesial community that they were making their demand. He writes as if a group of fallen Christians considered themselves to be the Church and to grant reconciliation, without any martyrs included in their ranks, whose sufferings could alone atone for their fall (1.2).

The second certainly did contain martyr confessors, but acted in accordance with his view that his decision as bishop was the final one, and the certificate was therefore merely a request (2.1).

Cyprian makes it clear (1.1) that his divine law (*lex diuina*) that regulates church order is in fact Mt 16.18–19. His words here however imply that each individual bishop over his own diocese exercises the office of Peter, which is not confined therefore to the bishop of Rome alone.

1.1 In setting out the place of honor for the bishop and the ruling principle of his Church in the gospel, our Lord (whose precepts we ought to hold in awe and to observe) speaks these words to Peter: "I say to you, you are Peter, and upon that rock will I build my Church, and the gates of the underworld will not conquer it, and to you I will give the keys of the kingdom of the heavens, and those things that you bind on earth will have been bound even in the heavens, and whatever you loose upon earth will have been loosed even in the heavens" (Mt 16.18–19).

From this principle, the ordination logically follows of each bishop in temporal succession, and thus the ruling principle of the Church. According to that ruling principle, the Church is founded on the bishops, and every movement of the Church is steered through the governance of those same presiding bishops.

2 Since we have what is founded by divine law, I am amazed that certain anonymous people have been willing to write to me with so bold a presumption as to publish a letter in the name of the Church. They have so done on their own initiative against the principle that the Church has its basis in the bishop and in the clergy, and in all who remain constant in the confession of the faith.

It is out of the question that the compassion of the Lord and his unvanquished power should allow that a band of fallen lapsed could be called the Church. After all, it is written: "God is not of the dead but of the living" (Lk 20.38). We desire that all will be made alive, and we pray that our prayers and cries of mourning may restore them. If however certain of those who have fallen wish to become themselves the Church, and if the Church is with *them* and in *them,* all that is left is that they should receive *our* petition that they will deem *us* worthy for *them* to admit *us* to the Church.

But on the contrary, rather they, mindful of their sin, should be both submissive and peaceful and patient. They ought to appease God's anger, and not concoct a letter in the name of the Church when they should discover that it is rather for them to write *to* the Church.

2.1 But also recently certain from amongst the fallen have written to me humbly and gently, and shaking with fear, but holding God in awe. These have always acted with a high degree of religious devotion in the Church, with just pride, and they have never claimed credit from the Lord for their work, knowing that he has said: "And when you have done all these things, say: 'We are superfluous servants because we have done what we were obliged to do'" (Lk 17.10).

The latter in the light of these reflections have written to me with a petition. They recognize their sin and are conducting a true penance, even though they have received a certificate from the martyrs. Nor do they approach reconciliation haphazardly or with unseasonable haste, but they are awaiting our presence, saying that such reconciliation would be far sweeter for them when it can be received from us when we can be present.

The God who has deigned to reveal what servants of this kind and quality merit from his goodness is my witness of the extent to which I congratulate them.

2 I have recently received these letters, and I have read another that you have written. I request that whoever you are who have now sent me these letters make your requests specific, and that you add your names to the document, and that you forward the document with those individual names to me. For it is important to know first to whom it is that I should have to reply. Then I shall write back addressing the individual points that you have written, taking the moderate position in our course of action. I wish you, brothers, to fare well and to exercise conduct that is peaceful and at rest in accordance with the discipline of the Lord.[1]

---

[1] A reference to the violence of some of the fallen in seeking readmission to communion; see also Cyprian *Laps.* 16 and *Ep.* 59.2–3.

The Confessor Aurelius Is Ordained Reader

Here we meet with the first of Cyprian's ordinations of confessors who had stood fast but escaped the death of final martyrdom. In so acting, he studiously avoided any mention of an alternative theology of ordination according to which, if a confessor had physically suffered more than the kind of beating appropriate to a slave or schoolboy, he had no need for imposition of hands for the presbyterate or diaconate.[1]

Cyprian does not lose the opportunity here of extending the concept of martyrdom beyond merely physical suffering to exile and confiscation of goods, while stressing that Aurelius comes in both categories (1.2).

Although he proposes ordination to a minor order of reader, he leaves open the future possibility of their becoming presbyters, but only through his approved route (2.1). Thus he proposed by his acts to suppress any kind of ecclesial order that was not under episcopal control. Paradoxically, he partly grants the case for confessorship as a self-authenticating ministry since he has to apologize for circumventing the usual procedure for normal ordination, namely the consent of clergy and people (1.1–2).

Cyprian to the Presbyters and Deacons, and to the Holy General Laity

1.1 In the ordination of clerics, dearest brothers, we are accustomed to consult you, and to appraise the moral behavior and merits of individual cases in common council. But we cannot wait on human testimonies when God's vote in favor has already taken place. **2** Aurelius our brother, a distinguished youth, has already won the Lord's approval and is dear to God, until now tender in years, but

---

[1]Pseudo Hippolytus, *Trad. ap.* 9; see also A. Brent, "Cyprian and the question of *ordinatio per confessionem*," StPatr 36 (2001): 327–32.

advanced in years through the merit of his courage and faith, less in what is natural at his age, but greater in honor. He has been a contester in a double athletic contest,[2] he has been twice a confessor and twice won glory through the victory of his confession.

He was victor in the racecourse when he was sentenced to exile. He was victor when next he boxed in a tougher match only to celebrate a triumph and to be victor in a fight that cost him the pain of suffering.[3] As often as the Adversary wished to challenge the servants of God, just as often Aurelius both fought as the keenest and bravest soldier and also overcame. The previous conflict, in the course of which he was being made an exile under the gaze of the few, had been as such too little an achievement. He deserved also to enter the conflict in the Forum with a courage that was more open to view, so that after finishing off the magistrates he overcame the proconsul; after suffering exile, he rose above torture.

3 It is beyond me as to what quality I should describe in him, the glory of his wounds or the modesty of his moral behavior, the courage for which he is honored with distinction or his demeanor praised by his admirers? He has matched his excellence in esteem with the humility of his submissiveness. Thus it would appear that he has been preserved, by God's intention, to be an example to everyone for their own Church discipline. The servants of God should, after making their confession, be as prominent in their morals as they were for their courageous acts in making their confession.

---

[2]The process involving both exile and then actual torture has been much discussed, for a summary of which see Clarke, *Letters of St Cyprian*, 2.181, n. 9. He may have been exiled but did not remain quiet and was too public in his proselytizing, or there may have been a deliberate policy to bring back people from exile after a suitable period in order to try once again to impose imperial *disciplina*, by enforcing the offering of pagan sacrifice.

[3]Taking my cue from the unambiguous reference to "athletic contest (*agon*)" and "in the race course (*in cursu*)," I have, unlike Clarke, *Letters of St Cyprian*, 2.52, continued the athletic references by translating *certamen* ("match"), *pugnare* ("box") and *proelium* ("fight") in their nonmilitary, athletic sense.

2.1 A person of this quality would normally merit the higher grades of clerical ordination, and greater advancements that should be calculated, not from his years, but from his merits. But meanwhile we resolve that he should begin with the office of reader, since there is nothing more suitable for a voice that has confessed God with such a glorious public proclamation than that it should resound with the divine words that are to be sung with praise.

After his sublime words that have spoken forth his witness to Christ, it is fitting that he read the gospel of Christ from whence martyrs are made. After the magistrate's dock he should approach the pulpit.[4] The former was the place where the crowd of pagans gazed on him, the latter where the brothers gaze on him. The former is where he had been listened to with the amazement of the people who stood around, the latter where he is listened to with the joy of the brotherhood.

2 This man, you are therefore informed, most beloved brothers, has been ordained by me and by my colleagues who were present.[5] For I acknowledge that you will both gladly embrace and request for as many of such men as possible to be ordained in our Church.[6] Since joy always inspires one to move quickly, and happiness cannot bear delay, Aurelius has meanwhile been reading the lesson for us on

---

[4]I translate *catasta* as "magistrates dock," even thought it usually and more strictly refers to the platform on which slaves were exposed for sale.

[5]The word "with colleagues (*collegis*)" does not imply fellow bishops in Cyprian's place of hiding as Clarke, *Letters of St Cyprian*, 2.184, n. 16 suggests, but some of the presbyters who were present who would normally join the bishop in ordaining a presbyter (Pseudo Hippolytus *Trad. ap. 7*). There the presbyters shared in the bishop's office like the Jewish presbyters did that of Moses, which is what the Latin word *collega* implies. Clarke indicates that "nowhere else does Cyprian use *ordinare* for appointing to the lower clerical orders." As pointed out in the preface to this letter, Cyprian was here emphasizing the presbyteral character of Aurelius' "ordination" to the office merely of reader to compensate him for forgoing what his confessorship entitled him according to the Church of the Martyrs, namely immediate admission to the presbyterate without an episcopal act. See also Brent, "Cyprian and the question of *ordinatio per confessionem*," 333.

[6]And not, we might add, otherwise swell the self-authenticating ministry of the Church of the Martyrs.

Sunday, that is to say he performs the ceremony of giving the peace whilst he blesses the reading.[7]

Remain constant in petitions frequently offered, and strengthen our prayers with your prayers, that the Lord's mercy may favor us, and restore soon both their priest to his people, and the reader who is a martyr along with the priest. I beseech you, dearest brothers, that you may always fare well.

[7]Clarke, *Letters of St Cyprian*, 2.53 translates "performs the ceremony of giving the peace (*auspicatus est pacem*), whilst he blesses the reading (*dum dedicat lectionem*)," as "he has given us an omen of peace to come by inaugurating his duties as reader." On p.185, n. 18 he sees the allusion to Aurelius' act presaging peace after persecution with a return to normal liturgical life in contrast to the warfare as a confessor, which I find far-fetched. I have followed here J. H. Strawley, *The Early Church and the Liturgy* (Cambridge: Cambridge University Press, 1913), 132.

Celerinus Joins Cyprian's Side and
Is Made Reader

Celerinus, as we learned in Cyprian (Celerinus) *Ep.* 21, had sought absolution from Lucianus, *antistes et minister* of the Church of the Martyrs. Here we find, like Aurelius (*Ep.* 38), he is made reader and promised advancement to the presbyterate to which his confessorship entitled him, in the eyes of Lucianus' group, by virtue of his martyr-sufferings alone. But here, in addition, we have mention of the payment that he is to receive as if he were fully one of Cyprian's presbyters. The bishop as *patronus* clearly fulfilled his obligations to his clients, with the resultant power that he thus came to possess.[1]

In 2.3 we have a clear example of Cyprian adopting the discourse of the glory of martyrdom whilst denying its sacramental power, as was the case also with Aurelius (*Ep.* 38.2.1). He will speak like Lucianus and his group in claiming that through his physical sufferings as confessor, Celerinus has a particular right to represent Christ in Church (4.1), but will insist that this is as a reader and not, at least for the moment, as a presbyter (4.2). Nevertheless, he is to receive a presbyter's income, and, when of sufficient age, to sit with the presbyteral circle at the Eucharist as *conpresbyteri* with the bishop (5.2).

*Cyprian to the Presbyters and Deacons
and to the General Laity, the Holy Brothers*

1.1 Those divine benefits must be acknowledged and embraced, most beloved brothers, by means of which the Lord has deigned to illuminate and adorn his Church in our times, by granting leave

---

[1] For bishops as patrons, see Cyprian *Ep.* 13.7 and bibliography in n. 7.

from duty[2] to his good confessors and glorious martyrs. As a consequence, those who have made so high a confession of Christ should only at a later time form the adornment of the Church's ministries. Rejoice, therefore, and be glad with us when you read our letter by which I, and my colleagues who were present, commend to you Celerinus our brother.

His glory is in his acts of courage, as well as in his moral behavior. He has been joined with our clergy, not as the result of us taking a purely human vote in his favor, but because God has revealed his worth. **2** Though Celerinus was hesitant about consenting, he felt compelled not to say no to what we were urging on him as a result of a vision by night, as well as through the admonition and exhortation of the Church herself.

The Church herself granted her permission and determined the outcome. That he should be without ecclesiastical honor was clearly not in accordance with divine law nor was it fitting for one whom the Lord had thus honored with the dignity of heavenly glory.

2.1 Celerinus was first in our time in joining the battle. He was leader of the vanguard amongst the soldiers of Christ. Amidst the savage beginnings of the persecution, he joined in combat with the leader and instigator himself of the attack. Because he overcame the adversary by his unconquerable steadfastness in this encounter, he made a path for the rest that they might overcome. He was thus a victor, not by limiting his wounds, but as one whose triumph was through long involvement in suffering, and in which he persisted in the remarkable course of his long struggle.

2 For nineteen days he was constrained by the prison's guard and chained in the stock. But though his body was placed in chains,

---

[2] "Leave from duty" = *commeatus*. Here Cyprian is suggesting that the fact that he requires them to wait till later ("only at a later time" = *postmodum*) to perform presbyteral functions ("*adornment* of the Church's ministries") is not an affront to their dignity as martyrs, as Lucianus' group might claim, but should be rather be "spun" as God acting like a general giving a soldier a leave from duty.

his spirit remained unfettered and free. His flesh was wasting away as the hunger and thirst were prolonged, but God nourished a soul that lived by faith and courage with spiritual food. He was stronger than those tortures, though he lay prostrate in the middle of being racked. Though imprisoned, he was greater than those who imprisoned him. Though prostrate on the ground, he stood higher than those who stood upright. Though overcome, he was more resistant than those who overcame him. Though he had been sentenced from the dock, he stood higher than those who sentenced him. Although his feet were shackled in the stock, the Serpent was crushed underfoot and trodden down and overcome (Gen 3.15; Lk 10.19).

3 The resplendent marks of those wounds shine in his glorious body. Their deep impressions have left clear and striking patterns in his bodily members, and in limbs that have wasted away through his long deprivation. These are great deeds, they are marvelous deeds of courageous acts for which he is praised as the brotherhood listens.

And if someone like Thomas comes forward,[3] who tends to believe less from what he only hears, there is no lack of visual evidence for him even to see what he hears (Jn 20.24–29). In the case of this servant of God, the resplendent fact of his wounds confirms his victory, and the record of those scars preserves in our memory that resplendent fact.

3.1 In the case of Celerinus, our most beloved brother, his commemorative tablet is neither incomplete nor recent.[4] He is following the footsteps of his kinsfolk, he is matching his forebears and near relations with a rank of honor similar to theirs, granted by God's

---

[3]Clearly someone who was released was always subject to the suspicion that they had in fact apostatised but were covering things up.

[4]For *titulus* as meaning a "commemorative tablet" detailing a person's career, and so forth, see Horace *Carm.* 4.14.4: "What responsibility of the senators . . . will immortalise your acts of courage (*uirtutes*) for eternity, O Augustus, by means of commemorative tablets and festal calendars (*per titulos memoresque fastus*)." The *uirtutes* of Celerinus are being recorded here as part of a Calendar of Saints, including former members of his family.

choice. His grandmother Celerina already long ago was crowned in martyrdom.[5] Likewise his maternal and paternal uncles Laurentinus and Egnatius, themselves in the army, though once marching in the armies of this world, were nevertheless true and spiritual soldiers of God. They earned by their renowned passion the Lord's palms of victory when they laid the Devil low by their confession of Christ.

We always offer sacrificial Masses on their behalf, as you will recall, as often as we celebrate the passions of the martyrs and their day at their annual commemoration. **2** Examples of courage and of faith came to him from his own household, and he could not therefore be inferior in his bloodline to them. The value of a family of noble birth encouraged him to follow their examples. If to be patrician is worthy of commendation and of fame in a family of this world, how much the more is it worthy of greater fame and honour to be made of noble birth through heaven's commendation?

I cannot discover whom I should call more blessed, whether it is those ancestors of his for their famed descendant, or himself because of his glorious family from which he had descended. In that family we see the ebbing and flowing of God's approval in equal measure. In consequence, both the worthiness of the descendent adds luster to the crown of the ancestors, and the eminence of his kindred intensifies the radiant glory of their descendent.

4.1 So, most beloved brothers, Celerinus comes to us with so great an approval from the Lord, renowned for his witness that caused the amazement of the magistrate who had persecuted him. And so, where else should he be placed than upon the pulpit, that is to say on the magistrate's dais of the Church?[6] In this way, supported by his more elevated position, and visible to the general congregation

---

[5]Celerina may have been one of the Scillitan martyrs of North Africa, see Victor Vitensis *Historia* 1.9, but see Clarke, *Letters of St Cyprian*, 2.190, n. 14.

[6]"Magistrate's dias of the Church" = *tribunal ecclesiae*, used generally for any officer but in particular, the *tribunus militum*. Note here Cyprian's tendency to equate the structure of Christian society with that of the secular, political sphere.

as befits the fame for which he is thus honored, he might read the precepts and gospel of the Lord that he has bravely and faithfully followed.

In these tasks his voice that has confessed the Lord should be heard daily in the words that the Lord has spoken. **2** It is for the future whether there might be a higher grade in the Church to which he can progress. There is nothing in which a confessor profits the brothers more than that whoever is listening should imitate the faith of the reader while the gospel reading is being heard from his mouth. **3** It had been right that he be joined in the office of reader with Aurelius, with whom he has been joined in the company of the divinely honored, with whom he has been united in all the marks of courage and of praise. Both are equal together and, each like the other, in so far as they are exulted in glory as they are humble in their deference, so far are they brought forward by God's approval as they submit in their serenity and peace.

They provide comparable models for individuals both of courageous acts and of moral behavior, and are suitable for both a time of war and of peace. They are to be praised on the one hand for their fortitude, and on the other for their modesty.

5.1 The Lord rejoices in servants of this character, he glories in confessors of this kind. Their discipleship and conduct so contribute to the praise of their glory that it provides instructions in discipline to the others. For this end Christ has wished that they be here in his Church. This is the purpose for which he has kept them without harm, having drawn them out of the midst of death and clothed them with what might be called a kind of resurrection.

In consequence, the brotherhood should follow them and become their companions, since the brothers will discern a no more exalted example of honor, and no one of more submissiveness in humility. **2** You are thus informed that these have been appointed readers for the time being, since their lamp ought to be placed on a lamp stand from where it can illuminate all, and their glorious countenances be found in a higher position. There, regarded by every one who gathers around, they can inspire zeal to obtain glory in those who view them.

Nevertheless you should note that we have considered them worthy already of the honor of the presbyterate. In consequence, they are both receiving an honorary monetary allowance with the presbyters and a monthly allocation in kind of an identical amount to the latter. They are destined, in the future, to take their seats with us[7] when their years have progressed to maturity. However, no one who has brought to perfection his youth through the courage that gained him glory can be regarded in any way as lacking in maturity.

My prayer for you my dearest and most beloved brothers is that you will always fare well.

---

[7]For the physical construction of places for the clergy in African chancels, see J. B. Ward Perkins and R. G. Goodchild, "The Christian Antiquities of Tripoli Tania," *Archaeologia* 45 (1953): 63.

§2 The Unity of the Church and the Nature of Schism

LETTER 43
The Origin and Character of the Schism of Felicissimus

Cyprian writes before Easter (23 March, 251), with the persecution almost over but before he considers it safe to return (7.2). He is appealing to the laity and loyal presbyters, against the rapidly organizing laxist group around Felicissimus, which feeds for its growing influence on the grudges of the presbyters who originally opposed Cyprian's episcopal election (1.2 and 3.2). But as his delicately drafted introduction reveals, there is considerable sympathy for this group amongst the clergy who stayed and ministered, rather than with Cyprian who fled.

Cyprian insists that he shows them like care through the medium of his letters (1.1). When characterizing the schism of Felicissimus, his primary focus is that of Roman political rhetoric. They are a "conspiracy (*coniuratio*)," a "faction (*factio*)," acting with "treachery (*perfidia*)" and engaged in "plots (*insidiae*)," against the lawful authority of a bishop appointed by due process (1.2). Proconsular authority is grounded upon authority or *imperium* exercised within the sanctified boundary (*pomerium*), so that rebellion becomes sacrilege (2–3). He insists, as in *Fallen* 14, that quick absolution will destroy rather than heal a disease that requires longer treatment (4).

There is one Church founded by Christ's promise on Peter (5.2). Cyprian carefully sanitizes his pagan and secular political concepts by duly glossing them with Old Testament imagery from the Deuteronomic tradition according to which Jerusalem afforded in its Temple the one sanctuary and the one valid priesthood. All other were pagan pretences (5.2). This letter is an important background to the composition of Cyprian's treaties *On the*

Fallen and *On Unity of the Catholic Church*, now in draft form but nearing completion.

Cyprian to the General Laity, Holy Brothers

1.1 Dearest brothers, the most faithful presbyter, Virtius, has integrity, and likewise also Rogatian and Numidicus, as presbyters, who made their confession and shine with the glory of God's favorable approval. I include also the deacons, good men and fully committed to the Church's management through their acts of allegiance. They, with the remaining ministers, continue to afford you their care by being present.

They do not fail to strengthen you individually with continuing words of encouragement, but they also remold and direct the minds of the fallen with health-giving counsels. However I, as much as I am able, advise, and, in the way that I can, I visit you through my letter.

2 I am speaking through a letter, dearest brothers, because it is the achievement of the malice and treachery of certain presbyters that it has not been granted me to come to you before Easter Day. They have kept the memory of their conspiracy and its old poison against my episcopal office, and also against your votes and the judgment of God. They have recommended their ancient battle against us, and renewed again their sacrilegious designs in their all-too-usual plots.[1] **3** And of course they have paid as the penalty the punishments that they deserve, not because we wished or desired it, but because of the providence of God. We had been prepared to forgive and keep silent.

[1]Cyprian's language here shows an assimilation of his understanding of ecclesial order to that of Roman, pagan order. An emperor is, theoretically, formally elected by the Senate, who therefore give their "votes (*suffragia*)," with the consent of the people. The gods express their judgment (*iudicium*) by awarding him the palm in the war that brings him to power, as was so often the case in the age of Decius and before. A supernatural sign of divine approval comes from heaven. Conspiracy and rebellion in consequence are "sacrilegious machinations (*sacrilegas machinationes*)."

In consequence, they expelled themselves rather than that it was we who expelled them. It is they who have passed the sentence upon themselves according to their own conscience, consistent with your divinely inspired decision.[2] The criminal conspirators have of their own free will expelled themselves from the Church.

2.1 The source of Felicissimus' faction has now become transparent along with its roots and supporting strength. These people at one time used to provide inducements and encouragement to some of the confessors to end their concord with their own bishop, and not to hold fast to ecclesiastical discipline in trust and calmness, according to the precepts of the Lord. Thus they failed to preserve the glory of their confession by a corrupting and staining association. **2** It was not enough for them to have corrupted the minds of some of the confessors, and to have aimed at providing a remnant of a fractured brotherhood with weapons against the sacred episcopate of God. Now and in addition, they engage themselves in securing the baleful ruin of the fallen by means of the poison of deceit.

They lure away from the remedy for their wound those who are sick and injured and too incapacitated and faltering to embrace stronger advice about the disaster of their collapse. They allure them into a pernicious recklessness by lying to them about a deceptive reconciliation. They have ceased from the prayers and petitions by means of which the Lord needs to be expiated in a long and unbroken atonement.

3.1 But you, brothers, be watchful against the artifices of the Devil, and keep careful watch against his deceit that leads to death, anxious for your salvation.

---

[2] Of course the clergy and people of Carthage had made no such synodical decision, amongst whom there was clearly much sympathy for pastorally caring clergy who had remained in danger. Cyprian is at his most disingenuous in claiming that because he was originally elected, any opposition to him is an opposition to those who elected him, albeit they elected him then as a bishop who was present and not as one now in hiding.

This is another persecution, another time of trial. Those five presbyters are no different from those other five men of prominence who were so recently grouped by the Edict with the magistrates with the purpose of overthrowing our faith. In this way they have lured the simple hearts of the brothers into their deadly snares in their violation of the truth.

2 The method is now the same. Once more the same process of subversion, the intention of which is to overthrow their salvation. Such is the project being conducted at the hands of the five presbyters grouped with Felicissimus. God is not being petitioned because he who has denied Christ cannot pray for forgiveness from the very Christ whom he has denied. The opportunity for penitence is taken away after the blow of guilt has fallen.

A person who has fallen does not then gain forgiveness from the Lord through his bishops and priests, but he has abandoned the priests of the Lord. There arise in their place a new succession based upon a sacrilegious doctrine against the moral order of the gospel. It has been resolved that there should be no new policy in the case of the fallen without our convening as one body. On that occasion we will engage ourselves in comparing our considered opinions and devising a tariff[3] that would be moderated equally both by concerns with discipline and with mercy. It is not only our resolution but also that of the confessors and clergy of Rome, and likewise of every bishop holding office whether in our province[4] or beyond the sea. It is against this decision of ours that they have rebelled. These divisive

---

[3]"Tariff" or "sentence (=*sententia*)." Since Cyprian once again assimilates the deliberations and decisions of an ecclesiastical synod to the operation of a Roman court, comparing them with the considered opinions (*consilia*) of judges, I have tried to give a suitable forensic flavor to the translation here.

[4]"Province (=*prouincia*)," which referred to the geographical sphere (*imperium*) that set the boundaries within which a proconsul or governor exercised legal and constitutional authority. Since the boundaries of the city were purified by a sacrifice of a pig and a bull (*suotaurovilia*), the exercise of legitimate political power was sacred, and to infringe or usurp it was sacrilege; cf. 1.2 (*sacrilegas machinationes*). Cyprian now defines ecclesiastical authority by analogy with this pagan model; see also Cyprian *Ep.* 55.21.1, n. 20.

conspiracies are challenging every priestly authority and power to their very foundation.

4.1 What pains I am now suffering, dearest brothers, for not being able to come to you face to face, to confront each of you individually, to encourage you myself with the direction of our Lord and of his gospel. I have been an exile now for two years. My sorrowful separation from your countenances and your sight has not been enough, shaken as I have been in my loneliness without you by my continual sorrow and tears in the course of my interminable grief.

My tears have been shed by day and night for my inability to greet you and be clasped to your embrace. This has not been granted to the bishop whom you appointed with so great a love and yearning.

2 Here a greater sorrow assails my melting heart because I am unable myself to rush back to you in view of my anxiety about a crisis of this magnitude. At this time we must exercise caution about the threats and plots of the treacherous in case on our arrival a worse riot may in consequence occur. Since a bishop is under obligation to make provision that there be peace and calmness in all things, he ought not to be seen himself to have been the cause of sedition and to have aggravated a renewal of persecution.

3 So it is for this reason, most beloved brothers, I give you warning as well as advice that you do not carelessly trust destructive voices, that you do not reach an easy agreement to suit your own convenience because of the language of deceit. Do not choose the shadows of darkness for light, night for day, hunger for food, thirst for drink, poison instead of an antidote, and death instead of salvation. Neither their years, nor their authoritative bearing, should deceive you. They are the counterparts of the ancient iniquity of the two presbyters, just like those who tried to corrupt and violate chaste Susanna (Dan 13.1). Just like them, these presbyters are trying to corrupt with their adulterous doctrines the chastity of the Church, and to violate the truth of the gospel.

5.1 The Lord proclaims his declaration: "Do not listen to the words of the false prophets, since the visions of their hearts delude them. They speak, but not from the mouth of the Lord. They are addressing those who reject the word of the Lord" (Jer 23.16–17). Those who do not themselves have reconciliation are now offering reconciliation. Those who have departed *from* the Church promise that they will lead back and reclaim the fallen *to* the Church. **2** God is one and Christ one, the Church one, and the Chair founded on Peter by the voice of the Lord is one. It is not possible to found another altar nor to create a new priesthood against the one altar and the one priesthood.[5] Whoever gathers elsewhere scatters.

It is a counterfeit act,[6] it is impiety, and it is a sacrilege. It is what originates from human frenzy with the purpose of violating what is of divine appointment. Depart from the contamination of this kind of men and their arguments, just as you insist on carrying on living when you drive away disease and pestilence. Act according to the counsel of the Lord who says: "They are blind leaders of the blind. When a blind man leads a blind man they both will fall into a ditch" (Mt 15.14).

3 They are intervening against our prayers that you as well as us pour out to God by day and night, with the object of satisfying him with a payment that is fair. They intervene against our tears by which you wash away the charge of an offence that has been committed. They intervene against a reconciliation for which you ask, truly and faithfully, to come from the mercy of the Lord. They know not that it is written: "That prophet has spoken who dreams a dream in order to make you wander from the Lord your God" (Deut 13.5).

[5]There is clearly here an allusion to the one altar and sanctuary of Deut 12.5–12, and to the rebel altar erected on the bank of the Jordan by three tribes in Josh 22.10–20.

[6]"Counterfeit" = *adulterium* usually translated "adultery." If that is its meaning, then the reference is to OT associations of sexual immorality with idolatrous worship, as in Cyprian *Unit. eccl.* 6–7. But Felicissimus' act, like that of Novatian, according to Cyprian, is to counterfeit the true Church, so that it is in this sense that I translate the word here; see further Cyprian *Unit. eccl.* 6, n. 10; see also Cyprian *Ep.* 55.24.1, n. 25.

4 Let no one cause you, brothers, to wander from the ways of the Lord. Let no one snatch away you who are Christians from the gospel of Christ. Let no one rob the Church of its sons. Let them perish alone by themselves who are thus willing to perish, and let them remain alone outside the Church who have departed from the Church. They who have rebelled against their bishops are alone and not with those bishops. Let them alone submit to the punishment for their conspiratorial uprising as a result of your decision in the past,[7] and now as a result of the judgments of God. They have merited receiving sentence for conspiracy and their malice.[8]

6.1 The Lord admonishes us in his gospel with the words: "You reject the commandment of God in order that you may establish your tradition" (Mk 7.9). Let those who reject the commandment of God, and are trying to establish their own tradition, be strongly and firmly spurned by you. Let the fallen be allowed only one disaster. Let no one hurl down by their tricky maneuver those wishing to rise up. Let no one knock around on the ground and repress with greater injury those who are already lying there, for whom we pray that they may be raised by the hand and arm of God. Let no one turn away from all hope of salvation those who are half-consciously pleading that they might receive back their original salvation. Let no one extinguish every light on the road to salvation from those who waver in the darkness of their fall.

2 The Apostle instructs us with the words: "If anyone should teach otherwise and not repose in the sound words of our Lord Jesus Christ and his doctrine, elated by lust, depart from this kind of person" (1 Tim 6.3–4 and 11). And again he says: "Let no one deceive you with empty words. For the wrath of God comes upon the sons

---

[7]He is referring to their decision to elect him as bishop, which he claimed they had unlawfully opposed.

[8]We have already seen how, in *On the Fallen*, Cyprian is to conduct his argument in a forensic style, judiciously weighing the merits of the three sides: rigorist, laxist, and Cyprian's middle position; see especially Cyprian *Laps.* 13–19.

of those who reject a verdict.[9] Be therefore unwilling to be their accomplices" (Eph 5.6–7)

It is not that you should begin to be accomplices of their wickedness because you are deceived by their empty words. I beg you, depart from such people and find comfort in our advice. We pour out daily unceasing prayers for you in our desire that you be recalled to the Church through the Lord's pardon.[10] We pray for the fullest reconciliation from God, first for the Mother and then for her sons. Join your supplications and prayers with our prayers and supplications, and join also your tears with our copious weeping.

Shun the wolves who divide the sheep from the shepherds, shun the poisoned tongue of the Devil who, from the beginning of the world, as a liar and deceiver, lies that he might deceive, seduces that he might cause harm, promises good things so that he might deliver evil, holds forth the hope of life in order that he might bring life to an end. His words now are transparent and his poisons are brought to light. He holds out the promise of reconciliation precisely that he who sins should not come to salvation. He guarantees you *a* Church, when by so acting that he who trusts that pledge will wholly perish *apart from* the Church.

7.1 Now is the time, most dearest brothers, that you who have stood firmly should persevere. You should preserve with eternal fortitude your glorious constancy to which you held fast in persecution. As well, you who have fallen when your adversary cut you off, should, in this second testing, be faithfully concerned with your hope for your

[9]I have translated *contumacia* as "verdict" in the sense of "willful disobedience to a judicial order," as the sense in which Cyprian reads this verse; see, Pliny *Ep.* 10.57. Someone condemned to perpetual exile, if he returns, is to be sent in chains to the Pretorian Prefects: "For it is not good enough for him (*Neque enim sufficit*) to be remanded for the same punishment (*eum poenae suae restitui*), which he has avoided by ignoring a verdict (*quam contumacia elusit*)."

[10]Note that Cyprian here suddenly regards those who support the fallen as fallen themselves rather than, as up to now, exhorting them to treat the fallen with the bitter medicine that will heal them.

reconciliation. You should not withdraw from the priests of the Lord if you want the Lord to pardon you, since it is written: "Whatever man so acts with arrogance that he does not obey priest nor judge, whoever he shall be in those days, that man shall die" (Deut 17.12).

2 This is the most recent and final test of that persecution that will itself soon pass when the Lord soon grants me his protection so that I can be present with you together with my colleagues after Easter Sunday. When they are present we will be able to prescribe and together sketch those things that are to be resolved, according to your opinion and the shared counsel of us all, as the already agreed method of proceeding. But if anyone recoils from doing penance and propitiating God, and submits to the party of Felicissimus and his accomplices, and joins himself to a heretical faction, let him know that it will not be possible for him afterwards to return to the Church, and to receive communion with the bishops and laity of Christ.

I pray you, dearest brothers, that you may always fare well and remain constant in ceaseless prayers with us, petitioning the mercy of the Lord.

LETTER 55

The Origin and Character of the Novatian Schism

Cyprian writes to Antonianus in the course of AD 251, a bishop whose exact see is unknown, but is probably in Numidia, and who is wavering in his support for Cyprian's opposition to Novatian (1). Cyprian defends himself against the charge that he has changed his position from one that was close to Novatian's own, on the grounds that he was always of the opinion that the final decision was that of an episcopal council at the end of the persecution (2–4).

Cyprian then records in the course of the letter the proceedings of the two councils of that year, in Africa (6.1) and in Italy (6.2). Here we read not only a clear statement of the resolutions of those councils, but also Cyprian's account of both Novatian and Felicissimus and the character of their movement in the light of his understanding of church order. Cyprian, in defense of Cornelius (8), does not attack the orthodoxy of Novatian, which is not in question. Rather he makes the question of the validity of Cornelius' office purely that he occupied the chair first and when it was vacant, having been elected by clergy and people. Thus he invades the sacred space or *imperium* and commits sacrilege (8.4–5).[1] Cornelius is acquitted of further charges that he had generally communicated with those who sacrificed directly (*sacrificati*) (10 and 12), except for the special case of Trophimus who had been deprived of his priesthood (11).

Cyprian now goes on to argue that the fallen cannot be placed in a single category (13–14). Those who are sick to the point of death may be readmitted to communion and then recover. He cannot be blamed if this so happens (13.1). His argument now becomes pastoral (15–19).[2] He then turns to a judicial precedent in the case of adultery decided by an earlier gathering of

---

[1] See also Cyprian *Laps.* 8–9; 13–19; *Ep.* 43.3.2, n. 4; and Introduction §2.1.

[2] For Cyprian's pastoral model, see G. Dunn, "Infected Sheep and Diseased Cattle, or the Pure and Holy Flock: Cyprian's Pastoral Care of Virgins," *JECS* 11.1 (2003): 1–20.

115

bishops in council in Africa (20–21). He then produces two chapters of biblical exegesis in defense of that council and his own position (22–23). He then turns to his considered reflections on Novatian and his group (24–29).

This letter is long but of utmost importance as Cyprian's considered and mature defense of his own actions and ecclesiology.

Cyprian to Antonianus, My Holy Brother

1.1 I am in receipt of your letter, my dearest brother, that was firm in its maintenance of the mutual agreement of the sacred episcopal college, and which held fast to the unity of the Catholic Church. In this letter you pointed out that you held no communion with Novatian, but that you followed our resolution, and held to our united agreement with Cornelius our fellow bishop.

2 You have also written that I should forward a copy of the above-mentioned letter to Cornelius our colleague with a view to relieving him of every disquiet with the information that you are in communion with him, that is to say with the Catholic Church.[3]

2.1 However, more recently your other letter has arrived conveyed by hand of Quintus our fellow presbyter, in which I have observed that your opinion has begun to waver, urged on by Novatian's letter. For though you had expressed in definite terms your previous considered opinion, you sought in this letter that I should write in clarification of the decision[4] as to what heresy Novatian had introduced, and on what argument Cornelius had admitted Trophimus and

[3]Cyprian may mean here that Cornelius' church in Rome is the Catholic Church, which is the body that he shares communion with there, although, prior to his argument with Stephen, it may mean an acknowledgement of a primacy that he was later to deny. See the introduction to Cyprian *Unit. eccl.*

[4]I translate *rescriberem* "I write in clarification" in line with Cyprian's view of the ecclesiastical councils as courts. Like an emperor writing a *rescriptum*, Cyprian claims to be reproducing a solemn legal opinion; cf. Pliny *Ep.* 10.108.1: "On what rights you wish to prevail (*quid habere iuris uelis*) . . . I request, my Lord, that you should give your written decision (*rogo, domine, rescribas*)."

those who offered incense (*thurificati*) into his communion. **2** Now if your concern arises from an anxious care for the faith, and that concern leads you to search out the truth of a subject in which you have doubt, no blame attaches to you. Your disquiet comes from a heart that is in suspense because it is tossed about by a fear for God.

3.1 I observe, notwithstanding, that, after you pronounced your verdict in your first letter, Novatian's letter unsettled you. Therefore, my dearest brother, I put it to you in the first place that serious men, and those who are founded on a rock fixed solidly and unshakable, cannot be moved, I think, by wind and storm let alone by some gentle breeze. In shifting from a firm decision that it has reached in response to some lightweight criticism, a mind that wavers and is caused doubt in the face of varied opinions resembles the chaotic agitation caused by blasts of winds that so frequently rage. To avoid this condition, caused by the letter of Novatian in your case, and that of anyone else, I will in response to your request, my brother, set out for you a brief account of the matter.

2 In the first instance, since you seem concerned with my conduct and me, I must remove every taint from my role and motive. No one should think that I withdrew lightly from my considered position. At the beginnings of the dispute, I defended my concern for the strictness of the gospel. Subsequently I may seem to have modified my thinking from an extreme view of my previous administration of discipline. But I did not, in consequence, think that reconciliation should be easily granted to those who had besmirched their conscience by obtaining certificates (*libelli*), or to those who had actually performed sacrificial acts contrary to divine law. I did not act on either policy without a long considered and balanced reflection.

4.1 Appreciate that when the sword's blade was still flashing between fighting hands, and there was the glorious engagement in battle that was the persecution, there was need to rouse the strength of our soldiers with every exhortation to a complete attack. Most of all, the minds of the fallen had to be enlivened by our voice as a trumpet call so that they would seek the path to doing penance, not merely by means of prayers and expressions of grief, but also because they should be given the opportunity of returning to battle and winning back their salvation. They needed rather to be chided by the sounds of our voice, and challenged to desire to make their confession for the glory of martyrdom.

2 Then next, when the presbyters and deacons wrote to me on the subject of some of these people, that they had become unrestrained and were demanding admission to communion without delay, my decision in reply[5] was contained in my letter that is available. I added this sentence:

"If they are in such a hurry, they have what they demand within their own power, when the moment provides generously for far more than they demand. The battle is now in progress and daily a competition is staged in the arena. If they are truly and surely repentant about what they have done, and passion for the faith remains strong, he who cannot be deferred can be crowned."[6]

3 I did however defer what had to be decided in the case of the fallen. My intention was that when peace and calm had been granted, and God's favor allowed the bishops to assemble in one council, only then we should decide on what ought to be done. Our resolution of the matter could have been planned mutually, and given balanced consideration, with due comparison of opinions. If anyone, indeed, if anyone should be willing arbitrarily to receive the fallen to communion before our council, and before sentence was pronounced by the decision of us all, he himself should be subject to excommunication.

[5]"Decision in reply" = *scribens*, for which see n. 4 in this letter.
[6]Cyprian originally so argued in *Ep.* 19.2.3, not included in the present selection.

5.1 I even wrote to Rome, to the clergy then conducting its affairs without a bishop, and to the confessors, Maximus the presbyter, and the remainder who were held in prison but who are now in the Church, in full union with Cornelius. You are well able to find out what I have written about their formal responses. For in their letter they so declare:

> "Nevertheless on the main business with which you also are concerned we have resolved that the peace of the Church must first be upheld, and then we shall consider the case of the fallen by evaluating courses of action with the bishops, presbyters, and deacons, as well as the confessors and the unfallen laity."[7]

2 Novatian himself wrote an addition to that letter. The presbyter Moyses, who was then a confessor and now has become a martyr, appended his signature to what he wrote, when he read it out with his own voice: the fallen if they became sick or were at the point of death were to be granted reconciliation. This letter was sent throughout the whole world and was duly noted by all the churches and every one of the brethren.

6.1 According then to what had been previously laid down, a great number of bishops, whom their faith and the protection of our Lord had preserved unblemished and unharmed, met as a single body. It was possible for them to meet as a single body once the persecution was assuaged. After both sides had advanced passages from Scripture in a lengthy session, we reached a balanced compromise, whilst still exercising a healthy restraint.

Our intention was that the fallen should not be entirely denied hope of restoration to communion and reconciliation. They should not on the one hand be so weakened with despair that they should seek again this world and live the pagan life only because the Church

---

[7]Cyprian *Ep.* 30.5.3, not included in this selection.

doors had been closed against them. On the other hand, the moral order of the gospel should not be weakened by their rushing back haphazardly into making their communion. Rather their penance should extend over a long period, and the Father's clemency should be petitioned in a spirit of mourning.

The cases of each individual were to be examined, what influenced them, whether voluntarily, or under constraint, in accordance with what is to be found in the official report,[8] which I trust has reached you, in which the summary of each individual decision is recorded. 2 Lest the African bishops seemed in number less satisfactory, we sent our opinion on this matter to Rome, to Cornelius our colleague, who himself gave his consent to the selfsame judgment that we reached. He added equally his weight and sane balance, following a council that he held with very many of his fellow bishops.[9]

7.1 It has been necessary for me to write this to you so that you can grasp that I have not acted flippantly, but in accord with what I had previously included in my letters: all decisions were deferred for the moment until the shared verdict of a council. There should definitely be no prior admission to communion of any of the fallen when there was still opportunity that any one of the fallen could win not only pardon, but also a martyr's crown.

2 However we are now after all this. We have to comply with the necessity of the new situation, as required both by the mutual agreement of the college, and in the interest of a brotherhood that needed closing of their wounds[10] and healing. We have considered that we have to make provision for the salvation of the many. We

---

[8]"Official report" = *libellus*, translated in a judicial sense as in the case of a brief given to an advocate as in Quintillian *Inst.* 6.2.5: " . . . in briefs (*libellis*) . . . which a litigant compiled (*quos componit . . . litigator*).

[9]These councils are recorded in Cyprian *Ep.* 44 and *Ep.* 49.

[10]Clarke, *Letters of St Cyprian*, 3.36 translates *colligendae fraternitatis* as "gathering our scattered brethren together." In view of the clear medical context, I have translated *colligere* in its sense of binding up a wound; see Pliny *Nat.* 35.51.180–181: "Babylonian bitumen . . . stops the blood (*sanguinem sistit*), binds up wounds (*volnera colligit*)."

must not now draw back from our resolutions, passed decisively in our council and reached by a common decision, in the face of sentiments bandied about and voiced by many people. These include those deliberate lies flaunted against the priests of God, and emanating from the Devil's mouth, the intention of which is to fracture everywhere the bond of the unity of the Catholic Church.

3 But you ought, as a good brother, and a priest of one mind with us, to consider seriously what the moderate and serious men that are your colleagues have produced from their examination of church life and discipline. What evil and apostate men trip easily from their tongues should be of no concern to you.

8.1 I come now, my dearest brother, to the character of our colleague, Cornelius, that you may share with us a more accurate knowledge of Cornelius. Forget about the falsehood of his slanderers and detractors. Look to the judgment of God who made him bishop, and to the testimony of his fellow bishops, on which the united body of whom, one throughout the whole world, has expressed its agreement in the concord of one mind.

2 What commends our dearest brother to God, Christ, and his Church, is the public commendation of his entire fellow priests who have praised his worth. This man did not come suddenly to the episcopate, but was promoted through all the ecclesiastical offices. Having gained the Lord's favour through his administration of divine worship, he climbed to the highest step through every grade of religious practice.[11]

3 Secondly, he neither asked, nor wished, for the episcopal office itself, nor did he storm in like others, inflated by their swelling conceit and pride.[12] Rather, he remained unruffled, as at other

---

[11]Unlike, of course, Cyprian himself and Ambrose after him, who were ordained to all the lower ranks in a matter of days, and which was part of the offence felt by the five presbyters who had good grounds on this point, as Cyprian himself shows in his comments here; see also n. 13 below.

[12]See the comments on the position of Lucianus in the introduction to Cyprian *Ep.* 39 above. See also Cyprian *Unit. eccl.* 14, n. 20, and the case of confessors marching

times, and decorous. Such are the qualities they have by custom who are divinely chosen for this position. Think of his virginal chastity born of his self-control, and of his submissive attitude, maintained and nurtured in him by his inborn modesty. Indeed, he applied no violence in order to become bishop, but he himself suffered violence when he received the bishop's office by compulsion.[13]

4 Our many colleagues who were then present in the city of Rome created Cornelius bishop. It was they who then sent to us letters that honored and praised him. The distinctive mark of those letters was the clear testimony of their public proclamation of his ordination. Cornelius therefore was created bishop by the decision of God and of his Christ, by the testimony of almost all the clergy, and by the supporting election of the laity that were then present.

The assembled college of bishops consisted of men of an age of experience and of moral worth. No one had been created bishop before him, when the rank to which the sacred Chair gave entitlement was vacant. The place occupied by Fabian, that is to say the position of Peter, was unoccupied.[14] 5 Once however it was filled, and confirmed by the will of God and the consent of us all, anyone who wished to be made a bishop could necessarily only be made so *outside* the Church. He who does not maintain the Church's unity has not the Church's ordination. Whoever this man may be, and granted that he will boast much of himself and even more justify himself, he is an alien and he is a foreigner: he is on the outside. And since after the first there cannot be a second appointment, whoever is created after the first one (of necessity the only one!) is not really the second one but no one at all.

in and demanding, by virtue of their physical wounds, the right to act as presbyters and to offer the Eucharistic sacrifice.

[13]Cyprian refers here to the formal and ritual expectation that a candidate for the bishop's office should show theatrically an unwilling resistance; see Pseudo Clement *Homilies* Ep. to Jas 3. For Cyprian himself, see Pontius *Vita* 5. See also Paulinus *Vita Ambr.* 7.

[14]Remember that Peter's place was to be found not only in the See of Rome but also in any episcopal see; see Cyprian *Ep.* 33.1.1; *Unit. eccl.* 4–5.

9.1 Cornelius neither canvassed for the bishop's office nor acquired it by extortion, but received it by the will of the God who creates priests. Thus the greatness of his courage in his acceptance of his episcopate, the greatness of his strength of mind, the quality the firm texture of his faith surely of necessity follows?

We simply have to acknowledge with total sincerity, and to praise the fact that he took his seat on the high-priestly Chair at Rome unflinching. That was the very time in which an aggressive tyrant was making threats that were humanly lawful but divinely not so. The latter at that time was prepared to listen to the news that a rival emperor had arisen with greater patience and toleration than that a sacred bishop of God had been appointed at Rome.[15]

2 This man, dearest brother, must surely be specially recommended with the greatest testimonial to his courage and faith. He must surely be assigned to the ranks of the glorious confessors and martyrs, who took his seat during such a crisis while fully expecting the butchering of his very body, and the avenging fury of the raging tyrant. These were perfectly able either to attack Cornelius with the sword, as he made his resistance to the savage edicts and spurned both threats and tortures and the rack with the resilience that comes from faith. On the other hand, they could have impaled him on a cross, or scorched him with fire, or tore to pieces his limbs and internal organs with some unheard of kind of punishment.[16]

---

[15]Who such a rival emperor was in AD 249 is not clear. Suggestions have been made regarding such minor figures as Julius Valens Licinianus, or Julius Priscus, and for these and other possibilities see Clarke, *Letters of St Cyprian*, 3.178–180, n. 40.

[16]Cornelius never suffered martyrdom in any strict sense, despite the construction of a later martyrology. He died in exile at Centumcellae on his way in June AD 253 to be tried; see the Chronographer of 354, whose entry records him as "falling asleep in glory (*cum gloria dormitionem accepit*)." Cf. Th. Mommsen, Chronica minora I, Saeculum IV, in *Monumenta Germaniae Historica*, Auctores Antiquissimi 9 (Berlin, 1892). Cyprian here is anxious to extend the concept of martyrdom to those who, by suffering in blood, could claim the right to absolve the fallen, without formal ordination. See also above n. 12.

The sovereignty of the Lord our protector and his goodness now protected the sacred bishop whom he had willed to create. Nevertheless Cornelius, in the sense of his being ready to be a sacrifice, and in the fear that was the companion of that readiness, did suffer whatever he was able to suffer. The fact is he first vanquished the tyrant by his own sacred office as bishop. It was only subsequently that the tyrant was vanquished in war by an armed fight.[17]

10.1 Do not be amazed that there are dishonest and evilly intended accusations being bandied about, for you should know that this is always the Devil's work. It is his intention to savage the reputations of God's servants with lies, and to slander their glorious name with false opinions. His intention is to besmirch with unfounded gossip those who stand resplendent in the light of their clear conscience.

2 I must inform you that our colleagues have conducted an examination of the matter. Their most secure finding is that the aforesaid Cornelius has not been stained with the dishonor of a certificate of sacrifice, as some assert. More to the point, he has not engaged in sacrilegious intercommunion with bishops who have sacrificed. He is only in communion with those who are in communion with us following the hearing of their case, and the proving of their innocence.

11.1 Even in the case of Trophimus, about whom you requested my written reply, the facts do not fit the rumor of the spiteful lie that has reached you. Our dearest brother has bowed to necessity, just as our predecessors often have done, when the brothers needed binding together. **2** Because the largest section of the laity broke away in the company of Trophimus, now that Trophimus has returned to the Church, his prayers have been heard once more.

This follows his making amends and confessing his former error with full acts of humility and amendment for which he did penance

---

[17]Decius and his son died in battle against the Goths at Abrittus in the middle of AD 251.

to obtain clemency, and his subsequent recall to the Christian community that he had so recently split into parts. It is not so much Trophimus himself, but the large number of the brethren who were with Trophimus, that has been allowed back. All of these would not have returned to the Church unless they had come in Trophimus' company.

3 In summary, Trophimus has been received back following a discussion over here with a large number of colleagues. The return of the brethren and the restoration of salvation to many constituted an act of atonement made on his behalf. Nevertheless Trophimus was admitted on condition that he received communion as a layman, contrary to what the letters of spiteful people have proclaimed, namely that he is in illegal possession of the status of a sacred bishop.

12.1 The report that you have that Cornelius is accustomed to receive into communion those who have offered pagan sacrifices is the product of the invented rumors of the apostates. Those who depart from us are unable commend us. We cannot therefore expect that we can placate them who, in their displeasure with us, and as rebels against the Church, are in the violent business of leading the brothers away from the Church. For this reason, dearest brother, you should not give a ready ear to whatever opinions are bandied about regarding ourselves nor believe them.

13.1 If any are overwhelmed by sicknesses, we so resolved that they should be supported as they are in mortal danger. Nevertheless, after such assistance has been granted, and reconciliation given to those in danger, we cannot throttle them or smother them. We cannot force their death by the strength of our hands, on the grounds that if reconciliation is granted them because they are dying, it is necessary that they die once they have received reconciliation.

It reveals a clear indication of divine forgiveness and a father's gentleness that those who reap the pledge of life in being granted reconciliation should continue the path of life once reconciliation has been reaped. For that reason, if God grants a leave of respite when reconciliation has been received, no one ought to bring charges against the sacred bishops because they have resolved to grant support to the brothers who are at death's door.

2 You should not however consider, dearest brother, though some might think it, that those who have obtained certificates (*libellatici*) should be considered as equivalent to those who have offered sacrifice (*sacrificati*).[18] Even in the case of those who have sacrificed, their position and their reasons are frequently quite diverse. There is no way each particular case can be considered equivalent. One of them jumped eagerly into making a sacrilegious sacrifice voluntarily and readily. Another struggled against and offered strong resistance, and only came to perform the act that brings death under compulsion. Then there is someone who handed himself over with his whole family, but someone else who approached the dangerous situation on his own on behalf of them all: he thus protected his wife and children and his whole house by his compliance with a risk to himself alone.

Then there is someone who forced his tenants and his friends to an evil act, and someone who spared his tenants and their wives even to the extent of welcoming into his own house and hospitality many Christian brothers who were fleeing under banishment of exile. At the expense of his own single injured soul he prays for pardon for many souls. He spreads before and offers to God those many alive and unharmed.

14.1 There is therefore a great difference between those very persons who have offered sacrifice. To class those who have sacrificed (*sacrificati*) with those who have acquired certificates (*libellaciti*) is sheer brutality and harsh to excess. His certificate accepted by the magistrates, he might say:

---

[18]With his statements here, cf. Cyprian *Laps.* 8; 13–19; and 27–28.

"I previously read and also knew from my bishop's preaching that there should be no sacrifices to idols, and the servant of God should not address images in prayer. It was for that reason that I avoided doing what was not allowed, when an opportunity of having a certificate presented itself. I would never have accepted the certificate (*libellus*) if the opportunity had not opened up. I went to the magistrate myself, or, conversely, through someone else who went for me, I conveyed the message that I was a Christian, that it was not permitted me to sacrifice, that I could not approach the altars of the Devil, that for this reason I was paying a bribe to avoid doing what was not permitted me."

2 Nonetheless, even though his hands are pure and his lips undefiled by the touch of the deadly food, he who is defiled by receiving a certificate ought not to have done this after what he had learned from our exhortations: his conscience is defiled. He is now in tears after hearing our words, and he shows remorse and he is admonished about what he has done wrong. Now that he has been put right and morally prepared, he can call God as witness that he was deceived when he wandered into an act of error rather than a deliberate crime.

15.1 We cannot reject the penitence of those have acted in good faith on what their conscience allowed. If we do, in response they will allow themselves to be swept away into heresy or schism at the Devil's continuing invitation, taking with them their wife with their children whom they had sought to preserve unharmed. And it will be inserted into the account against us on the Day of Judgment that we have not cared for the sheep that was injured, and that we have lost the many that were whole on account of the one that was wounded.

The Lord left the ninety and nine who were well, and sought the one that wandered and was exhausted. He carried the wanderer on his arms when he had found him (Lk 15.4–5). Unlike the Lord, we would not only have not sought those worn down with exhaustion, but even when they came to us we held them back. Though false prophets now never fail to lay waste and tear asunder the flock of Christ, we would have given the dogs and wolves their opportunity so that those whom the intensity of persecution failed to destroy, we destroyed by our harshness and inhumanity.

2 What will be our position, my beloved brother, regarding what the Apostle said: "I please everyone through everything, not seeking what is profitable for me but what is profitable for the many that they may be saved. Become imitators of me just as I am of Christ" (1 Cor 10.33–11.1). And again: "I am weak for the weak that I may gain the weak" (1 Cor 9.22). And again: "If one member suffers, all the other members also suffer with it; and if one member rejoices, all the other members also rejoices with it" (1 Cor 12.26).

16.1 The argument of the philosophers and Stoics is a different one, dearest brother. They say that all sins are equal, and that a man of seriousness ought not to be moved easily.[19] However, there is a great gulf between Christians and philosophers. This is because the Apostle says: "Take care that no one robs you through philosophy and empty deceit" (Col 2.8). Those acts are to be shunned that do not come from the mercy of God, but which originate from what a harsher philosophy framed as a contrary argument.

2 About Moses we read in Scripture that it was said: ". . . and Moses was a very gentle man" (Num 12.3). And the Lord in his gospel says: "Be compassionate, just as your father has had compassion on you" (Lk 6.36). And again: "Those in health need not a physician

---

[19] For an example of such a Stoic view, see Cicero *Parad.* 3. Although before his conversion Cyprian had enjoyed a pagan education, he makes almost no reference to pagan literary sources, unlike Clement of Alexandria and Origen. The reason that he makes specific reference to Stoic philosophy here is that he can compare its strictness with that of Novatian, and thus claim that Novatian's motivation is ultimately pagan. See also Cyprian *Ep.* 60.3.1 and that of Cornelius recorded in Eusebius *Hist. eccl.* 6.43.8.

but those who are sick" (Mt 9.12). **3** What kinds of medicine can the kind of doctor practice who says: "I care only for those who are well, who have no need of a doctor"? We ought to apply our labor, our healing treatment, to those who have wounds. We should not consider them to be dead, but rather that those whom we observe struck with wounds from the deadly persecution lie comatose. Confessors and martyrs will never subsequently be created from those who are stone dead.

17.1 There still lives in them something that can be revived following penance. From penitence comes the strong armor that protects faith and moral strength. **2** But someone cannot be so armed if he is lacking in hope, if insensitively and cruelly he is placed apart from the Church and turns back to pagan ways and the practices of this age. This equally applies if he is expelled from the Church and should pass over to the heretics and schismatics.

In his death he will not be able to receive the martyr's crown even in the case where he is slain subsequently for the sake of the Name. This is because his position is *outside* the Church, and broken off from its unity and bond of love. **3** For this reason it was decided, my most beloved brother, in the first instance, to allow back those who obtained certificates (*libellatici*) subsequent to the examination of individual cases. Otherwise, those who had sacrificed (s*acrificati*) were to be granted our aid when at the point of death because there is no opportunity for confession for those in hell.

We cannot compel anyone to make an act of repentance if we take from him the fruit reaped from a penitent act. If warfare should first come, he will be found armed by us with the strength that we have supplied. If alternatively, before such a war, he were to be overwhelmed by sickness, he can depart this life with the comfort of the sacrament of reconciliation, and of receiving communion.

18.1 If on Judgment Day the Lord will find the repentance of the sinner full and what justice required, he will then have confirmed what we here have decided. Thus we are not preempting here that future judgment. If, in truth, someone has deceived us by a pretended penitence, the God who is not mocked, and who examines the human heart, will pass his sentence on our imperfect perception of such acts. The Lord can correct the sentence passed by his servants.

We ought in this matter to bring to mind, brother, that it is written: "A brother who gives aid to a brother will be exalted" (Prov 18.19) and that the Apostle also has said: "You should consider one another lest you yourselves be tempted, bear each other's burdens and thus you will fulfill the law of Christ" (Gal 6.1–2). This selfsame Apostle, convicting the proud and restraining their arrogance, declares in his epistle: "He who thinks that he stands should take heed lest he fall" (1 Cor 10.12) and in another place he says: "Who are you who judge another's servant? By his own master he stands or falls. He will however stand, for God is able to cause him to stand" (Rom 14.1).

John also proves Jesus Christ our Lord to be the advocate and propitiator of our sins when he says: "My little sons, I write these things to you that you do not sin: and if anyone will sin, we have an advocate with the Father, Jesus Christ the righteous, and his is the propitiation for our sins" (1 Jn 2.1–2). And Paul the apostle also in his epistle declares: "If while we were still sinners Christ has died for us, by much more will we now be, justified in his blood, freed through him from wrath" (Rom 5.8–9).

19.1 Pondering our Father's care and mercy, we ought not ourselves to be insensitive and inhumane in nurturing our brothers, but grieve with those who grieve and weep with those who weep (Rom 12.5). We should to the best of our ability stand them upright with the help and consolation of our love. We should not, on the one hand, be so harsh and unyielding that we impair their ability to repent. But, on the other hand, we should not be so lax and pliable that we should without good cause relax the conditions for granting them communion.

2 You see your wounded brother laid low and injured in the line of battle by the Adversary. When the Devil tries to slay him whom he has wounded, Christ instead pleads that he whom he has redeemed should not completely perish. To which of these two sides do we belong, in whose ranks do we stand? Do we support the Devil so that he can wipe a brother out and do we pass him by lying prostrate and half-alive as the priest and the Levite did in the gospel? (Lk 10.30–32) Or rather do we, as sacred bishops of God and of Christ, imitating the pattern of what Christ both taught and did, snatch him who is wounded from the jaws of the Adversary in order that we may preserve him over whom we have exercised care for the judgment of God?

20.1 You should not think, dearest brother, that the result will be that the moral fiber of the brothers will be diminished, or that martyrdoms will end, because penitence is not begrudged those who have fallen, and because the hope of reconciliation is offered those who are penitent. The strength of the faithful will truly remain unshaken, and an unmoving and strong probity will endure with those who fear and love God with all their hearts.

2 We allow a period of penance even in the case of adulterers, after which reconciliation is then granted. Virginity has not as a result become absent from the Church nor has the glorious practice of chastity languished through the sins of others. The Church's wreath of victory blossoms with so many virgin flowers, and chastity and continence preserve their sustained course to glory. The strength to be chaste is not crushed, simply because penitence and pardon is not begrudged to an adulterer.

3 It is one thing to stand waiting for pardon, another to attain to glory; one thing not to return from the prison where one has been sent until he has paid the last farthing, another to receive at once the reward of his faith and moral courage. It is one thing to be made pure after being wracked for one's sins through a long process of grief and to be purified for a long time by fire, another to have purified all one's sin by a martyr's suffering.[20] Finally it is one thing to pay the penalty on the Day of Judgment at the sentence of the Lord, another thing to receive the martyr's wreath of victory at once from the Lord.

21.1 Certain amongst our predecessors, bishops at that, here in our province,[21] did not consider that reconciliation could be granted to adulterers. Accordingly they completely excluded any room for penitence for acts of adultery.[22] However, they did not withdraw from the college of their fellow bishops or fracture the unity of the Catholic Church by a stubborn adherence to a rigorist principle. For that matter they did not stubbornly adhere to their belief in their own right to prescribe conditions of membership.

In consequence, a bishop who did not grant reconciliation to adulterers did not have to separate himself from the Church because another of them had granted it. **2** So long as the bond of concord is maintained, and each inseparable solemn episcopal oath of unity[23] continues in force, each individual bishop administers and directs his own actions, having in view his account that he will render to the Lord.

22.1 I am amazed, however, that there are some who are so stubborn that they do not think that penance should be granted to the fallen, and they consider that pardon should be denied those offering

[20]"A martyr's suffering" = *passio.* The martyr is believed to be, in some sense, an icon of the suffering Christ, although Cyprian will deny that for that reason he can absolve. Nevertheless, as this passage makes clear, his sufferings are at least expiatory for his own sins.

[21]"Our province" = *prouincia nostra,* showing the assimilation in Cyprian's mind of his episcopal position with that of the Roman governor of North Africa, with a geographically defined sphere (*imperium*) within which his legitimate authority is exercised. See also Cyprian *Ep.* 43.3.2 and n. 4.

[22]For the relevance of this council to the earlier debate between the Hippolytan school and Callistus, of which Tertullian was cognizant, see Brent, *Imperial Cult,* 409–39.

[23]"Solemn oath of agreement or unity" = *sacramentum*; see Cyprian *Laps.* 7, and n. 7; *Unit. eccl.* 6, and n. 13, and associated references.

penance. This is against what is written: "Remember from where you have fallen and perform penance and do the first works" (Rev 2.5). This verse is directed particularly at him who has been established to have fallen, and whom the Lord is exhorting to rise up again by performing works. After all, it is written: "Alms-giving frees from death" (Tob 4.10). The reference is not to that death which the blood of Christ once for all has wiped away, and from which the grace of our baptism of salvation and of our redeemer has set us free. Rather is it from those postbaptismal sins that creep in.

2 In another place opportunity for penitence is given, and the Lord gives this solemn warning to those who do not do penance. "I have," he says, "many things against you, because you allow your wife Jezebel to teach, who says that she is a prophet, and to seduce my servants, to commit fornication and to eat from the sacrifice, and I gave her opportunity that she could do penance, and she did not wish to repent of her fornication. Behold, I am sending her to her bed and those who have committed fornication with her into great tribulation, unless she does not perform penance for her works" (Rev 2.20–25). Obviously the Lord would not have encouraged them to do penance if he did not promise pardon to the penitent.

In the gospel the Lord pronounces: "There will, I say to you, thus be more rejoicing in heaven over a sinner doing penance than over ninety-nine righteous persons who have no need of repentance" (Lk 15.7). For since it is written: "God does not cause someone to die and does not rejoice in the destruction of the living" (Wis 1.13), obviously God who wishes none to perish desires sinners to do penance and through penitence to return anew to life. Accordingly, through Joel the prophet God issues this proclamation: "Now the Lord your God says: return unto me with your whole heart accompanied by fasting, weeping, and mourning, and rend your hearts and not your garments, and return unto the Lord your God, since he is compassionate and fatherly and long suffering and of great mercy, and who redirects his sentence concerning the evil that he has ordained" (Joel 2.12–13). We also read in the Psalms of both the judgment and mercy of the God who at the same time threatens as he spares, of the God who punishes in order that he might set right, and who preserves when he has set right. "I will visit," he says, "their misdeeds with a rod, and their sins with scourgings. My mercy however I will not scatter from them" (Ps 88.33–34).

23.1 The Lord also in the gospel reveals the fatherly duty of God the Father and says: "Which man of you whom if his son asks for bread will offer him a stone, or if he demands a fish, will he offer him a snake? If therefore you, though you have no reason, know how to give good gifts to your sons, how much more will your heavenly Father give good gifts to those who ask him?" (Mt 7.9–11) **2** Here the Lord compares side by side a father of flesh and the eternal and munificent fatherly goodness of God the Father. Suppose the worthless father on earth just mentioned is gravely offended by a son who is a sinner and evildoer. Suppose nonetheless he will see his son subsequently reformed. He has now laid aside the misdeeds of his past life and been directed through his penitential mourning to the paths of moderate and good behavior and to an innocent character. The father rejoices and is made glad and receives again into his embrace with the votive prayer of a father's joy the son whom previously he had cast out. How much more will that one and true Father, good and compassionate in his fatherly duty, indeed in himself goodness and compassion and fatherly duty, rejoice in the penitence of his own sons.

He will not threaten wrath to those who are penitent, nor punishment for those who grieve and mourn. Rather he would promise pardon and forgiveness. **3** Therefore the Lord in the gospel calls blessed those who grieve, since he who grieves is invoking mercy, but he who is haughty and proud is causing to mount up the wrath against him, and the punishment of the judgment that is coming. **4** And accordingly, for that reason, most dearest brother, we decided on a total prohibition from all hope of receiving communion and reconciliation those who failed to do penance and to testify with their whole heart to their sorrow for their sins in a publicly expressed grieving. This applied even in the case when someone in sickness or mortal danger started pleading for reconciliation. In that case they were making their petition under duress and as a result only of the suggestion of an imminent death. Repentance of their sin was not the moving factor. A person who has never reflected that he is destined to die is hardly worthy to receive consolation at the point of death.

24.1 I come now, dearest brother, to the subject of Novatian himself.

You requested that I state in writing what heresy he had introduced. Understand, in the first place, that we ought not to be curious about what he is teaching, since he teaches from *outside* the Church. Whoever Novatian is and whatever kind of person he may be, he is not a Christian because he is not in the Church of Christ. He might boast even of philosophy in projecting in speech eloquence expressed in exalted language. But, nevertheless, he who has not maintained the bond of fraternal love nor the unity of the Church has lost that which previously he had been.

2 Ignore then the fact that Novatian was made a bishop in the Church by seventeen fellow bishops. You could after all regard no one as a bishop who contrived by seeking the office of his own accord[24] to become what was in effect a counterfeit[25] and foreign bishop, created by those who were themselves runaway bishops. There is one Church that comes from Christ's body divided into many members throughout the whole world. For precisely the same reason there is one episcopate widely spread in a harmony of concord between

[24]"By seeking the office" = *per ambitum. Ambitus* usually means "canvassing for an election." The principle of *nolli episcopari,* by which the candidate is expected to refuse the bishop's office that has to be forced on him, predominates in patristic sources. See also n. 13 above.

[25]"Counterfeit" = *adulter,* usually translated "adulterer," can also mean "counterfeiter," so that Cyprian is able to use the term in both senses; see *Unit. eccl.* 6–11; *Ep.* 43.5.1, n. 6.

many corporations. Despite this, Novatian is attempting to create a Church of human origin, in place of what God has handed down, in place of the unity, fastened and universally joined together, of the Catholic Church.

Novatian is sending forth his own new apostles through a large number of cities, with the intention of setting up more recent foundations for his own teaching. Already long ago bishops have been ordained throughout all the provinces, and throughout individual cities, who are venerable in age, unimpaired in their faith, proven in tribulation, proscribed in persecution. Despite their already being in existence, Novatian has the audacity to try to create in their place other false bishops.

3 As if he could travel the whole world with his determined effort for his new scheme, and to sever the joints of the ecclesiastical body by the dissemination of his new discord! He is ignorant that while schismatics are always on fire at their first beginnings, they are able to neither increase nor cause to grow the movement that they have unlawfully begun. Rather they immediately start diminishing due to their rivalries that lead to dissolution.

4 Novatian could not however have claim to the episcopate even if he had previously been made a bishop, but then had departed from the body of his fellow bishops and from the unity of the Church. For the Apostle admonishes by his words that we should support one another lest we secede from the unity that God has established: ". . . supporting one another in love, striving to preserve the unity of the Spirit in the bond of peace" (Eph 4.2–3). This person therefore who preserves neither the unity of the Spirit nor the bond of peace but separates himself from what binds him to the Church, namely from the college of sacred bishops, is not able to have the legal power of the bishop nor the honour due to his rank. He has no intention to hold to the unity of the episcopate nor to be in communion with it.[26]

---

[26]"To be in communion" = *tenere pacem*, which is literally "to hold to the peace." *Pax* in Cyprian is used of reconciliation through penance and the receiving back into communion.

25.1 Consider next, how swollen is his arrogance, how forgetful of the claims of humility and gentleness, how arrogant his vaunted claim. He is claiming that a man should dare to do or believe that he is able to do something that the Lord never allowed the apostles. I mean that he should think the he can separate the tares from the wheat. The bearing of the winnowing fan and the purging the threshing floor was not a sole concession to him alone, nor that he should undertake of himself to separate the chaff from the wheat (Mt 3.12). **2** He flies in the face of what the Apostle says: "In a great house there are not only golden and silver vessels, but also wooden and earthenware" (2 Tim 2.20). But he appears to choose the golden and silver vessels, and so to despise the wooden and earthenware ones, to throw them aside, to condemn them, when only on the day of the Lord will the wooden vessels be reduced to cinders by the fire of God's passion, and will the earthenware ones be smashed by him to whom is given the rod of iron (Rev 2.27).

26.1 He has appointed himself as a judge (and not God), as the one who examines the heart and the reins (Rev 2.23). Let him therefore judge with equity in every case. He knows that it is written: "Behold, you have been made well, do not now sin lest something worse should happen" (Jn 5.14). He should then separate from his side and from his company embezzlers and fornicators.[27]

Fornication is far more serious and a worse sin than a case of receiving a certificate (*libellaticus*). The latter sins because he has to, the former of his own free will. The former is deceived by an error when he considers that it is enough if he does not actually make a sacrifice. The latter assails the marriage bond of another, or he enters the sewer and slimy chasm of the brothel, and violates his body that had been sanctified as the temple of God with a defilement that is

---

[27]Novatian's associates, Nicostratus and Novatus, had been accused of embezzlement in Cyprian *Ep. 50.1.2 and 52.1.2 and 52.2.1, but not fornication. But these are standard, rhetorical jibes use to stereotype any schismatic or heretic. See also Clarke, *Letters of St Cyprian*, 2.201, n. 120.

subject to a curse. That is why the Apostle says: "Every sin whatever a man has done, is outside the body: however, he who commits fornication, sins against his own body" (1 Cor 3.16 and 2 Cor 6.16–18).

2 Yet even to these very sinners penance is granted, and there is left to them the hope that they can publicly grieve and make atonement according to the very Apostle who says: "I fear lest coming to you I might cause grief to many of those who previously have sinned and have not practiced penance in the impurities which they have committed as well as the fornications and acts of lust" (2 Cor 12.20–21).

27.1 The new heretics should not flatter themselves in this regard by saying that they do not have communion with idolaters. Instead they keep company with adulterers and fraudsters, who are convicted of being guilty of idolatry. The Apostle identifies them: "Know this and understand that every fornicator or impure person or fraudster, because it is idolatry, has no inheritance in the kingdom of Christ and of God" (Eph 5.5). And again: "Accordingly, put to death your members which are on earth, laying aside fornication, impurity, and evil lustful desire and greed, which are the service of idols, on account of which the wrath of God is coming" (Col 3.5–6).

2 For because our bodies are members of Christ, and we are as individuals the temple of God, whoever violates the temple of God by an act of adultery violates God. He who sins in serving daemons and idols does the will of the Devil. For evil deeds do not come from the Holy Spirit but from the inspiration of the Adversary. From the impure spirit sinful lusts are born and compel action in the service of the Devil and contrary to God.

It is they who claim that one person is stained by the sin of another. Their constantly asserted argument is that idolatry of the wrong doer passes over to him who does no wrong. As a result, according to the claim that is their very own, they cannot acquit themselves from the charge of idolatry. This is because it is established from the conclusive argument of the Apostle that the fornicators and fraudsters with whom they are in communion are idolaters.

3 Our truer argument is compatible with both the faith and the doctrine of what has been divinely proclaimed. Each and every person is himself to be held responsible for his own sin, and it is not possible for someone to be made guilty for another. The Lord, after all, gives advance warning of this and says: "The judgment for the just will be upon him and the wickedness of the wicked will be upon him" (Ez 18.20). And again: "The fathers will not die for the sons, and the sons will not die for the fathers. Each and everyone will die in their own sin" (Deut 24.14).

When we read and grasp this, we come to think that no one should be held back from the fruit of making atonement and from the hope of reconciliation. After all, we know, according to the confidence given by the divine Scriptures, by the very God who is its author and who encourages it, that sinners should be constrained to conduct acts of repentance, and that pardon and forgiveness should not be denied to those who are penitent.

28.1 Novatian's claim is that we should exhort to acts of penance in order to make atonement, but that the act of atonement itself should be deprived of any curing medicine. This is his mockery that causes obstacles to the brothers. This is his cheating[28] deception inflicted on those who have sorrowed in their grief. This is his empty tradition, without validity, his creation of a heretical foundation. He proposes saying to our brothers:

> "Beat your breasts and shed tears, and sigh for days and for nights, and perform generous and frequent acts to obtain washing and cleansing for your sin. But after all those things you will die outside the Church. You should do whatever is

---

[28]"Cheating" = *caducus,* in its legal sense of inherited property that cannot be taken up by the heir to the estate. Justinian (Gaius) *Inst.* 2.150: "By that law goods are to be made caducary (*ea lege bona caduca fiunt*) and are ordered to be delivered over to the People . . . if the departed should have no heir (*et ad populum deferri iubentur, si defuncto nemo heres . . . sit*).

proper for receiving reconciliation but you will receive none
of the reconciliation for which you are looking."

That would, would it not, be enough for someone to drop dead at
once, to expire from the very hopelessness his position, to give up
immediately any intention of expressing grief?

2 Do you imagine that a peasant farmer could possibly engage
in labor if you were to say to him:

"Exercise on the field your every skill at farming, carefully
apply yourself in preparing the ground, but you will reap no
harvest, you will press no ripe vines, you will not gain the
fruit of your olive trees, you will pick no orchard fruit from
your trees."

3 Or would you say to someone whom you were urging to buy
and set ships to work:

"Buy material from the most excellent of forests, my brother,
construct your ship's keel with the strong and choice oak-
wood, labor so that your ship should be built and armed
with a tiller, with ropes, with sails, but when you will have
done these things, you will not see any fruit from its trade
and voyages."

29.1 Their purpose is to block and cut off the path of sorrowful
mourning as well as the way to acts of repentance. Apparently penitence itself is to be eliminated while the fruitful reward for penitence
is to be snatched away through our hardheartedness and cruelty,
even though, in the sacred Scriptures, the Lord God fondly encourages people to return to him and to be penitent. Our conclusion
is that no one should be prohibited from doing penance, and that
through his priests reconciliation can be granted to those who earnestly pray for it and implore the mercy of the Lord. God is merciful,

and with a father's love, so that we must allow the laments of those who beat their breasts in sorrow, and not deny to those thus grieving the fruit of their penitence.

2 Those who have departed this life have no opportunity for professing their faith nor for public confession where they are. In consequence, those who have repented with all their heart and have made their petition ought, while in this life, to be received into the Church and be preserved in it for their Lord. Christ is destined to come to his Church and will pass his judgment on those whom he will find on the *inside*. Apostates, of course, who otherwise are deserters or adversaries and enemies, who fragment the Church of Christ, cannot be received, according to the Apostle, in admission to the Church's rite of reconciliation. Even if they are cut down for the name of Christ, they will still be on the *outside* when they maintain neither the unity of the Spirit nor of the Church.

30.1 I have, for the moment, dearest brother, briefly run through, to the best of my ability, some few points amongst many. By my comments, I intend to satisfy your urgent request and to unite you more and more to our episcopal college and to the fellowship of being part of our body.[29] If, however, the opportunity and the means present themselves to you for visiting us, we will then be able to discuss together and treat both fully and completely the many matters which affect the concord necessary to salvation.

I pray, dearest brother, that you may always fare well.

---

[29]Clearly Antonianus is to be left in no doubt of the ecclesial and sacramental consequences of his siding with the Novatianists, in accordance with Cyprian's theology of Church order; see Introduction, §3.

Troubles with Felicissimus:
Cyprian Criticizes Pope Cornelius

Cyprian writes to Cornelius in AD 252 in reply to two letters from him, the first of which recorded the expulsion of Felicissimus and his party from the Church, and the second reports Cornelius' climb down from this position subsequent to threats and violent behavior (2.1). Those who believed with Felicissimus that they should be freely absolved without participating in the theatrics of public penance were clearly moved by a feeling of desperation, and a lack of sympathy with Cyprian's understanding of penance in terms of the requirements of a quasi-juridical process (2.2). Cyprian describes their often-violent demands, and likens them to those of the pagan mob (2.3–5). Cornelius must follow Church discipline without fear (3.1–2), and realize that his opponents are Antichrists (3.3). A bishop is a priest, against whom sacrilege is being committed (4). His opponents are rebels who are setting up a rival authority not legitimated by God's command (5).

Cyprian then describes his own experience of pagan persecution following the implementation of Decius' Edict in 251 (Introduction §2.1). The pagans attacking him as bishop were *outside* the Church. Those rebels now attacking him must be like the pagans *outside* the Church. Satan is behind both groups (6). These can now be identified with various parallels from Scripture (7–8). Cyprian can then describe the consecration of Fortunatus, called by him a "pseudo bishop," along with the excommunication of him and the five presbyters. Felicissimus, involved in an embassy to Rome on behalf of his claims, has also been excommunicated by an African episcopal council (9.1). Cyprian reveals the emergence of a due process in identifying and dealing with schism. Bishops write letters to one another in order to cement unity in practice. It is essential for each bishop to be clear on the name from whom one should receive a letter, and what name on a letter (such as Novatian's) should lead to its rejection without reply (9.2–3).

Felicianus and Perseus were the bearers of Cyprian's letters, but bad weather and the pressure of other business had delayed their setting sail.

Felicissimus had thus reached Rome and Cornelius first, and put his side of the case (9.4–10.1). Cyprian now accuses the party of Felicissimus as being stained with idolatrous sacrifices, and as consecrating bishops with a very small number of consecrators (10.2–11.1). His consecrators were, despite their lies, only five (11.2), and not twenty-five (11.3). A somewhat contrived list of their sins now follows, for which not to allow repentance before readmission robs the sinner of forgiveness (12–13). They have now compounded their offence by creating a pseudo bishop (14–15).

Cyprian now describes how Felicissimus' delegation managed to reach Rome before that of Felicianus, his representative (16). He concluded by rehearsing once again the implications of readmitting those using threats and violence against what he considers to be a council of bishops exercising jurisdiction by divine right in a court administering the New Law (17–20).

Cyprian to His Holy Brother Cornelius

1.1 I have read your letter, dearest brother Cornelius, which you sent by the hand of our brother, the acolyte Satyrus.[1] The contents of that letter were both about the love of the brotherhood, and ecclesiastical discipline, and priestly oversight. You demonstrated therein that Felicissimus is no new enemy of Christ, but has already been restrained on account of many serious charges against him. It is his condemnation, not only by my verdict but also that of the majority of my fellow bishops, that has lead you to make him an outcast.

2 You recounted that, when he came with a gang and a conspiracy of desperate individuals as a bodyguard, you made sure that

---

[1] The office of acolyte was ranked higher than that of exorcist, below which came that of reader. It would appear that Satyrus held the latter post in AD 250. In Cyprian *Ep.* 35.1.1 he had been sent to Rome in order to establish the validity of the consecration of Cornelius. For minor orders in Rome at this time see also Cornelius' criticism of Novatian in Eusebius *Hist. eccl.* 6.43.11: "This so-called vindicator of the gospel was ignorant of the fact . . . that in a catholic church there must be one bishop in which nevertheless there are forty-six presbyters, seven deacons, seven sub-deacons, forty-two acolytes, fifty-two exorcists, readers, and door keepers, upwards of five hundred widows along with down and outs . . ."

he was expelled from the Church in the exercise of the full force
of the episcopal prerogative—from the very Church from which
previously already he had been expelled with those like him by the
exercise of the sovereignty of Christ our Lord, and by the uncompromising act of our court. We so acted that the person responsible for
a schism, and for a ruptured community, should not further violate,
by the shameful appearance of his presence and by the accompanying contamination with immorality and unchastity, the bride of
Christ who is incorrupt, holy, and chaste. He was a fraudulent user
of money entrusted to him, a sexual abuser of young maidens, and
the destroyer and corrupter of many marriages.

2.1 However, I have read your other letter, brother, which you
enclosed with your first missive. I am shocked on observing that
the threats and terror tactics of those who arrived have shaken you
considerably. According to what you have written, they attacked you,
uttering threats from the depths of their despair to the intent that, if
you did not accept the letter that they delivered, they would read it
out in public, and their mouths would issue vile and abusive threats
typical of them.

2 It is not the case, my dear brother, that evil men should get
away through sheer brazenness born of desperation with what they
cannot achieve from a fair sentence of our court. Were the effrontery of the morally worthless to so frighten us, there would need to
be serious questioning of the strength of will of the episcopate, and
of our exercise of the supreme and divine power of governing the
Church. We are unable to endure or even exist as Christians, if what
it has come to is our being scared by the threats and subterfuges of
the lost.

3 Both pagans and Jews and heretics are issuing their threats,
and all those whose hearts and minds the Devil has occupied bear
witness today from their wild voices to a mad savagery with its own
poison. We cannot simply yield to them because they make threats.
The Adversary and enemy does not become greater than Christ

by such methods of claiming and arrogating to himself so much in this present world. Our faith should remain like an unshakable and immovable oak, dearest brother. Our courage should possess the physical strength of a massive, obstructing rock. It should stand unshaken, blocking the course of the roaring waves as the tide comes bursting and rushing in.

4 It is of no importance to a bishop from where terror or danger might come. His life is exposed to terrors and to dangers, but he is nevertheless made glorious by those terrors and dangers. Of course we ought not to reflect upon and examine only the threats of the pagans and of the Jews. Why, we see the Lord himself was held prisoner by his brothers, and betrayed by one amongst the apostles whom he had himself chosen.

Even at the beginnings of the world, none other than his brother killed the righteous Abel. Jacob became a fugitive under persecution from a brother that hated him. It was the destiny of the boy Joseph to be sold with his brothers acting as the salesmen. In the gospel we often read that it has been foretold that it is rather those of one's house who will be one's enemies, and thus in consequence those who have been previously bound by the solemn obligation to remain united will be those very betrayers.

It makes no difference who is the betrayer or who is enraged, since it is God who allows our being betrayed and winning the crown. We do not find it a degradation to be made to suffer by our brothers what Christ has suffered. They have no glory for doing what Judas did.

5 Why do they push themselves forward in this way? Their boastfulness is empty, for all the threats of their inflated pride. Why did they threaten me over there in Rome, when I was not present? It is over here in Carthage where I am present where they could have me in their power.

6 We do not fear their insults with which they tear themselves and their lives daily into shreds. We do not cringe in terror at the clubs and stones and swords that they are brandishing at us, with

the words that threaten the murder of we who are their own kindred. Their character is such that they are murderers in God's sight. But they cannot murder us unless the Lord allows them to murder us. Although it is appointed to us once to die, they nevertheless are causing us to perish daily through their anger and their words, and their sinful deeds.

3.1 That we are repeatedly attacked with insults and shaken by their acts of terror is no ground, dearest brother, for abandoning the discipline of the Church nor for relaxing the high-priestly, episcopal judgment of their case.

Divine Scripture confronts and admonishes us when it says: "The man who is presumptuous and proud, boasting in himself, will achieve nothing at all even though he has extended his soul to fill the underworld" (Hab 2.5). And again: "Do not fear the words of a man who is a sinner, since his glory will be in his excrement and in its worms. Today he will be exulted and tomorrow he will not be found. When he has returned to his own dust, thought of him will perish" (1 Mac 2.62–63). And again: "I saw the impious exalted and lifted up above the cedars of Lebanon. And I went by, and behold, he was not. And I looked for him and his place has not been found" (Ps 36.35–36).

2 Exulting oneself, and an inflated ego, and arrogance, and proud boastfulness, are born not from the authority of Christ who teaches humility, but from the spirit of Antichrist, against whom the Lord expresses his disapproval through the prophet in these words: "You have said in your heart: 'I will ascend into heaven, I will set my seat above the stars of God, I will take my seat on a high mountain in the North above the high mountains. I will ascend above the clouds, I will be like the most High'" (Is 14.13–14). But he adds these words: "Regardless, you will descend to the place of the departed into the depths of the earth, and those who will see you will be amazed because of you" (Is 14.15–16). Therefore divine Scripture threatens a like punishment to such people in another place and states: "For the day of the Lord of Hosts is upon all the careless and proud, and everyone who is haughty and lifted up" (Is 2.12).

3 Accordingly, each and every one is betrayed by his own words, and whether he has truly Christ or Antichrist in his heart can be uncovered from that which he speaks. Just as the Lord says in his gospel: "Offspring of vipers, how are you able to speak good things, when you are morally worthless? For your lips send forth from the abundance of your heart. The good man produces from his good treasury good things, and the morally worthless man produces the morally worthless from a morally worthless treasury" (Lk 16.19–25).

Likewise, the rich man who was a sinner that begged help from Lazarus was scorched by the raging fire of the burning flames and racked by their tortures. But he paid the penalty with his lips and tongue more than all other parts of his body because he had sinned far more with his tongue and lips. Lazarus was placed in Abraham's bosom, and assigned to a place of cool relief.

4.1 In consequence it is written: "Neither shall evil doers attain to the kingdom of God" (1 Cor 6.10) and again the Lord in his own gospel says: "He who will say to his own brother, 'O fool,' and will say 'Racha,' he will be found guilty for the gehenna of fire" (Mt 5.22). In consequence, how are they who perpetrate such things to escape the judgment of our avenging Lord, not only for wrongs against the brothers, but also against the priests to whom so great an honor has been granted by God who deigned them worthy?

Remember, whoever did not obey God's priest who acted as judge for a time here on earth was at once executed. In Deuteronomy the Lord addresses this point when he says: "And whatever man will so act with arrogant pride that he does not listen obediently to the priest or judge, whoever he shall be in those days, that man shall die. And all the people when they hear shall fear, and they shall not continue to conduct themselves with impiety even as now" (Deut 17.12–13).

2 Similarly, when the Jews reject him, God says to Samuel: "They have not rejected you but me" (1 Sam 8.7). And the Lord also in his gospel adds: "He who hears you hears me, and him who sent me, and he who rejects me, rejects also him who sent me" (Lk 10.16). And when he had cleansed the leper, he said: "Go and show yourself to the priest" (Mt 8.2–4). When afterwards, at the time of his Passion, he had received from the servant of the priest a blow of the hand, when he said to him: "Do you thus reply to the high priest?" (Jn 18.22) the Lord said nothing of a threatening nature to the high priest, nor did he detract anything from the honor of a priest. Rather he asserted and demonstrated his innocence with the words: "If I have spoken wrongly, convict me of the wrong, if however well, why do you beat me?" (Jn 18.13)

3 Likewise afterwards, in the Acts of the Apostles, it was said to the blessed Paul the apostle: "Do you thus assail a priest of God by your slander?" The Lord had now been crucified, and those Jews had begun their course of sacrilege and impiety and bloodshed, and did not retain any fragment of sacerdotal honour and authority. Notwithstanding, even though the name of priest, in Paul's imagination, was an illusion and his form a shadow, Paul said: "I did not know, brothers, that he is the high priest. For it is written: 'You shall not slander the prince of your people'" (Acts 23.4–5).

5.1 There are also other precedents, of very great number and of considerable quality, in terms of which God confirms with his approval sacerdotal authority and power. In their light, what kind of people do you think them to be who are not frightened by the terror promised by the Lord in his forewarning nor by the punishment of the Judgment to come? They are surely enemies of the sacred bishops and rebels against the Catholic Church.

The only source from which heresies arise that give birth to schism is disobedience to God's sacred bishop, in failure to note that there is one bishop in a church and one judge in Christ's place at one time. **2** If their whole sacred fellowship renders him obedience in accordance with God's governance, no one should start any uprising against the college of sacred bishops. No one should make himself that judge following God's decision, following the election by the laity, following the consent of his fellow bishops. Otherwise they would then be not acting against those bishops but against God.

Let no one split the Church of Christ by rending apart its unity, let no one, taking pleasure in himself and with swelling pride, found a new heresy outside and apart from it. It could only be so if a sacrilegious boldness and a self-destructive mentality so took possession of someone that he should imagine that he could be made a priest apart from God's decision.[2] The Lord in his gospel says: "Are not two sparrows sold for a farthing and neither of them falls to the ground without the Father's willing it" (Mt 10.29). When Christ claims not even the smallest things can be done apart from God's will, does anyone consider that what is of the highest and greatest importance can be done in the Church apart from either the knowledge or the permission of God? Sacred bishops, that is to say God's stewards, are not ordained apart from his judgment on their ordination.

3 To maintain the contrary is not to hold the faith by which we live. Such a view does not honor the God whom we know and believe to rule and govern all things by his direction and determination. Clearly only in the case of those who have been so made outside the Church are bishops not made by the will of God. But they are so when they are made according to what is set out and handed down in the gospels. This is the Lord's principle laid down and enunciated in the Twelve Prophets: "They established for themselves a king, and not through me" (Hos 8.4). And again: "Their sacrifices are like the bread of sorrow, all who eat them will be defiled" (Hos 9.4). And through Isaiah the Holy Spirit proclaims and says: "The Lord says this: 'You have held a council, not through me: and you have made an assembly, but not through my Spirit, to add sins upon sin'" (Is 30.1).

---

[2]It is arguable, of course, that Felicissimus' party would have responded that it was the grace of martyrdom that often marked their claims to offer the Eucharist without formal ordination; see the introduction to Cyprian *Ep.* 38.

6.1 However, because I am challenged to speak, I speak with sorrow, I speak because I am forced to. My subject is the example of a bishop put in the place of the one who has died. He has been chosen by the vote of the whole laity in the bond of peace; he has been defended in persecution by God's aid. He is joined to all his colleagues in faith, and his own laity continues to approve of him in the course of an episcopate already having lasted four years.

This bishop has calmly served the cause of the practice of moral order. He was outlawed while the gale of persecution raged,[3] with the name of his bishop's office inserted and attached on the list.[4] So often they demanded him for the lion, honoring him in the circus, in the amphitheatre, by his witness to the Lord who deigned him worthy.

During these very days in which I am composing my letter to you, the outcry of the mob continually demanded him to be thrown to the lions in the circus, on account of the sacrifices that the people are under orders to offer by the Edict that was posted up. **2** When someone of this kind, most beloved brother, is seen to be under attack from certain groups, the attacker is seen to be, not of course the Christ who both appoints and protects his sacred bishops, but he who is Christ's Adversary and the enemy of his Church. Those groups are without hope and lost, having placed themselves outside the Church. This is the reason why that Adversary pursues with hostility this bishop who presides over the Church. The Adversary's design is to snatch away their helmsman so as to make the shipwrecked souls crash violently round and upon the churches.

7.1 But any person of faith ought to be mindful of the gospel and to remember the commandments of the Apostle. He ought not to be swayed in the light of the Apostle's forewarning of our situation. We thus expect that, in the last times, the proud and willfully disobedi-

---

[3]"Outlawed" = *proscribere,* or to have one's name officially posted up in the forum.

[4]This is a key text in the debate about whether Christianity as such was the object of Decius' legislation or whether Christians were simply persecuted in consequence of their refusal to sacrifice along with any other pagan religious leader who might refuse to do the same.

ent, and enemies of God's sacred bishops, intend either to depart from the Church or to act against the Church. Such kinds of people are here now, whom the Lord and his apostles previously predicted would come in the future. **2** Nor should anyone who presides as servant be surprised that he is being deserted by certain people. His own disciples forsook the Lord himself while he was performing mighty works and the greatest miracles, and confirming by the testimony of his deeds the moral qualities of God his Father. Even so, he did not chide them for withdrawing from him, nor did he issue serious threats, but rather he turned to his apostles and said: "Would you also wish to go?" (Jn 6.67) Of course he was observing the law under which a man has been left to his own freedom, and, resting on his own free will to decide, he seeks after either death or salvation.

3 Nevertheless Peter, upon whom the Church had been built by the same Lord, speaking as one on behalf of all, and responding with the voice of the Church says: "Lord, to whom shall we go? You have the word of eternal life, and we believe and know that you are the Son of the living God" (Jn 6.68).

What he means, of course, and demonstrates is that those who withdraw from Christ perish through their own fault, but that the Church which believes in Christ and which holds fast to his doctrine that it has come to know never withdraws from him in any way. Those who remain in the house of God are the Church. They are the seedbed planted indeed by God the Father. They are as such packed solidly together with the thick growth of the wheat. They are not, as heretics, like chaff blown about by the windlike spirit of the enemy who scatters them. John in his epistle speaks of them: "They went out from us, but they were not of us, for if they had been of us, they would have remained with us" (1 Jn 2.19). **4** Similarly Paul informs us that we should not be concerned when the wicked perish from the Church: our faith should not be made less because the treacherous have withdrawn. He says: "What if certain of them fall away from believing, will their faithlessness make faith in God empty? Far from it! For God is true, but every man a liar" (Rom 3.3–4).

8.1 Our principle concern, brother, is, in agreement with our conscience, to make the effort to prevent anyone perishing from the Church by our own fault. But if, on the other hand, anyone will perish as a result of his own offence, and is unwilling to undergo penance and to return to the Church, we cannot in the future on the day of Judgment be blamed. We have acted in the interests of obtaining their health.

2 The abuses of the lost ought not to influence us, in so far as we have not departed from the straight path and from our definite rule in the light of what the Apostle instructs us. His words are: "If I were to please men, I would not be Christ's servant" (Gal 1.10). The issue is whether we seek to gain the favor of men or of God. If indeed we strive and work towards being able to please God, we ought to reject with disdain human insults and slanders.

9.1 I did not write to you immediately about Fortunatus that pseudo bishop appointed by a few and familiar old heretics. This was because, dearest brother, the matter was not one warranting your fear that needed therefore to be brought hastily to your notice as though it were some big thing to be reported. This was especially the case since you already knew well enough Fortunatus' name. The man is one of the five presbyters who were already a long time ago in exile from the Church. They have been actually more recently removed positively by the sentence of our many fellow bishops and the most serious of men.[5]

These five presbyters composed a letter last year to you on this subject. You would recognize the name of the selfsame Felicissimus, as the standard bearer of the mutiny. He is also found in person in the same written proceedings of our fellow bishops sent to you in a previous letter. Not only have these bishops here excluded him, but you have also expelled him from the Church recently over there in Rome. **2** I trust fully that these matters have come to your notice,

---

[5]This was probably the council of 251, recorded in Cyprian *Ep.* 55.6.2.

and I know that they would be strictly consistent with your memory of them and your moral practice regarding them. I did not think it necessary that a quicker and more urgent report should be made to you about the foolish fripperies of heretics.

The effrontery that schismatics and heretics devise against the Catholic Church ought not to affect its majesty any less than its sense of worth. They are saying that the party of Novatian has created recently for itself here as its own pseudo bishop Maximus. He was the presbyter recently sent to us as an envoy by Novatian, and expelled from our communion. **3** I did not write to you about him either, when I had rejected with disdain the whole business, and I sent to you just now the names of our fellow bishops who have been appointed to their positions here. These are whole and healthy, and are preeminent amongst their brothers in the Catholic Church.

It was the general resolution of the council of us all that we write to you by way of making a summary of our proceedings in order for error to be refuted and truth to be carefully studied. It was also that you be informed to whom you and our colleagues ought to write, and from whom you should receive letters in reply.[6] However, if any one except those who we have included in our letter should presume to write to you, you are informed that he has either been defiled by offering a sacrifice or receiving a certificate, or is one of the heretics and is certainly perverse and profane.

4 I did however write to you from Africa on, amongst other matters, what needed to be brought to your attention in regard to Fortunatus. A favorable opportunity enabled me to do so in the person of Felicianus the acolyte, who is the friendliest of men and

---

[6]Clearly the "summary of proceedings (*conpendium*)" also contained a list of "valid" bishops, i.e. those in communion with Cyprian. It seems that we see here the growth of the practice of a bishop formally writing to the remaining bishops of his province, or of the wider world not present at his consecration, informing them that he had been consecrated, and summarizing his faith. These would then write back their letters of welcome into the episcopal college. Cyprian is taking Cornelius delicately to task for accepting letters from Fortunatus (2.1). "Our colleagues (*collegae nostri*)" refers to the Italian bishops that Cornelius is to inform.

a cleric, whom you sent with Perseus our colleague.[7] But whilst Felicianus our brother was either delayed by weather conditions or held back by ourselves because of our other letters that you needed to receive, he was overtaken by Felicissimus who raced on to you. So typical is it that guilty acts are always done in haste, as if haste is sufficient to prevail against the guiltless.

10.1 I gave you notice through Felicianus, brother, that Privatus had arrived at Carthage, that old heretic in the colony of Lambaesis, condemned some many years before for many and serious offences by the sentence of ninety bishops. That sentence of our predecessors, of which you are also aware, was taken severe note of in the letter of Fabian and Donatus.[8] Privatus stated that he was willing to conduct his case before us in the council that we held on 15 May last year. Despite that, he was not admitted. He then made this Fortunatus fellow, worthy to be in his own, private episcopal college, a pseudo bishop. **2** A certain Felix also had accompanied him, whom he himself once set up as a pseudo bishop outside the Church. Jovinus and Maximus, companions in heresy with Privatus, were also present, who had been condemned because of the sacrilegious sacrifices and crimes declared proven against them by the sentence of our nine colleagues. Also they had been confirmed as excommunicated by very many of us in the council of the previous year.

3 With these four is conjoined also Repostus of Sutunurca, who not only himself fell under persecution, but cast down the largest section of his laity by persuading them to commit sacrilege. These five, together with a small number who had either offered sacrifice or who were his evil fellow conspirators, chose for themselves as their colleague Fortunatus as their pseudo bishop. Their purpose

[7]Perseus must be, as Cyprian's and Cornelius' colleague (*collega*), an Italian bishop, as a member of the episcopal *collegium,* or college.

[8]Donatus was Cyprian's immediate predecessor at Carthage, and he died in AD 248. Fabian became bishop in AD 236. Cyprian claims here a joint episcopal letter, which is lost, and thus reinforces his claim that the episcopal order of the wider Church is collegial.

was of course that, when they had agreed together on their collective crimes, those who were guided would be of the same moral quality as their guide.

11.1 You can now understand, dearest brother, how from this source came the other lies which these men, without hope and lost, have brandished around over there with you. They who had come to Carthage were no more than five pseudo bishops, composed of those who had offered sacrifices (*sacrificati*), and heretics. They were mad enough to make Fortunatus their ally.

Nonetheless, as sons of the Devil, their outrageous acts are full of their falsehood so much so that you write their arrogant claim that twenty-five bishops were in fact present. This falsehood was their constant boast previously over here to our brothers, when they were saying that twenty-five bishops would arrive from Numidia with the intention of making them a bishop. **2** In consequence, their lie was exposed afterwards when five only assembled, shipwrecked and muddled souls, and whose excommunication we confirmed.

Then they sailed to Rome with their cargo of falsehoods, appearing to believe that the truth was unable to set sail after them and convict lying tongues with the proof of certain evidence. This is their real insanity, brother, not to reflect nor grasp that lies do not deceive for long, that there is night only for so long before a shining day break. When the day grows bright and the sun has risen, the shadows and darkness give way to the light, and those acts of violent robbery that have run wild throughout the night have to stop.

3 Finally, if you ask of them the names, they will not have any, or they give false names. Such is the shortage of evildoers amongst them that they cannot gather together to themselves twenty-five names either from those who sacrificed (*sacrificati*) or from the heretics. However, in order to deceive the ears of simple souls who were not there, they have blown up the number by lying. But even if this number were to be true, it would be a case of the Church being overwhelmed by heretics as well as justice by the unjust.

12.1 I ought not, dearest brother, to now join with them in hand-to-hand combat and to run over in my argument those wrongs they have committed and are continuing to commit up to this moment. After all, we should consider what God's sacred bishops ought to publish and write. With us it is not resentment that should do the talking but a sense of decency. As a result, I must not appear to be provoked into thrusting at them abuse rather than charges arising from their sin.

2 Accordingly, I hold my tongue about their actions in defrauding the Church. I pass over their conspiratorial meetings, their adulteries, and various kinds of offences. But I feel that I cannot keep silent about God's case—not mine nor that of human beings in general—against one of their crimes. Immediately, on the first day of the persecution, they did not hold themselves aloof from sharing communion with the fallen and thus stood in the way of their doing penance. It was then that the crimes of those who committed them were fresh, and not only the altars of the Devil were exuding the odour of sacrilegious sacrifices, but also the very hands and lips of those who were then falling.

God proclaims: "He who sacrifices to the gods shall be done away with, unless to the Lord alone" (Ex 20.22). And the Lord in his gospel says: "He who will deny me, I will deny him" (Mt 10.33). And in another place, in his indignation and divine anger, he does not keep silence but says: "You have poured out to them drink offerings and you have added to them sacrifices. Should I not be angry about these things? Says the Lord" (Is 57.6). Yet they stand in the way lest the God who has born witness that he is angry receives their supplication. They stand in the way lest the Christ who has asserted that he himself will deny the one who denies him should be asked to intercede through prayers and through acts of atonement.

13.1 This was the subject of letters we sent at the very time of the persecution and we have not been heard. We laid it down that the brothers should do penance, and that no one should grant reconciliation arbitrarily to those who were not prepared to do penance. Our decision followed a well-attended debate that issued not only in common agreement but also in a warning. Felicissimus' party made their departure from the Church and raised their fratricidal arms for their purpose. In their act they were committing sacrilege against God, and acting with a godless rage without consideration for God's priests. They are striving to accomplish the Devil's own work in support of his evil plan.

Their object is that God's mercy should not care for healing the wounded in his Church. **2** They spoil the opportunity for repentance of those who are in a wretched condition due to the false pretence of *their* deceptions, with the result that no atonement can be made to a righteous and angry God. Here is someone who previously blushed to be a Christian and afterwards feared to be. But he must not be allowed to search for Christ his lost Lord. *Their* object is to prevent a return to the Church on the part of someone who has departed from the Church.

There is no concern with redeeming one's sins by making atonement and by shedding the tears that are due. Wounds are not to be bathed clean with tears of weeping. The reconciliation that is real is taken away by the deceptive promise of a reconciliation that is false. A cruel stepmother blocks the path to the saving bosom of the mother. The sound of weeping and sobbing shall not be heard from the hearts and from the lips of the fallen.

3 In addition to the above, the fallen are still forcibly persuaded to be abusive to their sacred bishops with the very tongues and mouths by which they previously committed their sin on the Capitol. They pursue with words of insult and abuse the very people against whom there is no charge. These are the confessors and virgins, whose faith is honored with distinguished praise and who are glorious in the Church. It is not so much that these people are disparaging the self-effacement, humility, and modesty of those on our side, but more a question of the hope for life of their own people that is being torn apart.

You do not become contemptible because you hear abuse but because you speak it. In law the offender is not he who is suffers injury from a brother but he who inflicts injury. The guilty do injury to the innocent. But these, though they think that they are inflicting the injury, are in fact suffering it themselves. **4** In consequence, their minds are deadened; their hearts are hardened, their senses deranged. It is as a result of God's wrath that they do not grasp that they have sinned, so that an opportunity of repentance cannot follow. As it is written: "And God has given them a spirit that pierces them through" (Is 29.1) lest they be converted and cured, and made whole after their sinning by prayers of supplication and righteous acts of atonement.

Paul the Apostle in his Letter explains this when he says: "They have no love for the truth that they should be saved: and for this reason God will send upon them the working of error that they may believe a lie, in order that judgment may be passed on all who do not believe in the truth, but give themselves pleasure in injustice" (2 Thess 2.10–12). The first stage in the race on the course to blessedness is not to offend, the second is to recognize offences. From the first stage in the race innocence speeds on unblemished and unimpaired, and preserves us, from the second stage onwards the medicine that makes us whole takes its place.

Our opponents have missed both of these stages by their opposition to God. Consequently, they have lost the grace that they derived from the sanctification of their baptism. But the opportunity for repentance has not replaced it, through which the fault that they have incurred could be cured. Surely, brother, you can't think that offences against God become lighter, smaller, and insignificant because they are not the subjects of petitions before the majesty of the God who is full of righteous anger, because they are not the subjects of the fear of the Lord's Day of wrath and of fire?

Should an armed people be disarmed by an Antichrist that looms over them because he is robbing them of their energy and reverence for Christ? **5** The laity will make their own provision for how they should deal with this. A greater task is laid upon the sacred bishops in their responsibility to assert and expiate[9] the majesty of God. In consequence, we must not be seen to neglect anything in this category, according to our Lord's words of admonishment: "This commandment is against you, O priests, if you will not listen, and if you will not put it in your heart to give honor to my name, says the Lord, I will send upon you a curse, and I will curse your blessing" (Mal 2.1–2).

6 Is God honored when his majesty and judgment are disregarded? So much is this the case that when he pronounces his indignation and wrath upon those who offer sacrifice (*sacrificati*). He sternly warns about eternal punishments and everlasting penalties. But those who commit sacrilege seriously propose and keep saying that one should not ponder God's anger. God's judgment need not be feared, they should not beat upon the door of the Church.

Instead, robbed of any opportunity to be penitent, and without making any public confession for their offence, reconciliation should be declared by presbyters[10] using words that are deceptions. Thus they have treated the bishops with contempt and trampled them under foot. So the fallen (*lapsi*) cannot rise, or those whose place is now outside the Church return. Should communion be offered to those who are not in communion?

14.1 It was not enough for them to have departed from the gospel and to have robbed the fallen (*lapsi*) of hope of making atonement and offering penance. Whether entwined in the net of deception or deeply stained by acts of forging certificates,[11] or polluted with

[9]"Expiate" = *procurare,* used also for "to have charge of" or "to administer." See Cicero *Div.* 1.3: "Omens have to be understood and propitiation made to avert them (*monstris interpretandis ac procurandis*)."

[10]Note the implication here that Cyprian was resisting the claim of Felicissimus' circle that a presbyter could reconcile because, as Cyprian agrees, presbyters as well as bishops can offer the Eucharist. For reconciliation as simply the act of giving communion, and not through the imposition of episcopal hands apart from communion, see Cyprian *Ep.* 15.1.1 and n. 3.

[11]Literally "acts of adultery (*adulteriis*)"; see also n. 14 below.

their deadly touching of things sacrificed, they are not to petition God, they are not to make public confession in the Church for their offences. Thus they have been separated from every feeling of being penitent, and enjoyment of relief for so doing it.

Becoming outsiders, they have founded for themselves, outside the Church and against the Church, a cell of a breakaway group that is lost. Moving from there, a hive then swarmed together of those with a bad conscience, who both refused to petition God and to make atonement. Subsequently thereafter they accepted over them a pseudo bishop ordained by heretics. Then they had the audacity even to set sail to the Chair of St Peter and to deliver letters from schismatics and men outside our sanctuary to the primordial Church from whose source has arisen the united body of the sacred bishops.[12] They did not stop to think that there could be no access of treason into the presence of the Romans whose faith was extolled by the apostle who proclaimed it (Rom 1.8).

2. What case had they for coming and making an announcement of an act of pseudo bishops against true bishops? Either they still agreed with what they had done and were going to persist in their wickedness, or, if they no longer agreed and were departing from their original position, they were aware of the means of changing that position. It is an established principle with us all, and also one of fairness and justice, that a case of one and all be heard in that place where the crime has been perpetrated.

To each individual of the shepherds a share of the flock has been assigned, which each one rules and governs in the light of the account of his actions that he will deliver to the Lord. Therefore,

---

[12]"... to the primordial Church (*ad ecclesiam principalem*) from whose source has arisen the united body of the sacred bishops (*unde unitas sacerdotalis exorta est a schismaticis*)." Here Cyprian clearly has a higher view of the papacy (to which one *ms* reading of his work refers, namely the Received Text of *Unit. eccl.* 4–5) than that maintained later, in his controversy with Stephen of Rome. The bishop of Rome becomes the centre of the web of intercommunion formed by the mutual recognition of bishops throughout the world. Note in section 2 that follows, Cyprian will nevertheless claim the right to judge himself what has been committed "in the share of the flock assigned" to him in Africa.

those who are our charges have no right to run around generally causing conflict within the closely cohering concord of the bishops by an outrageous act of treachery and deceit. They should conduct their case in the place where they can find their accusers and witnesses to the offence with which they are charged. I suppose that you do not think that the authority of the bishops who are to be found in their places in Africa is less than that of a few desperate men on the way to destruction?

These bishops have already delivered their judgment on these men, and have condemned very recently, by a very serious judgment, their personal view of themselves, bound as they are by the snares of their many sins. Their case has been examined already, and already the sentence has been pronounced upon them. It is not fitting that the sacred bishops should be convicted of exercising their oversight with a looseness of conviction that vacillates and is without firmness. It is against this that the Lord teaches with his pronouncement: "Let your speech be, yes yes, no no" (Mt 5.37).

15.1 If we count the number of those, along with presbyters and deacons, who in the previous year passed sentence on them, we should find that those that took part then in the judgment and examination were very many more than those who now are seen to have been linked with Fortunatus.[13] You ought to know, dearest brother, that almost everyone deserted him after the heretics had made him a pseudo bishop. In the past his clever tricks had always had a veil drawn over them. He had made declarations that deceived them, in pretence that they were all on the point of immediate return to the Church. But after they realized that it was *outside* the Church that a pseudo bishop had been created, they admitted that they had been deluded and deceived. So then they came to and fro daily and beat upon the Church's door.

[13]Cyprian refers here to the African council that met in AD 251, with which the Roman council that met subsequently had been in agreement; see Cyprian *Ep.* 55.6.1.

But they are coming back to us who are to render an account to the Lord. We have as a result to weigh carefully and conscientiously in the scales those who should be received back and readmitted to the Church. **2** For with certain of them it is either their offences that are the obstacle or the obstinate or firm resistance of the brethren. They could in any event not be welcomed back with the danger of scandalizing very many people. For no rotten fruits should be gathered in at the expense of damaging those that are whole and incorrupt.

A shepherd is of no use and of any skill if he mixes amongst his flock sheep that are diseased and have been infected so that he contaminates his entire flock by inflicting upon it a malady that is hard to eradicate. **3** You should be able, my dearest brother, to take part with us here in the task when those deformed and twisted characters return from their schism. You would then realize what an effort it takes to urge forbearance upon our brothers, to agree to calm their heart's resentment, and to feel obliged to receive those marked by sickness and to care for them.

Of course they are glad and rejoice when those that return with lesser defect pass inspection. But for the same reason, they murmur against and express strong rejection whenever those who wander home to the Church are incurable and violent and contaminated, whether by acts of counterfeiting *libelli* or by sacrifices,[14] and yet even after these acts hold their heads high. The result is that they corrupt moral character within the Church. It is not so much a question of persuading the laity, but of forcing the issue with them, so that they will endure the readmission of persons of this kind.

---

[14]"Contaminated . . . by acts of counterfeiting" = *adulteriis . . . contaminati. Adulteria* is usually translated "adulteries," but it seems out of place here unless Cyprian is thinking in an OT context about idolatrous sacrifices as adultery; see Cyprian *Unit. eccl.* 18. Clearly what he also has in mind is either producing those false documents obtained by bribery that was a *libellus* for a sacrifice not offered, in contrast with the sacrifices themselves mentioned here, or the fact of the creation of a pseudo, and therefore, counterfeit bishop. See this use also in connection with Novatian in n. 11 above and Cyprian *Ep.* 55.24.1, n. 25.

4 The resentment of the fraternity has become more justified in the light of the fact that one or two who had been received back have turned out worse than they were previously: they were unable to maintain the faithful practice of penance because they had not come with a real desire to do penance. This happened through my leniency in the face of resistance from the laity and their voices of opposition.

16.1 But what can I say about those characters who sailed to you by ship accompanied by Felicissimus, who stands accused of every crime? They are the ambassadors sent by Fortunatus the pseudo bishop, who delivered letters to you that were as false as him himself: it is after all Fortunatus' letters that they carry. How many layers does the conscience of those sinners have, how is their life cursed, how vile, so that, even if they were in the Church, they ought with their character to have been ejected from the Church? **2** Furthermore, they are well aware of the state of their own consciences. That is why they do not dare to come to nor approach the threshold of the Church, but they wander around on the outside throughout the province in order to way lay and rob the brothers.

Everyone by now knows them for what they are. They have been expelled everywhere else because of their sins. So they have landed their ship with you. They cannot keep up their pretext of seeking to approach our court or to become litigants before us when the charges that the brotherhood has repeatedly brought up against them are so grievous and serious.

3 If they wish for the decision of our court, let them come and resort to a legal trial.[15] After all, if they can have any justification and defense, let us consider what feeling for the need to atone they may have, what fruit of repentance they may bring to court. The door of the Church over here is not closed to anyone, and the bishop is not

---

[15]"Resort to a legal trial" = *experiri,* as in Plautus *Poen.* 1408: "Although I appreciate that you merited losing (*quamquam ego te meruisse ut pereas scio*), I will not go to court with you (*non experiar tecum*)."

denied to anyone. Our long suffering and good nature and humanity are in immediate readiness for them to come. I pray that they all may come back to the Church.

I pray that all our comrades may be found within the camp of Christ and the habitations of God the Father. I absolve all sins, I turn a blind eye to many more in my zeal and devotion for my aim of binding the brotherhood together. Even those sins that have been committed against God I do not investigate with the full judicial examination that my sacred obligation demands. I myself am almost the wrongdoer in granting absolution for more sins than I ought. I embrace those who return in repentance with an eager and undiminished affection when they confess their sin, in an act of atonement, expressed with humility and simplicity.

17.1 If there are those who think that they can come back to the Church by means of threats and without prayer, they should grasp for the certain fact that the Church of the Lord stands closed against them for their character. They should not think that they could make their entrance with acts of terrorism, and not with expressions of sorrow and acts of atonement. Remember that Christ's army, unconquered and strong, and under the Lord's protection and safekeeping, does not yield to threats.[16]

The priest of God, maintaining the gospel of God and guarding the commandments of Christ, cannot be overcome. Zacharias, presiding priest[17] of God, furnishes and assists us with examples of moral discipline and of faith. When he could not be terrorized by threats and stoning, he was cut down in the temple of God,

---

[16]Cf. *Ap. Const.* 8.23.4 (= *Epitome* 14): "If a confessor not having received the imposition of hands shall forcibly steal for himself some such honor as this on the grounds that it is by his confession, he shall be thrust aside and cast out. For he is not, since he has denied Christ's ordinance and is 'worse than an unbeliever.'"

[17]"Presiding priest" = *antistes* normally used of a pagan priest superintending a cult, as in Livy 10.8.2: "The 'Ten men' with responsibility for making sacrifice (*decemviros sacris faciundis*) . . . the same who were high priests of the temple of Apollo (*antistites eosdem Apollinaris sacri*)." See also Cyprian (Celerinus) *Ep.* 21.3.1, n. 11.

proclaiming and crying those same words which we proclaim and cry against the heretics: "'The Lord is saying these words: you have forsaken the ways of the Lord, and the Lord has forsaken you'" (2 Chr 24.20).

2 We should not be neglectful of what is handed down to us from God because a few reckless and morally culpable people are forsaking the ways of the Lord that lead to heaven and salvation. The Holy Spirit has deserted them because their conduct is unholy. We cannot consider the wickedness of wild men to be greater than the sentence handed down by the sacred bishops, let alone judge that human efforts are able to oppose more forcefully than the divine protection that is our prevalent shield.

18.1 Is rather, dearest brother, the Catholic Church to be stripped of its status, as well as the faithful and uncorrupted grandeur of its laity found within it, along with the authority and power of its sacred bishop? That is what will be the case if those who have been found in the position of being *outside* the Church can keep on saying, as heretics, that they wish to make a judgment on the bishop who is placed *over* the Church. They are the stricken, making judgment on the one who is healthy. They are the wounded making judgment about the one who is whole. They are the fallen (*lapsi*) judging the one who has stood his ground, the guilty about their judge, those who have committed sacrilege about their priest.

All that is left is for the Church to yield to the Capitol. Pagan images and statues with their altars should move into the sacred and venerable assembly of our clergy while the priests depart, removing the altar of the Lord.[18] It is not merely a question of allowing the petition for readmission of those who had sacrificed and denied Christ publicly. Rather it is, in addition, their attempt to dominate us by force of their terrorism. More bountiful and fuller material evidence

---

[18]Clearly here Cyprian does not shrink from seeing the Christian table for communion as an *altare* that parallels the pagan "altar (*ara*)." For his views on the Eucharist as a priestly sacrifice, see *Ep.* 63 below.

than this could not have been given in support of Novatian as he makes his speeches against us and reproaches us so strongly.

2 If they are petitioning for peace, let them lay down their arms. If they are going to make atonement, why are they making threats? For if they threaten, they should know that they do not frighten the sacred bishops of God. Not even Antichrist, when he is at the point of coming, will gain entry into the Church simply by threats, nor will the Church yield to the violence of his armed forces simply because he proclaims that he will reduce to nothing those who resist him.

The heretics are arming us, even though they think that we are terrorized by their threatening behavior. They do not even begin to thrust us down when at peace, but rather lift us up and inflame us because they are making peace worse than persecution for the fraternity. **3** Our prayer is that their wild scheme, talked about in a wild frenzy of mind, will not find its fulfillment in a criminal act. May not those who sin with words that are treacherous and savage actually commit their offence in deeds?

We pray and intercede with the God whom they do not stop challenging and aggravating. Our prayer is that their hearts may be softened, that their minds, once their wild frenzy leaves them, may be restored to health. May their hearts, overspread by the darkness of their sins, recognize the light of penitence. May they seek for themselves from their presiding priest the outpouring of prayers and petitions, choosing this to the pouring out of the blood of their sacred bishop.

If, however, their wildly mad condition persists, and they savagely persist in their fratricidal plots and threats, no priest of God is so weak, none so prostrate and cast down, none so sick with the fragility of the limitations of the human condition that he will not be roused up by divine inspiration against the enemies and assailants of God. The strength and fortitude of our protecting Lord would not fail to breathe his strength into the lowness of such a condition and weakness. It is no concern of ours where or when we should perish, on our way to receiving the reward of our Lord for our dying by the shedding of our blood. It is the condition of those whom the devil makes blind for which we must weep and express our sorrow. Because they are not aware of the eternal punishments of hell, they would attempt an imitation of the coming of the Antichrist that is now hastening on.

19.1 Of course I know, dearest brother, because of the love that we share and which we demonstrate to each other, that you always read our letters over there to your excellent clergy who also preside with you, and to the most holy and fullest assembly of your laity.

Nevertheless my advice and my request is that you would do now at my asking what otherwise you would do of your own accord and out of respect. If the effects of contact with poisonous arguments and with diseased propaganda lurk in the background in your company over there, may it be entirely stripped from the ears and hearts of the fraternity by reading out this letter. Thus may the love of good things, entire and whole, be kept clean from every stain of heretical influence.

20.1 Our most beloved brothers will then turn aside with confidence from them in other respects, and will shun the words and discussions with those "whose words creep in like a cancer" (2 Tim 2.17) or, to use the Apostle's very words: "Evil conversations corrupt good characters" (1 Cor 15.33). And again: "avoid a man that is an heretic, after the first rebuke, knowing that this kind of person is perverse and sins, and is by his sin condemned" (Titus 3.10–11).

The Holy Spirit speaks through Solomon: "He who is perverted carries his depravity in his own mouth, and he hides with his lips his destructive fire" (Prov 16.27). He then next counsels with the words: "Hedge about your ears with thorns and do not listen to a wicked tongue" (Wis 28.24). Then again: "An evil person listens to the tongue of those of iniquity, but the just does not attend to false lips." (Prov 17.4). **2** Of course I know that our fraternity over there is well advised by your pastoral care as well as well protected by their own vigilance. They cannot fall prey to the poisons of the heretics nor be deceived by them. Their persistence in God's directions and commands is matched by their fear towards God.

Nevertheless it is our concerned, Christian love that influences us in writing, however superfluously, with the object of preventing you joining in exchanges with such characters, and mingling with evil persons in social events and discussions. We should remain apart from them whilst they are exiles from the Church, since it is written: "If he should treat the Church with contempt, let him be to you as though he were a pagan or tax collector" (Mt 18.17). The blessed Apostle not only advises but orders that we should withdraw from such people: "We command you," he says, "in the name of our Lord Jesus Christ, that you withdraw from all brothers who walk disorderly and not according to the tradition which they have received from us" (2 Thess 3.6).

There cannot be any common association between good and bad faith. He who is not with Christ, he who is Christ's adversary, he who is hostile to his unity and to his peace, cannot form the same association with us. If they come with prayers and with acts of atonement, let them be heard. If they wave placards of insults and threats, let them be spurned with abhorrence. My prayer for you, dearest brother, is that you will always fare well.

§3 Controversies on the Eucharist and Baptism

LETTER 63
The Nature of Holy Communion

This is the first treatise that has survived specifically on the theology of the Eucharist. It is addressed to Caecilius, who appears to be the bishop of Biltha mentioned in *Ep.* 67, condemning those who use only water without mixing it with wine in the celebration of the Eucharist. It was written sometime after the Decian persecution whilst Cyprian was contemplating the final struggle with Valerian who, as Antichrist, would presage the Second Coming (19.1).

Cyprian's argument contains all the features of a catholic Christian view of the priesthood,[1] such as:

1. Christ is the High Priest (14.4).
2. He has commanded that the Eucharist be done in remembrance of him (9.2).
3. The individual priest/bishop must faithfully and precisely do what he has done (2.1; 10.2; 14.1; 17.1; 19.1).
4. Christ at the Eucharist in offering the chalice and bread was performing a sacrifice (16.2; 14.4; 17.1).
5. The priest/bishop, in offering the chalice and bread, is also therefore offering a sacrifice in imitation of Christ (14.2–4; 19.2).
6. Wine is essential for Christ's saving presence (2.2; 9.3; 11.1).
7. The Eucharist joins the faithful with Christ into one body, in effecting which the signs of water mixed with wine and with bread are essential (13.1–3).

[1] J. D. Laurance, *The Priest as Type of Christ: The Leader of the Eucharist in Salvation History according to Cyprian of Carthage*, American University Studies 7.5 (New York: Peter Lang, 1984).

Cyprian, unlike Aquinas and his scholastic predecessors and successors, and unlike his contemporary, Clement of Alexandria, did not employ any arguments derived from contemporary philosophy in order to justify in what sense any of these propositions were so. Cyprian relies instead on a method of scriptural exegesis (or hermeneutic) that relies on a typology of allegory. Although this method was general, and shared with such writers as Justin Martyr, Clement of Alexandria and Origen, Cyprian in one respect has his own emphasis. Usually, Old Testament events and statements as types are considered vague foreshadowings of the New Testament antitypes that make them clear and expose their true character. Often in Cyprian it is the New Testament that contains shadowy allusions that can be made more definite by reference to the Old.[2]

13.1–3 shows that the practice of the mixed chalice presupposed for Cyprian a theology of the unity of the Church in Christ, since water mingled with wine represents the Church bound together in Christ, just as does the kneading of water with flour in the case of the one loaf. It is difficult to ascertain who precisely were those who celebrated the Eucharist with water alone, and against whom Cyprian has directed this letter. The Encratites were held to be such a group, but Cyprian does not mention any heretical sect outside the Church but writes as if directed against a practice within the Church. For them, the OT proof texts were those that contained commandments to drink water without mentioning wine. Cyprian must argue therefore that all such texts refer to baptism (8–9.1).

In 16 he makes reference to a mediating position taken by some, who claim that at the morning Eucharist they take water alone, but at an evening celebration they more appropriately drink wine. Clarke compares the language of 16.1–2 to *Donatus* 16, and believes that these were perhaps confusing deliberately a Eucharist with the whole gathered company of the Church, and an Agape that would have had a more private nature and would have been between a smaller circle of people.[3] Hence Cyprian makes his case by exposing the confusion of their argument.

[2]A. Brent, "Cyprian's Exegesis and Roman Political Rhetoric," in *L' Esegesi dei Padri Latini dale origini a Gregorio Magno*, in SEAug 68 (2000): 145–58.
    [3]Clarke, *Letters of St Cyprian*, 3.298–300.

Cyprian to Caecilius, His Holy Brother

1.1 Dearest brother, the very many bishops who preside, by divine acknowledgement, over the churches of the Lord in the whole world hold fast to the account of the gospel truth that comes from what the Lord has handed down. They do not desert for a human and new principle that which Christ our Master has commanded and practiced.

Despite this fact, some, in consecrating the chalice of the Lord and in administering it to the laity, are not doing, either through ignorance or through naivety, what the Lord Jesus Christ did and taught, who is the founder of this sacrifice and its teacher. I considered it a sacred obligation as well as a necessity to compose a letter in response to you on the subject. My intention is that anyone who is constrained by this error might, when he discerns the light of truth about it, be restored to the root and source of the Lord's teaching that has been handed down.

2 Do not think, dearest brother, that we are drawing up our own, human opinions, or that we have presumed to adopt this position out of personal preference. We maintain a moderate position as always, and with a humble restraint. But when a faithful servant perceives a principle under the inspiration and commandment of God, he must justify his position before all and show that he has taken on himself no task without due warrant. Since he feels compelled to fear offending the Lord if he does not do what he is ordered, he must then be submissive to the Lord.

2.1 You are aware that we have been exhorted to preserve the traditional practice of the Lord when we offer the sacrifice using the chalice. We should do no other thing than that which our Lord first did on our behalf. In consequence, the chalice that is offered in memory of him should be offered mixed with wine. For since Christ pronounces: "I am the true vine" (Jn 15.1) the blood of Christ without qualification is not water.

2 It is not possible for it to be regarded as his blood in the chalice, when the chalice lacks the wine. It is by means of this wine that we have been redeemed and made alive, because it represents the blood of Christ. This the sacramental promise (*sacramentum*) which is proclaimed by the witness of all the Scriptures.[4]

3.1 We find even in Genesis, in the pledge (*sacramentum*) given in Noah's example, that this same event has been anticipated: the allegory of the Lord's Passion stands out from the text. Noah drinks wine because he is drunk. In his house he is naked. He had reclined with his thighs naked and uncovered. The middle son pointed out the nakedness of the father, and reported it outside the house, although the nakedness was covered by the other two, the elder and younger son.

There are other details that it is not necessary to pursue. It is enough that this alone be grasped, that Noah, as depicting a type of the truth to come, will not drink water but wine, and thus will express an image of the Passion of the Lord.

4.1 Similarly, in the priest Melchizedek, we see the promised pledge (*sacramentum*) of the sacrifice of the Lord prefigured, in accordance with the spoken witness of divine Scripture: "Melchizedek, king of Salem, brought forth bread and wine. He was however priest of God Most High and he blessed Abraham" (Gen 14.18–19). Melchizedek was bearing an image of Christ, as the Holy Spirit declares in the Psalms when he speaks in the role of a father to a son: "I gave you birth before the morning star. You are a priest forever after the order of Melchizedek" (Ps 109.3–4).

This "order" is definitely one that comes and is derived from that very sacrifice. Melchizedek was priest of God Most High because he offered bread and wine, because he blessed Abraham. For who other is more a priest of God Most High than our Lord Jesus Christ, who

[4]I have endeavored to represent the sense of *sacramentum* as "oath" and "promise." For other meanings see also below, sections 12.1, 13.3–4, n. 9, 14.3.

offered himself as a sacrifice to God the Father, and offered the very sacrifice that Melchizedek had offered, namely bread and wine, that is to say his body and blood?[5]

2 In regard to Abraham, this blessing has ongoing application to us as God's present people. For if Abraham believed in God, and that was reckoned to him as righteousness, definitely anyone else who believes in God and lives by faith is found righteous. He is shown beforehand to be blessed and made righteous in faithful Abraham. The blessed Apostle Paul demonstrates this when he says: "Abraham believed in God and it was reckoned to him as righteousness. Know, therefore, that those who are of faith, they are sons of Abraham. For Scripture, foreseeing that God justifies the pagans by faith, announced beforehand to Abraham that all the pagans would through him receive a blessing. Therefore, those who have received their blessing from faith are in the company of faithful Abraham" (Gal 3.6–9).

Consequently, in the gospel we find the expression "to be raised up from stones" (Mt 3.9) which means "sons of Abraham, to be gathered from the pagans." And when the Lord praises Zachaeus, he says to him in reply: "Today salvation has come into existence for this house, since this man is also a son of Abraham" (Lk 19.9). **3** Therefore, in order that the blessing honoring Abraham through Melchizedek the priest might be celebrated according to a valid ritual, an image of the sacrifice was prefigured there, you see, given its configuration in bread and in wine.[6] It was this that our Lord completed and fulfilled when he offered up the bread and the

---

[5]It should be noted that Cyprian's argument is reinforced here by the Latin synonyms that he uses. There is a similarity between Melchizedek's recorded act of "bringing (*proferre*)" bread and wine, and Christ's "offering (*offerre*)" of the same, so that the first can be considered an allusion to the second.

[6]". . . image of the sacrifice . . . given its configuration in bread and in wine (*imago sacrificii in paene et in vino . . . consituta*). *Constituere* (*constituta*) means in some contexts "to be composed (or configured) from (ingredients or component parts)"; see, e.g., atoms in Lucretius *De rer. nat.* 1.821: "These same particles compose (in their configuration) the substance of the heavens, the sea, the land, the rivers, the sun (*eadem caelum, mare, terras, flumina, solem constituunt*)."

chalice mixed with wine. Then he who is the fullness fulfilled the truth of the image that was prefigured.

5.1 The Holy Spirit also indicated beforehand through Solomon a type of the Lord's sacrifice, when he made reference to a sacrifice consumed by fire. He also referred to bread and wine and also to an altar, and to the sending of apostles: "Wisdom," he claims, "has built for herself a house and supported it with seven pillars. She has slain her sacrificial victims, she has mixed in her bowl her wine and prepared her table. **2** And she has sent forth her servants, calling them together with a proclamation from on high to come to her wine bowl with the words: 'He who is simple minded, let him turn aside to me.' And to those who lack understanding she has said: 'Come, eat from my bread and drink from the wine which I have mixed for you'" (Prov 9.1–5).

She declares that the wine is mixed, that is to say she proclaims in advance, in the voice of prophecy, the chalice of the Lord mixed with water and with wine. Her purpose is to show clearly the events of Lord's Passion in what had been foretold before.

6.1 The same significance is found also in the Blessing of Judah where also there the figure of Christ finds expression. It is expressed in the fact that his own brothers consider him worthy of praise and esteem. It is expressed in the fact that he had been destined to press hard upon the backs of his enemies as they fled in retreat, with the very hands by means of which he endured the cross and conquered death. It is expressed in the fact that he is the very lion of the tribe of Judah, and that he lies asleep during his Passion but rises and becomes the hope of the pagans. The divine Scripture also adds to this exegesis when it says: "He will wash his robe in wine, and his clothing in the blood of the grape" (Gen 49.11). When, however, it says "the blood of the grape," what else is intended other than the wine of the chalice of the blood of the Lord?

7.1 The Holy Spirit certainly also bears witness in Isaiah when he says of the Passion of the Lord: "Why are your clothes and your garments so ruby red, and as though pressed down by treading in a full vat?" (Is 63.2) Surely water cannot make clothing ruby red, whether it is water in a winepress that is trodden under foot or is pressed out in a wine press? The reference to wine is therefore an exact one, and makes us understand by wine the blood of the Lord. The intention is that what is announced in prophetic foretelling might afterwards be made manifest in the chalice of the Lord.

2 I have assessed the meaning of "wine vat," and "treading down" and "pressing down," in view of the impossibility of coming to drink wine without bunches of grapes having been first trodden down and crushed. So also we would not be able to drink the blood of Christ without first Christ having been crushed, and first having drunk the chalice before administering this as a draft[7] to we who believe on him.

8.1 Baptism is proclaimed by the many references in Scripture to be in water alone. We can see from the reference in Isaiah: "Do not," he says "remember the former things, and do not ponder those of old. Behold, I am making new things, which are now arising, and you will recognize, and I am making a way in the desert, and rivers in a place without water, to refresh my chosen nation, my people whom I have sought that they may set forth my moral character" (Is 43.19–20).

In that place God announced beforehand through the prophet that, amongst the pagans, rivers would afterwards gush forth in places that had previously been waterless. They would flow upon the chosen nation of God, which means those made sons of God through being born anew in baptism. **2** Likewise again there is presaged and foretold in advance that the Jews, if they would thirst and seek Christ, would drink with us, which means they would acquire the grace of baptism. "If they will become thirsty in desert places,

[7]"Administering this as a draft" = *propinare* = "to give to drink as a medicine."

he will bring to them to water, he will bring it forth for them from the rock, a rock will be cleft and water will flow, and my people will drink" (Is 48.21). This is fulfilled in the gospel when the blow of a spear at the Passion cleaves Christ who is the rock. **3** Christ, making us mindful of what had been predicted before, spoke this proclamation: "If anyone thirsts, let him who believes in me come, and let him drink. Just as Scripture says: 'Rivers of living water will flow from his belly'" (Jn 7.37–38).

To make it even clearer that the Lord's words there do not refer to the chalice but to baptism, Scripture adds the words: "However, he said this regarding the Spirit whom they were destined to receive who believed in him" (Jn 7.39). For the Holy Spirit is received through baptism, and thus those who have been baptised and received the Holy Spirit are given the opportunity to proceed to drink the chalice of the Lord. **4** No one should be influenced by the fact that when divine Scripture speaks of baptism, it states that we are thirsty and drink. The Lord in the gospel also says: "Blessed are those who thirst and hunger after righteousness" (Mt 5.6).

The fact is that this means that what is grasped with a desire that is greedy and thirsty is consumed more fully and richly. Just as in another place the Lord addressed the Samaritan woman with the words: "Everyone who will drink of that water will thirst again. But he who will drink of the water which I will give, will not thirst everlastingly" (Jn 4.13). This in itself is a sign of the saving waters of baptism, which, once it is indeed completed, cannot be repeated again. On the other hand, the chalice of the Lord is always in the Church, and continues to inspire thirst and to be drunk.

9.1 We do not need a great many arguments, dearest brother, in order to prove that baptism is always indicated by the designation of water, and so we ought to understand it. The Lord, when he came, revealed the truth of baptism and of the chalice. He it was who commanded that the water for the believer, that water of eternal life, should be granted to those who believe in baptism.

Christ has taught, by his own example to the contrary as Eucharistic president, that the chalice should be mixed by commingling water and wine. **2** For taking the chalice on the day of his Passion, he blessed it and gave it to his disciples, saying: "Drink from this all of you. For this is my blood of the covenant which will be poured out for the many for the forgiveness of sins. I tell you, I will not drink in this manner of the fruit of the vine until that day when I will drink it new with you in the kingdom of my Father" (Mt 26.27–29).

In this section we find the chalice that the Lord offered to have been a mixed one, and to have been the wine that he called his own blood. **3** Therefore it is clear that the blood of Christ is not offered if the chalice lacks wine, and the Lord's sacrifice is not celebrated with the consecration required by the New Law if our offering and sacrifice does not correspond with the details of the Passion. How are we to drink from the fruit of the vine the new wine with Christ in the kingdom of his Father if we neither offer nor mix the chalice of the Lord in accordance with our Lord's teaching thus handed down?

10.1 The Apostle Paul was chosen by the Lord, and sent, and made a preacher of evangelical truth. Paul also lays down these very principles in his letter with the words: "The Lord Jesus, in the night in which he was delivered up, took bread and gave thanks, and brake it, and said: 'Do this in remembrance of me.' In like manner, he took also the cup, after they had dined, saying: 'This chalice is the New Covenant in my blood, this do as often as you shall drink it in remembrance of me.' For as often as you will eat this bread and you will drink this chalice you proclaim the Lord's death until he comes" (1 Cor 11.23–26).

2 If this is commanded by the Lord, and confirmed and handed on by his apostle, we should do that which the Lord also did as often as we will drink in remembrance of the Lord. We find that what he has commanded is only observed by us if we do expressly those things that the Lord did. We should not also, following an identical argument, depart from his divine direction by ourselves failing to mix the chalice.

3 We should not depart in any way from the commandments of the gospel. Those things that the master has taught and done, the disciples ought also to observe and do, steadfastly and firmly. This is what the blessed Apostle teaches in another passage with the words: "I am amazed that so quickly have you turned aside from him who summonsed you by his grace to another gospel, which is not another, even if there are some who disturb you and wish to overturn the gospel of Christ. But even though an angel from heaven should declare otherwise beyond what we have declared to you, let him be anathema. Just as we said above, even now I repeat: 'If anyone declare to you anything other than what you have received, let him be anathema'" (Gal 1.8).

11.1 Since, therefore, neither the Apostle himself, nor an angel from heaven, can make or teach any other declaration beyond what Christ once taught and his apostles declared, I am puzzled about from where this custom has come. My point is that it is against evangelical and apostolic practice that in certain places water is being offered in the chalice of the Lord that by itself cannot form an image of Christ's blood.

2 The Holy Spirit in the Psalms is not silent about a settlement of this case when he makes reference to the Lord's chalice. He says: "your cup though the finest is intoxicating" (Ps 22.5). Now a cup that causes drunkenness has usually been mixed with wine. Water is not able to make anyone drunk. **3** Thus the Lord's chalice intoxicates, just us even Noah, when drinking wine in Genesis, became intoxicated. But the insobriety of the Lord's chalice and his blood is not the same kind of insobriety of the wine of this age. When the Holy Spirit says in the Psalm: "Your chalice intoxicates," he adds "although the finest" (Ps 22.5). This of course means that the Lord's chalice makes those who drink of it intoxicated in the sense that they become sober, in the sense that it restores hearts back to a spiritual wisdom, in the sense that each person returns to his senses about his understanding of God from tasting the experience of this age.

The memory of the old man is laid aside as a result of drinking the blood of the Lord and his saving cup: we are made to forget our old form of life in this age. In the same way the mind is relaxed by ordinary wine, and the soul is soothed and all sadness laid aside. Our choking sins previously overwhelmed our breast, burdened with their grief and sorrow. But our breast is now relieved by the joy of God's forgiveness. In summary, drinking in the Church of the Lord is able to be the cause of joy on condition that what is drunk is consistent with the Lord's truth.

12.1 How reverse and opposite is this practice (to make wine into water) to when the Lord at the marriage made wine *out* of water. This act as the sign (*sacramentum*) of a promised, future reality ought to admonish and instruct us strongly that we should offer wine instead in the dominical sacrifices. For since the Jews had lacked the grace of the Spirit, they were also lacking wine: "For Israel was the vineyard of the Lord Sabaoth" (Is 5.7). **2** Christ, however, points in his teaching to the fact that a people from the pagans will take their place. We are to attain after them to the position that the Jews had lost. Thus he made wine out of water, which is a reference to the marriage of Christ and the Church, indicating that after the withdrawal of the Jews a more numerous people might flow together and assemble from the pagans.

Divine Scripture declares in Revelation that waters are a sign of peoples, where it says: "The waters which you have seen, on which that harlot is sitting, are the throngs and nations of the pagans and their tongues" (Rev 17.5). We perceive this, obviously, to be also the basis of the sign in pledge (*sacramentum*) of the chalice.

13.1 For since Christ was bearing us all when he was bearing our sins, we see in the reference to water to be understood the idea of a people. On the other hand, quite differently, wine is indicative of the blood of Christ. So when in the chalice wine is mixed with water, the people are united with Christ and the popular assembly of believers are linked and joined together in him in whom they have believed.

2 The resulting bond from this linking and joining of water and wine is so composed in the chalice of the Lord that it is not able to be separated from is constitutive elements. In consequence, nothing can pull apart the Church, that is to say the people assembled, and faithfully and firmly established, as the foundation of the Church. The love of each individual part of that foundation cleaves always to Christ and remains in him.

3 Thus water alone cannot be offered in consecrating the chalice of the Lord, but neither can it be wine alone. For if someone offers wine only, it begins to become the blood of Christ without us. But if on the other hand, it should be only water, it begins to become the gathered people without Christ. When however both elements are mixed and fused together by a unifying bond, joining them to each other, then a spiritual and heavenly pledge (*sacramentum*) is realized.

4 Just as the chalice of the Lord is not water alone, nor wine alone, in the absence of the intermixing of both, in the same way the body of the Lord is not able to be grain alone nor water alone, in the absence of both being united and joined and kneaded together into an organic structure.[8] **5** By this sworn bond (*sacramentum*) between parts,[9] we God's people are shown to be united together so that just as much wheat gathered and ground down and kneaded together forms one bread, so we recognize that there is one body in Christ, who is the bread of heaven, in which each one of us is joined and united.

[8]"Organic structure" = *compago*, otherwise "fastening" or "binding," but here in the sense of the structure of the human body as in Celsus *De medicina* 4.14.1: "From the structure of the body (*a compagine corporis*) we must pass on to the soft organs (*ad viscera transeundum*)."

[9]This passage indicates clearly the elasticity of the term *sacramentum* in Cyprian. Clearly its meaning here is of the oath or agreement that keeps individuals together within a single society; see n. 4 above. See also Cyprian *Laps.* 7, n. 17; *Unit. eccl.* 6, n. 13.

14.1 No one should consider following the custom of certain people who in the past thought that water alone should be offered in the Lord's chalice. We should seriously ask whom it is that they have followed. For if we should only follow Christ in the sacrifice that Christ has offered, it becomes certain that we should obey and do that which Christ did, and what he commanded was to be done.

In the gospel he says: "If you do what I command you then I do not call you servants but friends" (Jn 15.14–15). The Father bears witness from heaven that Christ alone should be listened to when he says: "This is my well beloved Son in whom I am well pleased, listen to him" (Mt 17.5). **2** Consequently, if Christ alone is to be heard, we ought not to give attention to what someone before us had thought should be done, but to what Christ who came before everyone did at first.

We ought not to follow the custom of man, but the truth of God. God speaks through the prophet Isaiah the words: "They worship me without reason, teaching the commandments and doctrines of human beings" (Is 29.13). The Lord in the gospel repeats this point when he says: "You have rejected the commandment of God that you may establish your tradition" (Mk 7.9). Also, in another place, he lays down this principle with his words: "He who will break one of the least of those commandments and will so teach men, he will be called least in the kingdom of heaven" (Mt 5.19).

3 We are not allowed to break one of the least of these commandments. How much more so is it with the great and weighty commandments that relate to the solemn pledge (*sacramentum*) itself of the Lord's Passion and of our redemption? It is contrary to divine law to violate these by changing a divinely established practice into something quite different.

4 Jesus Christ our Lord and God is himself the high priest of God the Father, and he first offers himself as a sacrifice to the Father, and commands this to be done in his remembrance. It follows then, of course, that the priest who truly acts in place of Christ is the priest who imitates that which Christ did, and offers a true and full sacrifice in the Church to God the Father. He does so thus on the condition that he proposes making a sacrifice in accordance with what he sees Christ himself to have offered.

15.1 In summary, the absence of the faithful preservation of what is spiritually instructed overturns the proper practice of all ritual and of its truth. I know that someone might be fearful, when attending the morning sacrifices, that as a result of sipping the wine he might smell of the blood of Christ. Thus originates in the fraternity the holding back from suffering with Christ in time of persecution, because they learn to be ashamed about his blood and flesh. **2** Furthermore, the Lord in the gospel says: "He who will be ashamed of me, the Son of Man will be ashamed of him" (Mk 8.28). And the Apostle also speaks with the words: "If I were to please men, I would not be a servant of Christ" (Gal 1.10). But how can we shed our blood for Christ's sake if we blush to drink the blood of Christ?

16.1 Is it possible that you could be persuaded to error by taking the view that, though water seems appropriately offered in the morning, however, when we come to dine, we should offer a mixed chalice? By the time when we dine, we are not able to invite the gathered people to our personal dining group with a view to celebrating with all the fraternity present the reality of the pledge (*sacramentum*). **2** They argue that the Lord offered the mixed chalice after supper and not in the morning. Surely we ought not to celebrate the Lord's sacrifice after dinner so that we then offer the mixed chalice amidst the throngs then having to gather for the Lord's sacrifice? It was obligatory that Christ should make his sacrifice at the eve of the day, in order that he may point, by the very hour of his sacrifice, to the sundown and evening of the world, just as it is written in Exodus: "And the whole assembly of the synagogue of the sons of Israel shall put him to death at evening" (Ex 12.6). And again in the Psalms: "the lifting up of my hands be evening sacrifice" (Ps 140.2). However, we celebrate the resurrection of the Lord in the morning.

17.1 Since we make mention of his Passion in every sacrifice that we make—for it is the sacrifice of the Lord that we offer—we ought to do nothing other than what he did. Scripture states that as often as we offer the chalice in remembrance of the Lord and his Passion, we are doing that which it is established that the Lord had done.

2 It may be, dearest brother, that someone amongst our predecessors, through ignorance or naïveté, may not have observed and held fast to this principle that the Lord taught us by his example and authority to do. It is possible that pardon be granted by the forgiveness of the Lord for his naïveté. But, on the other hand, it will not be possible for us, now under the Lord's exhortation and instruction, to be pardoned for not offering the chalice of the Lord's sacrifice mixed with wine just as he offered it.

On the subject of this matter we are addressing letters to our colleagues in order that everywhere the gospel law that we have received from the Lord may be preserved, and that there should be no turning back from that which Christ both taught and did.

18.1 For us now to continue treating this matter with contempt is nothing other than to encounter the Lord's rebuke who reproaches in the Psalms when he says: "Why do you set forth my judgments and profess my covenant with your mouth? But you hate morally ordered behavior, and you have cast behind you my words. If you should see a thief, you would rush to join him, and you would place your portion with adulterers" (Ps 49.16–18).

To expound, therefore, the judgments and covenant of the Lord, and not to do the selfsame thing that the Lord did, is nothing more than to cast aside his words and to treat the Lord's pattern of behavior with contempt. Are you not guilty of thefts and adulteries, not in their earthly but in their spiritual sense? He who robs the truth of the gospel of the words and the deeds of our Lord both corrupts and impairs the purity of the divine commandments.

2 It is written in Jeremiah: "What has chaff in common with wheat? 'Behold, on this account,' says the Lord, 'I am against the prophets who each plunder their neighbor of my words, and are leading astray my people in their lies and their own crooked paths'" (Jer 23.28–32). Another quotation from the same source is in a different place where he says: "And she has committed fornication with wood and stone, and in all these things she has not returned back to me" (Jer 3.9–10). We must take anxious precautions and keep watch with fear and awe over what bears the mark of theft or impairment lest even on us disaster should fall.

3 If we are priests of God and of Christ, I can find no one whom we ought more to follow than God and Christ. After all, Christ himself says with emphasis in the gospel: "I am the light of the world. He who will have followed me will not continue walking in darkness, but will have the light of life" (Jn 8.12). We ought therefore to avoid walking in darkness by following Christ and observing his commandments.

After all, in another place, when he was sending his apostles, he said: "All power is given to me in heaven and on earth. Go therefore and teach all nations, baptizing them in the name of the Father and of the Son and of the Holy Spirit, teaching them to observe all whatever I have commanded you" (Mt 28.18–20). 4 Therefore, if we wish to walk in the light of Christ, we should not depart from his commandments and exhortations.

We give thanks that, while he gives us instruction concerning what we must do in the future, he pardons for the past our mistakes committed in our naïveté. And since his Second Coming to us is hastening nigh, his kindly and generous regard for us begins to illuminate our hearts by the light of his truth.

19.1 Finally, dearest brother, when we have to mix and offer the chalice of the Lord's sacrifice, it befits our religious duty to safeguard the truth of what the Lord has handed down to us. The obligation of our rank as sacred bishop is accompanied by a sense of awe that adds to our sense of what is fitting.

We must correct, at our Lord's admonishment, what we see to be previously done in error amongst certain priests. Then, when Christ shall come in his glory and heavenly majesty, he will find us holding fast to that which he has exhorted us, and observing what he has taught, and doing what he did.

I pray, brother, that you may always enjoy good health.

Stephen and the Baptismal Controversy

This letter was written shortly after the council at Carthage in September AD 256, attended by 71 bishops, the proceedings of which can be found in *Ep.* 70. Since Cyprian had written *Letter* 59 to Cornelius, the latter had died in early June 253, on his way to making his confession before the magistrate. Lucius his successor died before completing his first year as bishop, and Stephen succeeded him in mid-May 254.

The question at issue was whether someone baptised in heresy or schism needed to be baptised afresh when being reconciled to the Catholic Church. Cyprian in his opening words carefully avoids using baptism of the schismatical rite to which he refers since for him it is "a defiling deluge of pagan water" (1.1). Heretics cannot be rebaptised since the rite by which they were admitted to their conventicles was never real baptism in the first place (1.2–3).

This is a short, highly diplomatic letter whose purpose is to enclose *Ep.* 70 and 71, that we have not included in our selection. *Ep.* 73 that follows contains the full account of Cyprian's theology regarding what is found there.

Cyprian and Others to Stephen, His Holy Brother

1.1 We have considered it a necessity, dearest brother, to deal with and clear up, by an investigation of our common council, certain problems. To this end so many sacred bishops convened in one place that we needed to find a place for them to assemble and to fill a council chamber in which we could advance and proceed with many solutions.

The chief reason for me to write to you and to seek the weight of your opinion on a grave matter was about one item on this council's agenda. The item is of great relevance both to the authority of the sacred episcopate and to the unity and to the honor of the Catholic Church. After all, such unity comes forth from God's ordering of affairs in his divine plan.

The question is about those who have been dipped in water outside of the Church's doors, and have been stained in the company of heretics and schismatics with a defiling deluge of pagan water. Whenever they would come to us and to the Church that is one, they ought to be baptised rather than experience an imposition of hands quite inadequate for them to receive the Holy Spirit in the absence of their receiving as well the baptism of the Church. **2** Only then finally and fully, on the condition that they are born from both rites of admission (*sacramenta*),[1] are they able to experience full sanctification and to be sons of God.

After all, it is written: "Unless someone be born of water and of the Spirit, he is not able to enter into the kingdom of God" (Jn 3.5). We discover in the Acts of the Apostles that this principle has been safeguarded and preserved by the truth of the saving faith. That was the case in the house of Cornelius when the Holy Spirit had descended upon the pagans who were present there. They were stirred up by the warmth of their faith, and believed in the Lord with all their heart, in the Spirit which filled them, and in which they blessed God in many different tongues.

Nevertheless the blessed Apostle Peter, mindful of God's command and of the gospel, commanded that those same people, who were already so full of the Holy Spirit, should be baptised. He could overlook none of the forms in which the apostolic teachings preserve in all things the law of God's commandment and of the gospel.

3 It is not baptism that the heretics are practicing. Nothing can be accomplished by Christ's grace in the case of those who are opposed to Christ. The point finds careful expression in the letter

[1] For the elasticity of the term *sacramentum*, see Cyprian *Ep.* 63.2.2 and references there in n. 4. Here, by the two "sacred rites of admission (*sacramenta*)," Cyprian means baptism and the imposition of hands as part of the baptismal rite. For *sacramentum* specifically as rite of admission, see Cyprian *Ep.* 73.5.2, n. 10.

on that topic that has been written to Quintus our colleague, who is found in Mauritania. The same point is also found in the letter that our colleagues previously composed to their fellow-bishops who preside in Numidia, copies of both of which letters I enclose.

2.1 We make an obvious addition and make a further point, dearest brother, agreed and authorized by us in common.

There may have been presbyters or deacons who had taken their stand as betrayers and rebels against the Church after their previous ordination in the Catholic Church. There may have been those instead who, following a sacrilegious ordination in heretical assemblies by the hands of pseudo bishops and Antichrists, were simply moved in against Christ's stewardship. Regarding both there is but one consequence. Both groups would have tried to offer, in opposition to the one divinely valid altar, false and profane sacrifices outside the Church. So, they can be received again on their return but on this condition: that they receive communion as laymen.

They should be grateful for being admitted to the sacrament of reconciliation at all since they have shown themselves to be enemies of reconciliation. Of course they ought not, when they return to us, still cling to their ordination for its esteem, and the protection that it gives them, when they have been rebels against us. **2** For it is necessary that priests and ministers who devote themselves to the service of altar and sacrifices should be without fault and blemish.

The Lord God confirms this principle in Leviticus: "The man in whom there will be a blemish and physically defect may not proceed to offer the gifts to God" (Lev 21.17, 21). To the same effect, he issues the same instructions in Exodus with the words: "Let the priests who approach the Lord God be sanctified, lest perchance the Lord abandon them" (Ex 19.12). And again, "When they approach to minister to the altar of the Holy One, let them not bring sin upon themselves lest they die" (Ex 28.43 LXX [= 30.20]).

But what can be a greater sin, or what more misshapen a blemish than to have stood against Christ, than to have shattered in pieces his

Church which he acquired and founded at the cost of his own blood? They have been forgetful of the reconciliation and love required by the gospel, and have, with a wildness of an enemy bent on dissension, engaged in battle against the people of God who are united with one mind and in concord. **3** Even if these people afterwards are seen returning to the Church, they cannot restore and reinstate those who have been lead astray by them, and whom death overtook while they were *outside* the Church.

These perished without an act of communion and the granting of reconciliation. Their souls on the Day of Judgment will be required from their very hands, when they have revealed themselves to be the instigators and leaders of an act of destruction. For that reason it is enough that pardon be granted to people of this kind when returning, but bad faith must not be encouraged in the household of faith. What would we have left for both the good and the innocent who, as such, have not departed from the Church if we should grant such a status to those who have departed from us and have taken a position against the Church?

3.1 We publish these points for your consideration, dearest brother, and in defense of our shared rank and the demands of indivisible love. Our belief is that it will be your decision too on what is both sacramental and true in defense of the truth of your sacramental practice and faith. However, we are aware that certain persons do not wish either to abandon or to change a course of action the justification for which they have swallowed whole. So long as the bond of peace and of concord is preserved between their colleagues, they maintain their own particular practices once they have adopted them. **2** In the matter under consideration, we are not seeking to apply pressure on anyone or to legislate on it. Each and everyone who presides as bishop over the government of a church should have freedom to judge for himself. He is destined to render an account to the Lord. We pray, dearest brother, that you will always keep well.

Rebaptism: the Novatian Dimension

Cyprian wrote in May/June AD 256 this letter as the expression of his fully developed case in his dispute with Stephen, and in further elucidation of the case made by the two previous Carthaginian councils on this issue.

Iubaianus raised an interesting point following the decrees of these councils. If heretics are to be rebaptised, does not this give Novatian his point when he claims from his point of view the right to rebaptise those who have received baptism in the Church from which he has broken away (2.1)? Cyprian will then argue that if this were the case, we would not perform any sacramental rite that Novatian invalidly and ineffectively celebrates (2.3).

Cyprian appeals to a former council in Africa, of indeterminate date, under Agrippinus, that had settled the matter (3.2).

Novatian has no status in this matter, so he can be ignored—but not because baptism outside the Church has validity as a sacrament. We can discern the opposite case being made against Cyprian from his criticisms of it. Forgiveness of sins is granted through the individual's faith that receives it, if it is at least in the name of Jesus (4.1). Cyprian (4.2–5.3) will argue that Marcion and the other heretics cannot validly baptise because baptism is in the name of the Trinity, and, furthermore, baptism in the name of Christ is not in the name of the same Christ as that of catholic Christianity. It is the creedal statement that determines the validity of the rite. But at this point Cyprian has entered the territory of what later Christendom was to define in terms of the "intention to do what the Church does" as the criterion of validity, and not the "intention to do what the Church believes." He clearly never applied this principle to what was later to be the sacrament of Holy Orders. Novatian's creed was orthodox as was that of Felicissimus. Their churches were sham churches solely on grounds of jurisdiction, and the principle that only one bishop could occupy the seat of authority in a defined geographical area.[1]

---

[1] See Cyprian *Ep.* 55.21.1 and n. 21.

Cyprian argues that to claim imposition of hands and not baptism as necessary to readmission to the Church actually gives him his point. If a heretic is truly baptised, then he has the Holy Spirit and does not need even this (6.2). He is convinced that baptism can only be administered by someone whose ordination is valid (7–8), and therefore clearly not by a layman, despite Tertullian's claim to the contrary.[2]

Imposition of hands for the receiving of the Holy Spirit was only for those who had already received the Church's baptism (9). Scripture shows that the saving fountain is within the Church alone (10–11). The sprinkling with water cannot be effective in the name of Jesus alone if the heretic means by this that the Father was not the creator, or that the Son was not divine (12–13). Paul's references to Christ proclaimed in envy and strife referred to parties *within* the Church and not *outside*, a distinction absolutely fundamental to Cyprian's theology of the Church (14). Both Christ and the apostles recognized heretics professing Christ's name as in fact enemies and antichrists (15–16). Jesus can only forgive sins because of his relation with the God the Father whom the heretics do not know and who cannot therefore know him. Baptism by Christ's command is in the name of the Trinity (17–19).

The heretics in returning in penitence to the true Church are seeking the grace of its sacraments, which Stephen and his supporters are denying them if they consider their rebaptism to be unnecessary (20). They are, furthermore, in effect claiming that baptism in water is stronger than the martyr's confession that leads to a baptism in blood that requires no baptism in water. But there are no true martyrs outside the Church (21.1). If we agree that this is so, then how can confession of faith in heretical baptism in water prevail when confession in blood did not do so (21.2). Baptism cannot therefore be common to heretics and the Church (21.3).

The example of a catechumen dying without baptism yet being saved for his confession as a martyr is irrelevant (22.1). But they are truly baptised: their baptism in blood is made real by their confession of the orthodox faith (22.2–3). Cyprian admits the force of tradition against him but claims that past but erroneous tradition ought not to be followed (23). Heretics are not being rebaptised since they were never baptised in the first place (24). The disciples of John received Christian baptism (24.3–25). Cyprian argues that if baptism is valid, it is unnecessary: if it is necessary, then so is rebaptism,

[2]Tertullian *Bapt.* 17.2.

which is really the true baptism of those never really baptised, as he previously argued in *Ep.*, 72.

Cyprian believes that nevertheless, despite his invective, the controversy needs calming down. No bishop should be prevented from doing what he thinks right (26.1). For this reason he compiled his treatise *On the Virtue of Patience*, to which we are otherwise referred (26.2).

Cyprian to Iubaianus, His Holy Brother Bishop

1.1 You have written to me, my most beloved brother, with a request that I give some indication of how my mind is reflecting on in what light we should consider the question of baptism by heretics. The latter are found located on the *outside* and have set themselves up *outside* the Church, and are claiming a prerogative for themselves that is neither within their right nor their power.

We cannot reckon this practice to be either valid or legitimate when it has been established that the law is not on their side. We have already in our letters written down firmly what we think on this subject. In consequence, I propose being brief. I have sent a copy of those very letters to you on the subject first of our decree passed when very many of us were present together in council. In the second letter I wrote my same considered, judicial opinion after that council, at the request of Quintus our colleague.

2 Now more recently, when we the bishops of the province of Numidia as well as of Africa gathered together in a common council, seventy-one in number, we confirmed once again this same conclusion that arose from our judgment. Our decision was that there is one baptism that has been laid down in the Catholic Church. There can be no rebaptism by means of this rite but only baptism performed by us. Whoever comes to us from a counterfeit and godless experiencing of water are to be washed clean of it, and are to be sanctified in the waters that save in reality.

2.1 We are not affected, dearest brother, by the claim with which your letter engages. You say that the Novatians rebaptised those whom they entice away from us. But it is of no relevance to us what the enemies of the truth are doing. We hold rather to the office that gives us our power, and to its foundation in reason and in truth.

Novatian, in the manner of apes who, though they are not human, try to imitate human characteristics, wishes to claim for himself the authority of the Catholic Church and its reality. But he himself is not *in* the Church, but, far more precisely than this, he has shown himself to be a rebel and an enemy *against* the Church. For because he knows that baptism is indivisible, he is seeking to claim for himself this one indivisible rite so that he can say that the Church is the possession of *his* party and thus make *us* the heretics.

2 We, however, hold to the head and root of the one Church. We know definitely and believe that it is unlawful for him to perform anything *outside* of the Church, and baptism that is the one baptism is *our* baptism. Why even he himself was first baptised there when he still held to the order and reality of a divinely ordained unity.

If Novatian considers that those who have been baptised in the Church ought to be rebaptised completely outside the Church, he ought to begin with himself. In consequence, he should first be rebaptised himself, with an extraneous and heretical baptism, since it is his opinion that they who are outside the Church and against it must be baptised in addition to the Church's baptism.

3 On what grounds therefore do we think that Novatian ought not to have done what he is daring to do? Why indeed does he? Why ought we to renounce our Chair simply because Novatian has taken possession of, on his own initiative, his position on the Chair of a sacred bishop? Novatian is striving to set up an altar and to offer sacrifices contrary to divine law. Because of that, we therefore do have to hold back from the altar and from sacrifices, fearing that we should be seen to be celebrating sacrifices that resemble and are like his? The argument is invalid and foolish. It implies the Church should abandon the truth because Novatian has laid claim outside the Church to the illusory appearance of truth.

3.1 It is no new and recent practice with us to judge that those who come to the Church from the heretics must be baptised. It is many years and therefore a long time ago since, under the presidency of Agrippinus, a man well remembered, a large number of bishops gathered in common assembly to decide this regulation. From that time to this day so many thousands of heretics in our provinces, on their return to the Church, have neither rejected the principle nor delayed its acceptance, but, seeing the reason, have more precisely even embraced it with joy.

They have in consequence acquired the grace of the baptistery of life, and of the baptism that saves. **2** It is not difficult for a teacher to inculcate what is true and valid in one who has paid the penalty for his heretical depravity and discovered the truth about the Church. After all, he is coming to the Church with the object of learning, he is learning with the object of coming alive. We ought not to make our gift to the heretics a foolishness that consents to provide them with our patronal support. Let them instead, without such an impediment, gladly and readily submit to the truth.

4.1 I find the clear statement in the letter that you have copied to me that one should make no inquiry as to who had performed the baptism. The argument is that he who has been baptised will be able to receive absolution from his sins according to the measure of his faith. I did not think it right to overlook this passage, particularly when I noticed that in the same letter mention is made of Marcion.[3]

---

[3]Marcion was a radical interpreter of the epistles of Paul: he claimed that the OT was the revelation of an imperfect (his detractors said "evil") God and that the God who sent Jesus and who appeared in his version of the NT (consisting of Luke's Gospel and the genuine letters of Paul) was a different and higher God. Irenaeus (*Haer.* 4), and Tertullian (*Marc.*) expounded this heresy in order to refute it.

The letter goes on to say that those who come from Marcion ought not to be baptised on the grounds that they clearly have already been baptised in the name of Jesus Christ. **2** So we must take into consideration the faith of those who are believers on the outside of the Church, and consider whether, in accordance with that faith, they are able to gain any part of grace. For if faith is a whole shared by us and by the heretics, grace can also be shared. If they confess the selfsame Father, the selfsame Son, the selfsame Holy Spirit, the selfsame Church as us—I mean the Patripassians,[4] Anthropians,[5] Valentinians,[6] Apelletians,[7] Ophites,[8] Marcionites[9] and the remaining murderous diseases and poison by means of which the heretics intend uprooting the truth— yes, well, in that case the rite of baptism can be shared in common on grounds that the faith is shared.

5.1 I will avoid wasting time running through the whole list of heresies, and examining their individual examples of silliness and madness. In any case, I have no pleasure in making statements knowledge of which may cause you to shudder and feel ashamed. Let our examination focus on Marcion alone, referred to in the letter that you sent on to us. Can we establish valid grounds for his baptism?

2 The Lord, when sending forth his disciples after his resurrection, instructed and taught them about the manner in which they

[4]*Patripassian* describes several groups of people, who in common denied any persons in the godhead, and thus were compelled logically to conclude that the Father himself (or, in or with his Son) suffered on Calvary. Noetus of Smyrna, Theodotus, and perhaps popes Zephyrinus and Callixtus I produced versions of this heresy (see Pseudo Hippolytus *Haer.* 9.7.1–3; Tertullian *Prax.* and Hippolytus *Noet.*).

[5]These, such as Artemon, denied that Christ was divine from birth, but as a mere man, was anointed at his baptism and therefore became the Christ; see Eusebius *Hist. eccl.* 5.28.2–3.

[6]Valentinus or his disciples taught a godhead of 33 persons called "aeons" (or emanations); see Irenaeus *Haer.* 1 and Tertullian *Val.*

[7]Apelles, a disciple of Marcion, believed that Christ's real body came not from the Virgin but from the stars; see Eusebius *Hist. eccl.* 5.13.1–7.

[8]Worshippers of the snake, or otherwise called Naasenes; see Pseudo Hippolytus *Haer.* 5.7.

[9]See n. 3.

ought to administer baptism with the words: "All power is given to me in heaven and on earth. Go, therefore, and teach all nations, baptizing them in the name of the Father and of the Son and of the Holy Spirit" (Mt 28.18–19). He is implying here the idea of the Trinity, by initiation[10] into which the nations should be baptised. But surely Marcion does not hold with this Trinity?

Surely he does not proclaim the same God as we do in God the Father the creator? He did not recognize Christ as the Son born of the Virgin Mary, who was the Word made flesh, who bore our sins, who conquered death by having to die. Then, as first of our race, began the resurrection of the flesh following his own resurrection, and so revealed to his disciples that they would rise in the same flesh. **3** Not only is this profession of faith far removed from that of Marcion but also from that of the rest of the heretics.

Of course those heretics have nothing to commend them but bad faith, blasphemy, and conflict that is hostile to soundness and truth. Therefore, in what way can it really be thought that someone who is baptised in their group has obtained absolution for their sins and the grace of God's pardon? Their profession of faith does not contain the truth of the faith itself.

If indeed, as some think right, someone can, from being on the *outside* of the Church, receive something in proportion to his faith, he receives exactly what he has believed in. Believing what is false, he cannot receive what is true, but rather he receives counterfeit and sacrilegious things, in which he is accustomed to state that he believes.

6.1 The prophet Jeremiah makes faint allusion to this category of sacrilegious and counterfeit baptism when he says: "For what reason do they prevail who make me sad? My affliction is unyielding,

---

[10]For *sacramentum* as "initiation," see Apuleius *De deo Socr.* 22.170, where he describes the "worship of the gods (*daimonis cultum*)" as none other than "a rite of initiation into philosophy (*philosophiae sacramentum*)." He does so on the grounds that pagan myths were allegories of philosophical truth. See also Cyprian *Laps.* 7, n. 17; *Ep.* 75.13.2.

from whence will I be made well? While it occurs, it has become for me like deceptive water that does not allow faith in it" (Jer 15.18). The Holy Spirit is referring through the prophet to the "deceptive water that does not allow faith in it." What is this water "deceptive" and "of bad faith?" It means the water that lies in giving the illusion of baptism, and which belies the grace that true faith provides by enshrouding it with pretence.

2 If someone could be baptised in separation *outside* the Church, he would be able to receive the absolution of sins from a defective profession of faith. Then, according to that same defective profession, he could also receive the Holy Spirit. But in that case it is not necessary to have hands laid on him when he returns in order that he should both acquire the Holy Spirit and receive the seal thereof. It is either that *both* can be obtained in separation, or that he who has separated receives *neither* of them.

7.1 Of course absolution of sins is what is granted in baptism. But it is obvious where and through whom it can be granted. For the Lord at the first granted that power to Peter, upon whom he has built his Church and founded and revealed the source of unity, that what is "unbound on earth the Lord should have unbound in heaven." **2** And after the resurrection, he accordingly spoke these words to the apostles: "'As the Father has sent me, so also I am sending you.' When he had said this, he breathed upon them and said: 'Receive the Holy Spirit. If you absolve the sins of anyone, they will be absolved them. If you have retained those of anyone, they will be retained'" (Jn 20.21–23)

From this statement we understand that it is unlawful for those who are not placed in authority in the Church to baptise or to grant absolution from sins. The authority of those who are so placed is founded on the law of the gospel and on what the Lord has laid down. It is impossible for anything to be bound or released in separation from the Church where there is no one who can bind or release.

8.1 We do not, dearest brother, lay down this principle without the support of the authority of divine Scripture. In consequence, we are asserting, on grounds of a definite law and passed in due form, that all things have been divinely ordered. It is not possible for anyone to abrogate to himself against the bishops and priests what does not exist according to legal right and legitimate power.

For, both Core and Dathan, and Abiron, attempted to abrogate to themselves the privilege of performing sacrifice against Moses and Aaron the priest. But they did not succeed in doing without punishment what they dared to do illegally. **2** The sons of Aaron, who placed strange fire upon the altar, were blotted out in the sight of God in his wrath. The same sentence remains for those who bring in strange water for a counterfeit baptism. The divine Judgment will avenge and exact reparation for the fact that heretics have performed against the Church that which it is unlawful to perform except for the Church alone.

9.1 An objection is raised from the case of those who had been baptised in Samaria. On their approach, the two apostles, Peter and John, merely laid hands on them for them to receive the Holy Spirit. Rebaptised, they were not!

But, dearest brother, we do not think that passage to be of any way relevant to the present case. In Samaria those former believers believed with a true faith, and were *within* the Church that is indivisible, and to which alone it is permitted to grant the grace of baptism and to forgive sins. They had been baptised by Philip the deacon whom the apostles had sent. It was by reason of the fact that they had acquired a legitimate baptism, and one that was of the Church, that there was no obligation to baptise them further.

Peter and John merely completed what was lacking by invoking the Holy Spirit, and offered for them a following prayer accompanied by the imposition of hands. As a result, the Holy Spirit was poured out upon them (Acts 8.5–17). **2** This is also now our practice with those who are baptised within the Church. They are brought before those in authority over the Church, and they acquire the Holy Spirit through the prayer we offer and the laying on of our hands. What they have acquired is finally crowned with this the Lord's seal.

10.1 So, dearest brother, it is not the case that we are of the opinion that heretics be granted the right of baptism. We do not think that baptism should be granted and transmitted to any other institution than the Church, one alone and undivided. It is the task of a good soldier to defend the camp of his own commander against those who rebel and are its enemies. The standards of his glorious leader are committed to him for their preservation.

It is written: "The Lord your God is a zealous God" (Deut 4.24). **2** We who have received the Spirit of God ought to have zeal for our divine faith. By such zeal Phineas pleased God, and, winning merit from him, soothed the anger of his wrath when the people were perishing. Why do we acknowledge with any credit practices that are hostile to the divine unity of which they are a counterfeited version and from which they are estranged? We are those who acknowledge only one Christ and one Church! **3** The Church reveals itself to be like Paradise, and encloses trees on the inside that bear fruit *within* its walls.

One of these trees not producing good fruit is cut down and cast into the fire. The Church waters these trees with four rivers, that is to say by means of the four Gospels, from which she lavishes the grace of baptism through its saving and heavenly flood. Surely someone not in the Church cannot draw water from the Church's fountains from the *inside*? Surely someone who has condemned himself to his own destructive fall cannot impart to anyone else the healing and saving draughts of Paradise. Rather he is cast out in exile from the fountains of paradise and he fades away parched by the dryness of everlasting thirst.

11.1 The Lord proclaims that he who is thirsty should come and drink from the streams of living water that have flowed from his bowels (Jn 7.37–38). Where is he to come who thirsts? Is it to the heretics where there is no fountain or stream of life-giving water at all? Or is it to the Church that is one, and has been founded on the one who received its keys at the invitation of the Lord's own voice. She is the one who holds and possesses all the legitimate power of her bridegroom and Lord.

2 In this Church we preside, we fight on behalf of her honor as well as her unity, we defend, by our commitment to the faith, her means of grace as well as her glory. We give water by divine consent to the people of God in their thirst. We guard the boundaries of her life-giving fountains. If we hold the right of occupation, if we acknowledge our sacred pact of unity, why do we present ourselves as in collusion with those in advocacy against the truth,[11] with those who are betrayers of our unity?

The water of the Church's sacrament is faithful, saving, and holy. It cannot be corrupted and counterfeited, just as the Church itself is incorrupt and chaste and modest. **3** If the heretics zealously attach themselves to, and are found in their places in the Church, they are able to enjoy both its sacrament of baptism and all other resources for salvation. If, however, they are not in the Church, but rather they work against the Church, whom are they able to baptise with the Church's baptism?

12.1 It would be no small and modest concession were we to recognize their baptism. The source of all faith and the saving entrance into the hope of life eternal flows from baptism. From that source comes the grant of God's favor to his servants in order for them to be purified and made alive.

2 Now if someone *could* be baptised in a heretical community, he definitely *could* receive absolution from his sins. If he has acquired absolution from his sins, he has been sanctified. If he has

---

[11]"In collusion with those in advocacy against the truth," translates *praevaricator (es)*, which means an advocate who acts in collusion with his opposing counsel to procure the mismanagement of a case. See also Cyprian *Unit. eccl.* 5, n. 7 (iii).

been sanctified, he has been made a temple of God. But I ask you: "Of whose God?" If of God the Creator, it could not have been of the creator in whom he did not believe. If of Christ, he could not be made his temple if he denies Christ to be God. If of the Holy Spirit, since the three are indivisible, how can the Holy Spirit be pleased to be in him who is the enemy of both Son and Father?

13.1 Some persons then put forward against us customary practice. But this is ineffective when they are being refuted by reason, as if customary practice could be of greater weight than the truth. It is definitely a fact that in spiritual matters what the Holy Spirit has revealed for the better has to be followed. It is possible to make allowance for someone who goes astray in his simplicity, just as the blessed Apostle Paul says of himself: "I was at first," he says, "a blasphemer and persecutor and cause of injury, but I was found deserving of mercy because I acted in ignorance" (1 Tim 1.13).

2 Someone nevertheless who continues fixedly in the path into which he has strayed after he has experienced inspiration and revelation is sinning without the possibility of pardon for his ignorance. What he does is to rest for support upon a kind of obstinacy and stubbornness in the face of overwhelming evidence. **3** Let no one keep saying: "What we have received from the apostles this we follow," when the apostles have delivered to us only one Church, and one baptism that is none other than that found established in the Church. We can discover no one to have been admitted by the apostles, and to have received communion from them, by virtue of the baptism with which he has been baptised in a heretical community. Thus you cannot say that the apostles thought it fit to approve of the baptism of the heretics.

14.1 Some cite a statement of the Apostle Paul as if it is of relevance to any vote in favor of the heretics: "Nevertheless in every way, whether by accident or by seeking truth, let Christ be proclaimed" (Phil 1.18). Here too we can find nothing in support of the plea of those who are voting to defend the heretics and cheering them on. **2** Paul in his epistle was not speaking about the heretics or their baptism. Thus it is demonstrated that his statement can have no relevance to this matter.

Paul is speaking about *brothers,* whether they are conducting themselves contrary to ecclesiastical discipline and order, or are preserving the truth of the gospel in the fear of God. And some of these, he asserts, had spoken the word of the Lord consistently and fearlessly, but certain others had engaged in envy and strife. Some had preserved a benevolent charity towards him, but others instead had engaged in strife out of ill will towards him. He nevertheless was patiently enduring all things. Whether in truth or by accident the name of the Christ that Paul was preaching would reach the attention of as many people as possible. The new and rough planting of the seed of the word would be made widespread by the preaching of those who proclaimed it.

3 Furthermore, it is one thing for those who are within and on the *inside* of the Church to speak in Christ's name, it is quite another for those on the *outside,* and acting against the Church, to baptise in Christ's name. Therefore, he who wishes to make a case for the heretics should not put forward Paul's statement about *brothers*, but he should rather show whether Paul is of the view that something needs conceding to a heretic. They need to ask whether he approved of heretical faith and baptism, whether he decided that those contrary to the faith and blasphemers were able to receive absolution from their sins *outside* the Church.

15.1 However, if we should take into consideration what the apostles felt about the heretics, we will find that they, in all their epistles, express detestation and abhorrence of the sacrilegious depravity of the heretics. When they say that their speech creeps serpent-like as a disease (2 Tim 2.17), how is it possible for that speech to grant absolution from sins which creeps serpent-like as a disease into the ears of those who listen? Since they say that there is no sharing of righteousness and iniquity, no communion of light and of darkness (2 Cor 6.14), how then can darkness bring light or iniquity righteousness? Since the apostles say that the heretics are not from God, but are of the spirit of Antichrist, how are they able to perform spiritual and divine acts? They are the enemies of God and the spirit of Antichrist possesses their hearts.

2 So, once we forsake the errors of human argument in favor of the authority of the gospel, we can return to the apostolic tradition with a sincere and reverent faith. We then understand that both Christ and his apostles grant to them legitimately nothing of the Church's saving grace. Christ himself calls those who scatter and assail the Church of Christ by the very name of "enemies," and the apostles call them "Antichrists."

16.1 No one can now produce Christ's name in order to escape the consequences of Christian truth and so say: "Wherever and however they have been baptised in the name of Jesus Christ, they have acquired the grace of baptism." This is because Christ himself speaks with the words: "Not everyone who says to me, 'Lord, Lord,' will enter into the kingdom of heaven" (Mt 7.21). Again, he gives advanced warning and instructions in order to prevent someone being easily deceived in his name by false prophets and false Christs. **2** "Many will come in my name," he claims, "saying: 'I am Christ,' and they will deceive many" (Mt 24.5). Afterwards he adds the words: "You should beware of them. Lo, I have predicted everything for you" (Mt 24.25).

From this it is clear that one should take up and hold on to acts performed in Christ's truth, and not to the words that are falsely uttered in Christ's name.

17.1 The concept of absolution from sins is informed by the name of Jesus Christ in the gospels, and in the epistles of the apostles. But this is not to indicate that the Son alone could be of benefit to anyone, either in separation from the Father, or in opposition to the Father.

Rather, it is there to demonstrate to the Jews, who were accustomed to boast that they possessed the Father, that the Father would be of no benefit to them unless they believed in the Son whom he has sent.

Those who knew God the Father as Creator ought also to have known Christ as his Son. They should not flatter themselves nor sing their own praises about the Father alone in the absence of any recognition of his Son, who also was accustomed to say: "No one comes to the Father but through me" (Jn 8.41–42). Christ himself makes clear that it is the knowledge of the two of them that brings salvation when he says: "This is life eternal, that they might know you the only true God and Jesus Christ whom you have sent" (Jn 17.3).

Since, therefore, according to Christ's own pronouncement and solemn witness, the Father must first be known and then next Christ who is sent, there can be no hope of salvation unless they are both recognized. How, in conclusion, without the knowledge of God the Father whom they blaspheme, can they be judged to have acquired absolution from their sins when they are reputed to have been baptised in the name of Christ in a heretical community?

2 There was a different explanation applying to the Jewish issue in the time of the apostles. The state of affairs regarding the pagans was also quite different. The Jews, since they had already received a very ancient baptism under Moses and the Law, had to be baptised in the name of Jesus Christ according to what Peter says to them in the Acts of the Apostles (2.38–39) with the words: "Repent, and be baptised, each and every one of you, in the name of our Lord Jesus Christ for the absolution of your sins, and you will receive the gift of the Holy Spirit. For to you is the promise and to your sons, and next to all whom the Lord our God will call." Peter makes reference to Jesus Christ, not because the Father is left out, but in order that the Son might be joined as well with the Father.

18.1 Finally, when after his resurrection the apostles are sent by the Lord to the pagans, they are commanded to baptise the pagans in the name of the Father and of the Son and of the Holy Spirit. How, therefore, do some say that a pagan can acquire absolution from his sins simply because he has been baptised in some way or other somehow in the name of Jesus Christ *outside* the Church and, moreover, in opposition to the Church?

It would be in the face of the Christ himself, who commanded that the pagans be baptised in the name of the full and undivided Trinity. **2** It could only be if he who denied Christ was in turn denied by Christ, but then he who denied the Father whom Christ confessed was not himself denied. The blasphemer against the Father, whom Christ called his Lord and God, cannot be rewarded by Christ and gain the absolution of his sins and the sanctification of baptism.

By what power can he when denying God the Father of Christ as Creator gain the absolution of his sins in baptism? Christ will have received that power itself by which we are baptised and sanctified from the selfsame Father, whom he claimed to be the greater, by whom he sought to be glorified, whose will he fulfilled to the full extent right up to the end by drinking the cup and undergoing death. **3** This claim is nothing more than a wish to defend being made an accomplice of heretics in their blasphemy. It is to assert that someone who seriously blasphemes and sins against Christ's Father and Lord and God is able to receive the absolution of his sins in Christ's name. Furthermore, what kind of contradiction is it that when he who denies the Son also does not possess the Father, but he who denies the Father is thought to possess the Son? The Son himself firmly testifies with the words: "No one is able to come to me unless it has been granted to him by my Father" (Jn 6.26). In consequence it is clear that no absolution of sins can be received in baptism from the Son that it is established that the Father has not granted, particularly when he repeats the same point further with the words: "Every planting that my heavenly Father has not planted will be uprooted" (Mt 15.13).

19.1 If the disciples of Christ are so unwilling to learn from Christ what adoration and honor they owe to his Father's name, let them learn from the earthly examples of things of the present age, and let them grasp that Christ has set before them the principle that is associated with the greatest of criticisms: "The sons of this age are more prudent than the sons of light in their age" (Lk 16.8).

Take as an example someone who, without moral order in his life, has made mockery of another's father, and has torn to shreds his sense of dignity and honor with insults. His son then becomes outraged and angry, and undertakes to avenge the injury to his insulted father with whatever strength he has. Do you think that Christ grants exemption from punishment to someone so unholy and sacrilegious, who has committed blasphemy against his own Father? Do you think that he will remove from such people their sins by baptism when it is established that they who have been baptised have so far waved their abusive claims in the face of the Father, and continue sinning with the wickedness of a tongue that cannot stop blaspheming?

Can the servant of God, can the Christian, either conceive of this in their heart or believe it in faith, or propose it as an argument in speech? **2** And where will come into all this the divine commandments of the Law which state: "Honor father and mother?" (Ex 20.12).

It cannot be that in the case of God the word "father" that commands honor in a human instance should be violated without punishment. What will become of what Christ himself laid down in the gospel with the words: "He who speaks evil of father and mother, let him die the death" (Mt 15.4)? Christ himself commands that those who speak evil of their parents in the flesh are to be punished and put to death. It cannot be that he himself will cause to live those who speak evil of their heavenly and spiritual Father, and are enemies of the Church that is their Mother. **3** The argument is therefore to be rejected with abhorrence, proposed again by certain persons, that the God who warns that he who will blaspheme against the Holy

Spirit will be found guilty of an eternal sin is claiming at the same time that the blasphemers against God the Father are sanctified with baptism for salvation.

So now for those who consider that the kind of people who come to the Church without its true baptism should receive communion. Are they not aware that they are in communion with the eternal sins of others when they admit without baptizing them those who cannot, in the absence of being baptised, lay aside the sins of their own blasphemies?

20.1 How without effect, to the point of perversity is it that, when the heretics themselves acknowledge the Church's truth, we seek to damage the rights and oaths sworn at baptism that bind us to the same truth? We are saying to those who come and are penitent that they are already in possession of absolution from their sins when they insist that they have sinned and on this account are coming for the Church's pardon. **2** For this reason, dearest brother, we ought to maintain steadfastly the faith of the Catholic Church and its truth, and to teach and to declare the pattern of divine order and unity found throughout all the gospels and the commandments of the apostles.

21.1 Surely the power of baptism is never of greater strength and force than the confession of one's faith itself, than suffering in the case of one who confesses Christ before men and is accordingly baptised in his own blood?[12] However, not even baptism in this case is of any advantage to a heretic.

Even though he has professed Christ, he has been slain *outside* the Church. The protectors of heretical interests and the spokesmen in their defense are wrong to give the title of "martyrs" to those

[12] In the early Church, baptism by blood in either martyrdom or confessorship (in which the confessor survived) was considered to be a proxy for water baptism that therefore produced the same benefit of grace, see Hermas *Sim.* 9.28.6–8, with which cf. Tertullian *Bapt.* 16.1 and *Paen.* 13.7.

heretics who met their violent end with a false confession of Christ. These are trying to assign glory and the crown of suffering to them. But they have the Apostle Paul's summary of the case against them, who states that it is of no advantage to them, even though they suffer the burning of the pyre and are cut down (1 Cor 13.3).

2 So, because there is no salvation outside the Church, if the baptism of blood consequent to a public confession of faith is unable to be effective for salvation, how much the more will there be no advantage to him if he feels on his skin a pretended washing with water in a cave or robbers' den. The pretence will not only fail to remove his sins from of old, but rather will collect together new and far greater ones than before.

3 For this reason, those who come from a heretical sect to the Church ought to receive baptism. They ought to be made ready for the kingdom of God by being born again from God by the legitimate, true and one and only baptism of Holy Church. They must be born from both signs. This is why it is written: "Unless someone is born of water and of the Spirit, he cannot enter the kingdom of God" (Jn 3.5).

22.1 On this topic some use the catechumens as a contrary case, as though they could, by presenting human arguments, empty the truth of what the gospels proclaim of its power. They ask whether this would mean that if any of the catechumens before his baptism in the Church would have been arrested and killed in the process of confessing the name, he would lose the hope of salvation and the reward of his confession simply because he had not first been reborn of water?

2 Let people of this kind, supporters of the candidacy of heretics and their encouragers, grasp in the first place the fact that those previously mentioned catechumens maintain the faith of the Church unimpaired and its truth, and go forth from God's camp in the war against the Devil in full and convinced acknowledgement of God the Father, and of Christ and the Holy Spirit.

In the second place, they are not deprived of the pledge of baptism on the grounds that they are baptised with the glorious and highest baptism of blood. Of this baptism the Lord used to say himself that he had another baptism with which to be baptised (Lk 12.50). The same Lord declares in the gospel that his Passion perfects them, when baptised and sanctified with his own blood, and that they acquire the grace that is divinely promised. At his own Passion he addressed the thief who believed in him, and confessed him, and promised that he would be with him in Paradise (Lk 23.43).

3 In consequence, we who are the authorities in matters of faith and of truth ought not to deceive and mislead those who come to faith and to the truth and request with an act of penitence that their sins be absolved. In order for us to set them right and restore them to the kingdom of heaven, they should be instructed in heavenly practices.

23.1 I hear someone saying: "What in this case should be done about these who have been over the course of time admitted without baptism when they come to the Church from heresy?"[13] The Lord is more than capable to grant pardon and not to separate from the gifts of his Church those who have been admitted into the Church in their innocence and have experienced death's sleep in the Church. **2** It is not however the case that we are always entitled to be mistaken because at one time we have made a mistake. It is fitting for those who are wise in God's fear to render without delay glad obedience to the truth when it is laid open before them and disclosed. They should not instead be fighting in their stubborn obstinacy the heretics' battle for them, against their brothers and against their sacred bishops.

---

[13]By admitting this objection, Cyprian is revealing that he is the innovator and that tradition is against him, so much so that he cannot draw the obvious conclusion that those who were readmitted without true baptism were not saved.

24.1 No one should form the impression that heretics can be held back from coming to the Church because our requirement of baptism is an obstacle to them, on grounds that offence is given them by the little word "second" baptism. **2** In fact in this very matter they are driven to regard returning as essential the more by our witness to the truth, once we have explained this to them and presented our evidence. For they *would* start thinking that they were in valid and legitimate possession of the Church, and of all other gifts of the Church, if they were, on the contrary, to have seen instead, as our judgment and sentence, that it was our decision and decree that baptism could be reckoned as valid and legitimately granted in their separated conventicle.

There simply will not be any reason for them to come to us once they start thinking that by possessing baptism they possess everything else. **3** But if, on the other hand, they come to recognize that there is no baptism outside the Church, their return will be a hurried one. Once they recognize that the absolution of sins cannot be granted on the *outside*, they will pursue the Church's one baptism more eagerly and more readily, beseeching the benefits and gifts of Mother Church. They will recognize that they are unable to reach with full assurance the promise of divine grace that is real without first coming to the reality of the Church. The heretics would not refuse to be baptised with the legitimate and real baptism of the Church once they have learned from us that those people who had already receive John's baptism were nevertheless baptised by Paul, as we read in the Acts of the Apostles (19.3–5).

25.1 At present, recognition of baptism performed by heretics is being advocated by some of our own number. Based upon a certain feeling of dislike of the practice of rebaptizing, they consider it to be a sacrilegious act to baptise after the enemies of God have already done so. They are asserting this even when we can see that those whom John had baptised were baptised again!

This John was held to be greatest amongst the prophets, filled with divine grace while yet in his mother's womb, strengthened by the support of the Spirit of Elijah and his power. He was no adversary of our Lord, but his forerunner and preacher. He did not only announce him beforehand in words, but he even revealed him to the eyes of men. It was he who baptised Christ through whom all others are baptised.

2 But if for this reason a heretic could acquire the right to baptise because he had got his baptism in first, baptism would then not be his who lawfully possessed it but his who simply made it his own. Baptism and the Church cannot be completely divided from one another and split in two. Anyone who was able to be the first to make baptism his own was also equally able to make the Church his own. You then begin to appear to such a person as the heretic for you have been made out to be the later person though you have precedence. By making this concession of surrender, you have forfeited the right that you had once received. **3** Holy Scripture declares how dangerous it is in affairs of God to surrender one's right and legal power. In Genesis Esau lost his first place and was not able to regain what he had once relinquished (Gen 27.30–40).

26.1 In our inadequacy and with brief words we write this letter in reply, dearest brother, without imposing any limitation[14] upon, or prejudgment upon, any of the bishops. Let each do what he thinks best, in possession of full power over his own decision.[15] **2** We for our part do not wish to fall out with our colleagues and fellow bishops on account of heretics. We maintain with them God's concord and the Lord's peace, particularly when the Apostle says: "If anyone should think that he should be quarrelsome, we do not possess such a custom and neither does the Church of God." (1 Cor. 11:16).

---

[14]"Imposing any limitation" = *praescribere* in its legal sense of "to enter an objection or limitation at the head of a *formula*."

[15]Thus his controversy with Stephen has lead him to defend the autonomy of each diocesan bishop again a nascent papal claim to the right to adjudicate. See also Introduction, §4 and §5.3.

May we preserve, patiently and gently, charity of spirit, and regard for our episcopal college, the bond of faith, and the concord of the episcopal priesthood. On this subject we recently composed a small book *On the Virtue of Patience*, despite our continuing inadequacy, with the Lord granting his permission and inspiration. This we are sending on to you as a token of our mutual affection. My prayer, dearest brother, is for your lasting good health.

Rebaptism: Firmilian's Approving Reply

Firmilian, bishop of Caesarea in Cappadocia (AD 230–268), has a well-established biography.[1] He writes in the autumn of AD 256, the year before Stephen's death and Cyprian's sentence to exile. Since Cyprian has written *Ep.* 73, Stephen has excommunicated those rebaptizing heretics, including large numbers of African and Eastern bishops (6.2 and 25.1–2). Firmilian will thus prey on the practice of the Eastern date for Easter as an example of episcopal differences that need not disrupt the bond of unity (6.1).

Firmilian was an important Eastern ally after the rejection of Cyprian's views on rebaptism in Rome. Firmilian adds no new theological insights into the views of Cyprian that he simply regurgitates (4–5; 8–9; 15–24). He mentions baptism in relation to the mortal sin of Adam (17.2). He reinforces Cyprian's argument with an example not used by Cyprian in his reference to bishop who had been deposed for heresy and whose subsequent baptisms were unrecognized (22.1).

Firmilian's letter illuminates how Stephen's acts and character appeared to Cyprian's sympathizers and contemporaries. He is a betrayer in the role of Judas (2.3). Stephen emerges as a player in a power game advancing the prerogatives of Rome so that Firmilian must in response appeal to Jerusalem as the primal see (6.1). Furthermore, we have the interesting portrait of the lady prophet exercising a sacramental ministry (10–11).

Also it seems that Stephen was acting in ways that lead to accusations that he was in a minority and endeavoring to exalt his See and its authority above the episcopal college as a whole. Firmilian is prepared to use the language of apostasy and schism in direct application to Stephen with a directness that Cyprian has not used (24.2). It is he who has broken communion with the bond of unity that is the mutual recognition and intercommunion of the whole episcopal college (25). But ecclesiastical bureaucrats always need a "hard man" in comparison with whom they can claim moderation

---

[1]Eusebius *Hist. eccl.* 6.27, 7.30.5; Gregory of Nyssa *Vita Greg. Thaum.* PG 46.905C.

in their strictures. The name-calling reaches its height (in 25.4) where, if Firmilian is to be believed, Stephen describes Cyprian as a false Christian, false apostle, and sly operative.

Firmilian to Cyprian, Brother in Our Holy Lord

1.1 We have received delivery from you through Rogatian, deacon most dear, of the letter that you composed to us, most beloved brother. We have given our grateful thanks to God for this act, because it is fitting that, though we are separate one from another in the body, we are united in spirit as though not only living in one and the same area, but as though dwelling in one and the same house.

2 It is a glorious pronouncement that the spiritual house of God is one. "For there will be revealed in the last days," he says, "the mount of the Lord and the house of God above the peaks of the mountains" (Is 2.2). Gathering together in this house we shall be joined together with rejoicing, even as also in the Psalm there is the prayer to the Lord that he dwells in the house of God for all the days of his life (Ps 26.4). It is furthermore shown in another passage that there is great filial desire amongst the saints for the wish to assemble in one house. "Lo," it says, "how good and desirable it is that brothers dwell together as one" (Ps 132.1).

2.1 Being united in peace and concord not only provides the greatest delight for faithful men who know the truth but also for the heavenly angels themselves, to whom God's word says that there is joy over one sinner who performs penance and returns to the bond of unity (Lk 15.7). **2** Obviously this would not be said of angels who have their customary life in heaven, had not they themselves also been united with us and rejoiced at our unity. Similarly and conversely they are clearly saddened when they see the hearts of some of us at variance amongst themselves, and their purposes divided. These people are not only not calling on the one and the same God, but, even worse, in their separation and division from each other, there cannot any longer be any discussion between them nor any common consultation.

3 We can at least commend Stephen with thanks for his one achievement in that through his incivility it has now come about that we can find at least in you an example of good faith and wisdom. It is not however that what Stephen has done deserves thanks for benefiting us. Judas, for example, in that case could be seen as worthy on the grounds that he provided the cause of all benefits by his own treachery and betrayal, worked in wickedness against the Savior. It was not thanks to him that the world and people of the nations would be made free as a result of the Passion of the Lord.

3.1 Let us now bypass Stephen's acts to avoid chastening ourselves with lasting grief over his unprincipled proceedings by mentioning his effrontery and insolence. But you mention, on the other hand, in recognition, that you have dealt with the issue that is now in question according to the rule of truth and the wisdom of Christ. We commend you with great joy and we give thanks to God. We have discovered amongst our brothers, though found far away from us, that they are of one mind with us in the faith and in the truth. **2** This is because God's grace is mighty in linking and joining, within the bond of Christian love and unity, even those parts that appear to be separated by a long distance across the world.

It is just like Ezekiel and Daniel who were divided by an interval of time, in a later age, from Job and Noah who had been in the earliest period. God's power joined them together in the bond of agreement, so that, although they were placed apart by a long course of time, they could have the same thoughts due to divine inspiration. **3** We note this same principle in your case.

Though you are now divided from us by locations so very distant, you are demonstrating that you nonetheless are joined with us in thought and in spirit. All of which is due to the operation of the principle of divine unity. For the one and the same Lord, who dwells in us, joins his own together from every place and unites them in the bond of unity. As a result, running swift of foot, blown by the spirit of unity, the sound of those who have been sent by the Lord has gone out into the whole world (Ps 18.5).

On the other hand, there is no advantage for certain others to be near to one another and physically joined to each other if they are in disagreement in mind and soul. Souls cannot at all be united when they have separated themselves from God's unity. "Lo," he says, "those who distance themselves from you will perish" (Ps 72.27). **4** Such people as these will experience God's merited judgment upon them because they are departing from Christ's words. He prayed to his Father for unity with the words: "Father, grant that in the way in which I and you are one, so all these will be one in us" (Jn 17.21).

4.1 So truly we have adopted your words written to us as though they were our own, and we are not reading them in a cursory fashion but we are entrusting them to memory by repeating them often. Nor is it an obstacle to their value for salvation to go back over their main points in order to confirm their truth, or to make certain additions to them in the interests of increasing their value as evidence.

2 If, however, we do make some additions, such additions are not to be understood as a correction to any deficiency in your statement of the case. We make them because theology is beyond the capacity of human nature, and one soul is unable to form a conception of it that is whole and complete. For this reason the number of the prophets is such a large one, because divine wisdom, in its multiplicity, has to be distributed among more than one mind. Therefore the commandment is given that the first to speak in prophecy is to keep silent if a revelation will be given by a second (1 Cor 14.30).

3 This is the reason why it is an essential practice with us that every year we the elders and the presiding authorities should meet in one body to manage those matters that have been committed to our care. Our common council can thus regulate any more serious issues. Thus fallen brothers, lying wounded by the devil after receiving the bath of salvation, can seek their cure through doing penance, not on the grounds that they are gaining absolution of their sins *from* us, but because *through* us they are being guided into the understanding of their sins, and are being constrained to make full atonement to the Lord.

5.1 Since however your delegate that you sent was in a hurry to get back to you, and the winter season was coming on, we are writing back our official reply to what you have written, to the extent that this allows us. **2** On the subject of Stephen's original statement, that the apostles did not allow those who had come from heresy to be baptised, and that they have handed down in the tradition a principle for posterity to safeguard . . . Your reply has been a full one: no one is so foolish to believe that the apostles handed down such a tradition when it is established that the heresies that came after them have stood out conspicuously for their accursed and detestable character.

We can unmask Marcion as the disciple of Cerdo, and show him a long distance in time after the apostles as bringing in a sacrilegious tradition that opposes God. Appelles also agreed with his blasphemy when he added many other new innovations threatening the faith and hostile to its truth. And for the period of Valentinus and Basilides it is also very obvious. They also, after the apostles, and after a long period of time, rebelled against the Church with their wicked lies. **3** It is established that the remainder of the heretics only later introduced their own breakaway groups and perverse inventions, as each had been lead by their error.

It is very clear that their very own acts have condemned all of them. They have pronounced their own sentence against themselves even before the Day of Judgment, from which no one is exempt. If anyone grants that their baptism is valid, what else can this be than to pass judgment upon and to condemn himself along with these by making himself a collaborator with persons of this nature?

6.1 Anyone can grasp from this example that those in Rome are not respecting in their every practice what the tradition hands down from its origin: their hiding behind apostolic authority is unfounded. For example, on the question of when the days of Easter are to be celebrated,[2] and on many other pledges of divine reality, it appears that they are guilty of other inconsistencies. They do not observe over there precisely the customary practices as in Jerusalem. This is the case too in many other provinces,[3] that there are many variations due to differences of local customs and nomenclature. But there is no reason here for any departure from the bond of peace and of unity of the Catholic Church.

2 Stephen has now the audacity to do what he is doing, and, in opposition to you, to rupture the peace that his predecessors together with you always safeguarded with a love and a respect that was reciprocated. He is even slandering the blessed Apostles Peter and Paul, on the grounds that they themselves handed down this principle in the tradition. To the contrary, they, in their epistles, have shown their repugnance towards the heretics, and warned that we should avoid them. From this it follows that it is a purely human tradition that the heretics are claiming, and are claiming in their defense that they possess the baptism that belongs to no one but to the Church alone.

7.1 Your reply was a good one to that section in Stephen's letter where Stephen is saying that the heretics themselves are in agreement with us on the question of baptism, and that "on either side,

[2]Firmilian as an Eastern bishop appears to be appealing to the Eastern practice of observing Easter on the Jewish 14 Nisan, irrespective of on what day of the week it might fall, instead of the Sunday following. Victor, much to the criticism of Irenaeus, had excommunicated the Quartodecimans in Rome; yet they could insist on the apostolic tradition from John. See Eusebius *Hist. eccl.* 5.24.9–16; cf. Brent, *Hippolytus*, 412–15.

[3]Note here that Firmilian follows Cyprian in assimilating the authority of a bishop over a territorial diocese with a unit of pagan, secular authority, so that he can assert that Stephen as bishop of Rome has no authority within the *imperium* of another; see Cyprian *Ep.* 55.8.4–5; *Laps.* 8–9, 13–19; and Introduction, §2.1.

when they come to their company, they do not baptise but only give communion."[4] As if we also were obliged to adopt this practice!

2 To this point we make a superfluous addition, even though you have already proved to be ridiculous enough the thought of following those who are going astray themselves. My thought is that it would not be surprising if the heretics conducted their business in this way. Even though they differ in some minor matters, they maintain their agreement on the one and the same great principle. This is that they should blaspheme the Creator, whilst they devise in their imagination dreams and fantasies of an unknown God. The general consequence of this is that they agree upon a baptism that is part of their own illusion, with the result that their agreement is the repudiation of the truth of the godhead.

3 It would be too distracting to make a point-by-point response to each of their arguments, whether they are wicked or simply invalid. It is enough to make a brief, verbal summary. Those who do not maintain the Lord and Father to be the true one are unable either to maintain the truth of the Son or of the Holy Spirit.

In the same way, those who are called "Cataphrygians" attempt to acquire new ways of prophesying, but do not have the Father or the Holy Spirit. If we inquire of them who the Christ is whom they proclaim, they will respond that they proclaim him who has sent the Spirit, who has spoken through Montanus and Prisca. Since we recognize that not the Spirit of truth but the spirit of error has been in them, we realize also that they are not able to possess Christ: they have laid claim to their false prophecy against the faith of Christ.

4 And all the rest of the heretics as well. They split themselves off from the Church of God and so are unable to possess any part of its power and grace. All power and grace have been placed in the Church, where the elders by birth hold office, and who possess the power of baptizing, of imposition of hands, of ordaining. It is unlawful therefore for a heretic to ordain and to lay hands, and, as well, either to baptise or to act in any sacred or spiritual role.

[4]Cyprian *Ep.* 74.1.2 and 4.1.

The heretic has no connections with spiritual holiness that can make him like God. **5** We have already previously established this entire matter on a firm basis when there was an assembly that came together in one body in Iconium, situated in Phrygia. It was gathered from Galatia and Cilicia, and the rest of the regions immediately close by. Our position was to be maintained firmly against the heretics, and our claim vindicated in the face of some doubt on this issue.

8.1 Stephen and his supporters are arguing that absolution from sins and the Second Birth is able to take place in heretical baptism. But they nevertheless themselves assert that the Holy Spirit is not found amongst heretics. They should consider and grasp that spiritual birth cannot exist without the Spirit: the blessed Apostle Paul baptised anew with a baptism of the Spirit those whom John had baptised before the Holy Spirit had been sent by the Lord.

To do this he laid hands on them for them to receive the Holy Spirit (Acts 19:1–6). **2** Since it is the case that we see that Paul had baptised John's disciples a second time after his baptism, should we doubt that we should baptise those who come to the Church from heresy following their illicit and invalid soaking? Can it be that Paul was of lesser power than these bishops that we have now? Is the result that these bishops are able to grant to heretics that come to them the Holy Spirit through the imposition of their hands by itself? Paul, however, had not been capable of granting the Holy Spirit to those baptised by John through the imposition of his hands alone, without first having baptised them with the Church's baptism.

9.1 It is absurd that they should not think to ask the question of the identity of the person that had performed a baptism. Their reason is that the baptised person will be able to acquire grace because of the invocation of the triune names of Father and of Son and of Holy Spirit. Here will be found the meaning of the wisdom Paul writes about in those who have been made complete (1 Cor 2.6). In consequence, they argue that he who has been made complete in the Church and is wise will defend and trust in this principle: the bare invocation of the names is sufficient for the absolution of sins and the sanctification of baptism.

But these results, on the contrary, only ensue when he who does the baptism has the Holy Spirit, and when baptism itself has been definitely established to be accompanied by the Spirit. **2** They also claim that some one who, in whatever manner, is baptised *outside* the Church can acquire the grace of baptism through his personal faith and intention. This is undoubtedly grounds for ridicule as it implies that a corrupt intention could bring down from heaven upon itself the sanctification of the righteous, or that belief in what is false effects the same reality that is experienced by those who believe in faith.

Not all who call upon the name of Christ are heard, nor is their invocation able to achieve any fruit of grace. This the Lord himself reveals when he says: "Many will come in my name, saying: 'I am Christ,' and they will deceive many." (Mt 7.21). There is no difference between a false prophet and a heretic. Just as the former deceives in the name of God and of Christ, so the latter deceives in making a solemn promise of baptism. Both rest on a lie in order to deceive humans about what their aim is.

10.1 I would like now to set out for you events that we experienced from a history that is relevant to this issue. About twenty-two years ago, after the reign of the emperor Alexander,[5] a great number of upheavals and tribulations befell us over here, whether shared by all humankind or confined only to Christians.

Very many earthquakes were of constant occurrence with the result that there were many subsidences throughout Cappadocia

---

[5]Alexander Severus died in AD 235, along with his mother, Julia Mammaea, during his Persian campaign. According to Eusebius *Hist. eccl.* 6.28, his successor, Maximus Thrax, launched a persecution against church leaders in Rome so that there is no need to be surprised that Firmilian does not mention this as a general persecution. But, see Clarke, *Letters of St Cyprian*, 4.263–64.

and Pontus. Even certain cities sank deeply into the earth that enclosed them, as the ground opened up and swallowed them. In consequence, a very serious persecution resulted against those who bore the name of Christian.

The persecution suddenly arose after a long period of peace, and its consequence was even more terrible in stirring up our people with fright at an unforeseen evil of which they had had no experience. Serenianus, a vicious and dreadful persecutor, was at that time governor in our province.[6] **2** The faithful, overcome by the chaotic confusion of all this, forsook their home countries and immigrated into the territories of other regions, fleeing here and there because of the terror from the persecution. The emigration was assisted by the fact that the persecution did not extend throughout the whole world but was local.

Some woman then suddenly arose over here, who proclaimed herself a prophet and was found in an ecstatic state. She thus conducted herself in the pretence that she was filled with the Holy Spirit. She was so controlled by the chief daemons by which she was overwhelmed that for a long time she caused the brotherhood deep concern. She deceived them by performing certain acts that were miraculous and supernatural.

She promised that she would cause the earth to move. It was not because her daemonic power was so great so as to move the earth, nor was it of so great a force that it was strong enough to shake an element about.[7] Rather it was because a spirit has unfailing foreknowledge and understanding of the future movement of the earth that she could pretend that she herself would do what she saw would

[6]Firmilian implies that the persecution was not general, in that it was organised from Rome. Rather it arose from perhaps the more usual reason for persecution, namely a feeling that the gods were angry at Christian unbelief regarding them. In this respect Serenianus' action was inspired by a groundswell of popular unrest on the part of the pagan population. See also the following section (*Ep*.75.10.1.2) and Cyprian *Demetr.*

[7]Earth was one of the four elements, together with fire, water, and air, in ancient cosmologies.

happen in the future. **3** The daemon controlled the minds of individuals by means of these lying, boastful assertions with the result that they became his subjects, and they would follow in whatever direction his commands led them. He even made his woman to walk with bare feet in a hard winter through the icy snow, and not to be troubled or injured by his possession of her.

The daemon would say that he and the woman were hurrying to Judea and Jerusalem, creating the illusion that he had come from there. **4** She succeeded in seducing one of the presbyters, an uneducated man, and similarly someone else who was a deacon, so that they had intercourse with this same woman. This was detected shortly following the event. One of the exorcists suddenly confronted her, a man of proven practical knowledge in matters of ritual practice in which he was always well versed. Urged on by the encouragement of many of the brothers, who themselves remained steadfast and of shining reputation in the faith, he asserted himself against that spirit who responded in vain to the attack. By means of a finely composed deceit, the daemon had even managed to predict a short while before that there would come an unbelieving opponent to test him.

Notwithstanding, that exorcist bravely resisted through the inbreathing of God's grace, and proved the spirit that was considered previously holy to be most fraudulent. **5** Accordingly the aforementioned woman, influenced previously by the tricks and deceptions of daemons to hoodwink the faithful, had dared even this trick amongst the many others which she had used on so many and so often. She even pretended, by making an impressive invocation, that she was consecrating the bread and effecting the Eucharist, and thus offering the sacrifice to the Lord without the guarantee of the customary formal liturgical preface. Also she performed many baptisms, even adopting the customary and valid words of the interrogatory formula in order not to appear in any way to conflict with the Church's rule.

11.1 What comment can we make on a baptism like this, in which a fraudulent daemon has performed a baptism through the agency of a woman? Surely Stephen and those who agree with him must particularly approve of a baptism that possessed fully both the creedal formula of the Trinity, and the Church's valid interrogation of it?

Can we trust that absolution from sins has been granted or that rebirth at the saving font has been validly effected when these have been entirely wrought by daemons effecting an illusion of their reality? The claimants on behalf of heretical baptism would have to argue that that a daemon has granted the grace of baptism in the name of the Father and Son and Holy Spirit. That very claim is without doubt erroneous in our circles, itself the very deception of daemons in the entire absence of the Holy Spirit amongst them.

12.1 But this is precisely the character of what Stephen intends. He wants to say that the presence and holiness of Christ are in those baptised in heretical conventicles. In that case, does not the Apostle lie with the words: "As many of you that have been washed in Christ have been clothed with Christ"? (Gal 3.27).

This would mean precisely that some one who has been baptised in their company has been clothed with Christ. If he has been clothed with Christ, he can receive the Holy Spirit whom Christ sent, and hands are laid on him without effect when he comes to receive the Holy Spirit. They cannot thus separate Christ from the Spirit so that in heretical circles some sort of Christ might exist but definitely not the Holy Spirit there with them.

13.1 In brief, with our dearest brother the deacon Rogatian eager to get to you in greatest haste, let us run through the remaining items that you have stated very fully and at great length. **2** My next point is that we have a right to inquire from those who are defending heretics whether their baptism is carnal or spiritual. For if it is carnal, it is no different from the baptism of the Jews. Their usage is to wash away only dirt in a shared and common bath. If however it is spiritual, how can there be a spiritual baptism in their group amongst whom there is not the Holy Spirit?

For this reason the water in which they are drenched is merely a carnal washing, not the solemn initiatory rite of baptism.[8]

14.1 If heretical baptism can possess the power of regeneration as a result of the Second Birth, people when baptised in their conventicles should be reckoned not as heretics but as sons of God. The Second Birth is that which in baptism gives birth to the sons of God.

However, if there is one bride of Christ that is the Catholic Church, she herself is the one who alone gives birth to God's sons. There are not many brides of Christ. It would be contrary to the statement of the Apostle: "I betrothed you as a holy virgin to one husband to assign you to Christ" (2 Cor 11.2). Also: "Listen, my daughter and look and bend your ear and forget your people because the king has desired your beauteous form" (Song 4.8). And: "I have entered into my garden, my sister, my spouse" (Song 5.1).

We see generally one person is put forward because there is only one bride. **2** The synagogue of the heretics however is not one with us, since the bride is an adulteress and a prostitute. Thus she is unable to produce sons for God, unless, as Stephen thinks, heresy not only gives them birth but also exposes them to die. The Church then, according to him, adopts the children thus exposed, and she nourishes along with her own children those that the adulteress did not spare.

But, to the contrary, the Church cannot be the mother of the sons of another person. For this reason Christ our Lord reveals that his own bride is one person, and declares the vindication of the claim[9] to that oneness with the words: "He who is not with me is against me, and he who does not gather with me scatters" (Mt 12.30). If Christ is with us, the heretics are not with us. The heretics are definitely

---

[8]For *sacramentum* as "initiatory rite," see Cyprian *Laps.* 7, n. 17; *Ep.* 73.5.2, n. 10.

[9]"Vindication of the claim" is another meaning of the slippery term *sacramentum*, and is most appropriate here.

opposed to Christ. If we gather with Christ, but the heretics do not gather with us, without doubt they scatter.

15.1 We must not overlook the point that you have stated as essential. The Church, according to the Song of Songs, is "an enclosed garden," and "a sealed fountain," "a paradise fecund with fruit trees" (Song 4.12–13). There are, however, those who have never entered this garden nor seen the paradise planted by God the Creator. How then will they be able to provide anyone with the living water of the saving font from a fountain that is enclosed and sealed up with God's seal?

2 The ark of Noah is truly none other than the promised pledge of Christ's Church. The ark then, when all on the outside were perishing, saved those alone who were within the ark. By this example we are clearly drawn to the careful consideration of the unity of the Church on the very grounds that Peter sets out with the words: "So also in the same way baptism saves us" (1 Pet 3.21).

Peter reveals that in the way in which those who were not in the ark of Noah were not only without purification and salvation through water, but they perished absolutely in the Flood. Correspondingly now, whoever are not in the Church with Christ will perish on the *outside* of it, unless they turn in penitence to the Church's one and only saving font.

16.1 This is truly the kind of error and the extent of the darkness of Stephen in claiming that absolution from sins can be granted in the synagogues of the heretics. He does not hold his ground on the foundation of the one Church that has been made firm once for all by Christ upon a rock. This conclusion can be learned from Christ's statement to Peter alone: "Whatever you will have bound on earth will have been bound also in heaven, and whatever you absolve on earth will have been absolved also in heaven" (Mt 16.18–19).

A second time in the gospel Christ breathes into the apostles alone with the words: "Receive the Holy Spirit. If you will forgive the sins of anyone, they will be forgiven them. If you retain those of any-one, they will be retained" (Jn 20.22–23). The power then of forgiving sins is granted to the apostles and to the Churches that they founded, when sent by Christ. That power is also granted to the bishops, who were their successors as a result of being ordained in their place.

2 The enemies of the one Catholic Church are in the process of setting up godless altars. They are the adversaries of we who are in the Church and the successors of the apostles. It is against us that they intend to lay their claim to priestly orders that are illegitimate. They are committing a sacrilege by a similar kind of sin that is no less than that of Core, Dathan, and Abiron. Will not those who share their opinion be destined to pay the same penalty that the latter incurred? Remember that those who then joined with them and supported them perished with them in the same mortal end.

17.1 I burn with righteous anger at Stephen's public and well-publi-cized stupidity on this topic in view of the fact that he glories in the location of his particular episcopate at Rome. He thus insists that he holds the succession from Peter on whom the foundations of the Church have been set. Yet he is bringing in many other rocks, and founding the constructions of so many new churches in defending by his authority the existence of baptism in them.

2 For without doubt those who are baptised are filling up the complete number of those in the Church. Whoever then gives approval to their baptism is trying to establish from the fact of their baptism that the Church is there with them. He understands not that he, in betraying and deserting unity, is darkening and smudging the real nature of the Christian rock.

The Apostle asserts that the Jews, though blinded by ignorance and constrained by their commitment of the most serious crime of all, have, in spite of this, a zeal for God (Rom 10.2–3). Stephen, who proclaims that he has the Chair of Peter through the apostolic succession, is not driven to oppose the heretics by any zeal at all. He is granting to them no small measure, but a very large one, of the

power of grace. He is saying and claiming that *they* wash away the
filth of the old man through the rite of baptism, that *they* pardon the
ancient mortal sins, that *they* create sons of God through heavenly
rebirth, that *they* restore to life eternal by the sanctification from the
divine font.

3 If Stephen thus grants and attributes to heretics the great and
heavenly gifts of the Church, can he do anything less than enter into
communion with them? His action is equivalent to defending and
claiming for them the means of grace. It is in vain that he says that
he is hesitant about agreeing and participating with them in all other
things. Thus he should meet with them and share the same prayers
with them, and join with them in setting up their altar and sacrifice
in which he, in consequence of his position, shares.

18.1 But, he must protest, his claim is that the name of Christ is
of great effect for making us confident that their baptism brings
sanctification. Consequently, whoever and wherever someone will
have been baptised in Christ's name, he acquires by that fact Christ's
grace.

We can here briefly confront his position, and with it our reply. If
baptism in Christ's name had power on the *outside* of the Church to
purge a human being of sin, the imposition of hands also in the name
of the selfsame Christ would have been able to prevail on the *outside*
also for the reception of the Holy Spirit. On this account, all other
acts amongst the heretics will begin to seem justly performed and
valid when they are performed in the name of Christ. You have followed through this point in your letter with the argument that only
in the Church, to which Christ has imparted the power of heavenly
grace through its unity, can the name of Christ avail.

19.1 The relevant strategy with which to refute this custom is to
expose its practitioners as opponents of the truth. Who is so lacking in substance that he should put custom in the place of truth,
or that he should fail to leave the shadows when the light sheds its

illumination? **2** The Jews were like that at Christ's Advent, that is the advent of the truth. The most ancient of custom availed for nothing in their case, in which they forsook the new way of truth and persisted in their ancient decay.

3 You Africans are able to reply to Stephen that, having found the truth, you have left the error of mere custom. Nevertheless, we combine custom with truth, and we set in answer to the custom of the Romans the custom of the truth. This principle we have maintained from the beginning because it has been handed down in the tradition from Christ and from the apostles.

We have no memory of how at any time the former practice began amongst us, since the observed principle here was always the case with us, namely that if we recognise the Church of God to be one, we cannot reckon baptism to be holy baptism if it is not that of the Church. **4** Obviously some were having doubts about the baptism of those who, despite welcoming adherents of the New Prophecy,[10] did so because they considered that they recognized along with us the Father and the Son. We assembled therefore together at Iconium and considered the matter with every care, and we confirmed that every baptism that had taken place outside the Church should be utterly repudiated.

20.1 They put forward an argument in defense of the heretics by claiming the Apostle's words in their support: "Let Christ be proclaimed, whether by accident or in truth" (Phil 1.18). Our response is that it is a loose argument. The Apostle has made it clear in his epistle why he has said this. He has made reference neither to the heretics nor their baptism, but has spoken only about *brothers*, who either are supporting his words with the intent to undermine him, or are continuing resolutely in the sincerity of faith. We are not required to engage in some long scrutiny with a lengthy examination, but we need only to read the epistle itself and thus to see that what the Apostle has said is about the apostle himself.

[10]I.e. the Montanist or Cataphrygian movement; see 7.3 above.

21.1 What therefore, they are asking, should happen in the case of those who have been admitted to the Church without the Church's baptism? If they have departed from this world, they are to be considered placed in the number of those who had received Christian instruction within our company, but who had met their death before they had received baptism. They had no small advantage from the truth, and from the faith to which they had attained, even though they had been prevented by death from gaining the final fulfillment of the work of grace. **2** Those of them who continue in this world should be baptised with the Church's baptism in order that they might gain absolution from their sins. They need to avoid dying without the final fulfillment of the work of grace through their persistence in their original error due to the obstinacy of others.

3 In other respects the character of the sin is identical between those who admitted heretics, and the heretics themselves who are admitted. They allow them to touch the body and blood of the Lord as a consequence of their demanding, without good reason, the right to receive communion, without their filthiness washed away in the Church's font or their sins put away there. Their answer is in Scripture: "Whoever will eat of the bread or drink of the cup of the Lord unworthily, shall be guilty of the body and blood of the Lord" (1 Cor 11.27).

22.1 We have made a judgment about those who were previously bishops in the Catholic Church, and afterwards baptised some others by still arrogating to themselves the power of their lost clerical order. Those so baptised are to be regarded as though they had not been baptised. This is the practice observed by us: that those who have received a drenching from them and come to us are baptised within our company with the one and true baptism of the Catholic Church, and gain the new birth from the life-giving font. We follow this practice on the grounds that they have been separated from us, and have gained nothing from such a drenching.

2 There is always a great distinction to be made between someone who succumbs unwillingly and coerced under the compulsion of persecution, and someone else who, with the deliberate intention of boldly committing sacrilege, becomes a rebel against the Church. Thus he blasphemes with unholy words against Christ's God and Father, and the creator of the whole world. Stephen has no shame in asserting that he can say that absolution from sins can be granted through those who are themselves found steeped in every sin, just as if a font of salvation can exist in the house of death.[11]

23.1 What will be the position of God's word written: "Abstain from another's water and you shall not drink of another's fountain?" (Prov 9.18 LXX). If you forsake the sealed fountain of the Church, and you acquire for yourself another's water instead of your own, you are defiling the Church from fountains outside the sanctuary. When you join in fellowship with heretical baptism, what else is it than, though you have been purified by the Church's sanctification, to drink from their polluted swamp and from its slime, and to defile yourself by touching the uncleanness of those who are separate?

2 Do you not fear the judgment of God when you provide heretics with a witness' testimonial in support of their case against the Church? You act against what is written: "A false witness will not be unpunished" (Prov 19.5, 9).

Moreover you are worse than all the heretics. For when many recognize their error and come over from their side to yours, with the intention of receiving the Church's light of truth, you are assisting the errors of those who are coming. You are increasing the darkness of heretical night by overshadowing the light of the Church's truth. When they confess that they are in a state of sinfulness and possess

---

[11]Thus, Firmilian argues that sacramental grace is granted according to what later became the principle *ex opere operantis*, or "by the sacramental act of the person who performs it," and not *ex opere operato*, or "by virtue of the sacramental act itself being performed." Note that the former view would have made the grace granted the particular gift of the minister and reflective of his personal sanctity, and not the gift and sanctity of Christ.

nothing of grace, and for this reason they are coming to the Church, you withdraw from them the absolution for their sins that is granted in baptism.

You are doing this as long as you are saying that they have already been baptised and acquired grace outside the Church. You do not understand that their souls will be required from your hand when the Day of Judgment will come. You have denied them the Church's draft of water to remedy their thirst. In the face of their desire to live you have been the cause of death to them.

And, despite all of this, you still claim to be angry with our position!

24.1 Consider in what way through your lack of refinement you have the audacity to hinder those whose struggle is for the truth against falsehood. Who has the greater right to unjust anger against another? Is it the one who speaks in protection of the enemies of God, or rather he who, in opposition to the enemies of God, expresses the Church's consensus in defense of her truth?

2 It is quite clear that those without refinement are especially highly unstable and given to anger. They turn so easily to anger because they lack wise counsel and speaking ability. So, you see, divine Scripture is talking about no one other than you when it says: "An unstable person keeps preparing law suits, and a man given to anger piles high his sins" (Prov 29.22).

How many lawsuits and disputes have you provided for the churches throughout the whole world? How great is the mountain of your sin when you have split yourself from so many flocks? Make no mistake about it, you have cut yourself off mortally. You are the real schismatic who has committed your apostasy from communion with the Church's unity.

While you think that you have the ability to place everyone apart from you, you are placed apart, and on your own from everyone else. **3** The commandments of the Apostle could have made you conform to the rule of truth and of reconciliation when he exhorts with the words: "I entreat you, in bonds in the Lord, to walk worthy of the calling in which you have been called, with the feeling of all humility and gentleness, upholding one another in love with patience, conducting yourselves in a manner sufficient to preserve the unity of the Spirit in the bond of peace. The body is one and the spirit is one, just as you have been called in one hope of your calling. One Lord, one faith, one baptism, one God and Father of all who is above all and through all and in all of us" (Eph 4.1–6).

25.1 How scrupulously has Stephen, preserving feelings of humility and gentleness from his supreme position, fulfilled these apostolic injunctions and exhortations that bring salvation! Could he be any more humble and gentle that when he disagreed with so many bishops throughout the whole world, upsetting the peace with individual ones by causing various kinds of discord, sometimes with Western bishops—which we are sure has not escaped your notice—and sometimes with southern bishops such as yourselves. With such patience and gentleness did he officially welcome the representatives of the latter bishops that he would not agree to even having a meeting with them for an informal discussion!

He was so conscious of the obligations of love and charity that he commanded the universal brotherhood not to receive the representatives into their home. The implication was that he was denying those representatives not only reconciliation and communion, but also even a roof and hospitality as guests. **2** So this is what the preservation of unity of the Spirit in the bond of peace is all about! One is to cut oneself off from the unity of charity, and to make oneself separate from the brothers in all things, and to rise up against the bond and solemn agreement of peace in the blind fury of discord.

Can there be with such a character one body and one Spirit when he himself is likely not to be of one mind and soul, his condition so changeable and unstable and unreliable? But his role in things we should now leave. **3** Our investigation is rather the chief subject of our inquiry.

The claim under investigation is that those who have been baptised by heretics ought to be welcomed as if they had acquired the grace of a valid baptism. But this is to claim that heretical baptism is one and the same between the heretics and ourselves, and differs in no respect. But what does the Apostle Paul say? "One Lord, one faith, one baptism, one God."

The heretics' faith is also one and inseparable from ours if their baptism is one and identical with ours. If, however, their faith is inseparable, their Lord, to be precise, is one and inseparable from ours. If there is one Lord, it follows that we say that there is God, one and inseparable. If, however, this unity, which cannot in any way be separated or divided, also pertains to the heretics, where does the argument lead?

Why don't we call those heretics Christians? Therefore, because there is not one God shared by us and the heretics, nor one Lord, nor one Church, nor one faith, it is obvious that there is neither one Spirit nor one Body: baptism cannot be shared between ourselves and the heretics, with whom we share nothing in common.

4 Stephen, nonetheless, is not ashamed to provide his advocacy for the benefit of the heretics against the Church, and to split the brotherhood by arguing in support of the heretics, and, on top of everything, to call Cyprian a false Christian and a false apostle and a sly operative. Stephen is aware that all these comments apply first to himself. He falsely throws accusations at some one else, to which he himself ought to give heed.

Our prayer from all of us is for your good health, in company with all the bishops who are in Africa, and from all the clergy, and from all the whole brotherhood. May we find you to be eternally of one mind and one opinion, united with us though long distances apart.

§4 The End:
Cyprian's Account of His Final Days

Valerian's Rescript

Cyprian writes after 6 August but before his arrest on 13 September AD 258, since the martyrdom of Sixtus on the former date in the Catacomb of Callistus is mentioned (1.4). His report is our only contemporary source for the details of Valerian's edict renewing the persecution, which was now unambiguously an attack on the Church as an institution (1.1). Bishops, presbyters, and deacons are sentenced to immediate capital punishment. Slow pressure is to be applied to distinguished lay Christians, with removal from senatorial and equestrian rank with loss of property as an initial punishment for nonconformity; with the death penalty for persistence; matrons to suffer confiscation of property and exile; with members of Caesar's household (*Caesariani*) to be in addition imprisoned (1.2). The persecution will begin when the imperial rescript reaches the province of Africa (1.3).

Cyprian to His Holy Brother Successus

1.1 One particular event is responsible for my not writing at once, my dearest brother, and that is that the clergy as a whole could not withdraw from Carthage because they had been living in danger of the blow of the persecution about to fall. All were with their hearts' commitment in a state of preparation for receiving God's heavenly victor's wreath of martyrdom. You should however now know that those whom I sent to Rome have returned. I sent them for the purpose of discovering and reporting to us the true facts about the published Edict that mentions us. I did this because different and ambiguous accounts were being breathed about in opinions that were expressed.

2 The truth of these matters is as follows. Valerian's rescript to the Senate read that bishops and presbyters and deacons should be proceeded against at once, senators certainly, and men of noble rank and Roman knights, should suffer confiscation of their goods and lose their status. If, even though their property has been removed, they persist in their Christianity, their punishment is to be capital. Matrons, with their goods removed from them, are to be assigned to exile. Members of Caesar's household, regardless of whether their confession of faith was made in the previous persecution or whether they would make that confession now, were to suffer confiscation of their goods and to be sent to the imperial estates in chains and duly placed on the official list.

3 Subjoined to the emperor Valerian's address is a copy of the letter that he has composed about us to the governors of provinces. This is the letter for whose arrival we live in daily expectation, standing fast in firmness of faith in expectation of bearing suffering, and hoping for the crown of eternal life from the Lord's bounteous resources.

4 You should know that Sixtus has been proceeded against in the Cemetery,[1] on the eighth day of the Ides of August,[2] in the company of four deacons. The prefects in the city of Rome are pressing on daily with this persecution, so that those who are brought before them are punitively dealt with and the treasury claims their goods.

2.1 My request in this letter is that its contents be brought to the notice of the remainder of our colleagues through you in order that

---

[1]I.e., Pope Sixtus II, successor to Stephen, in what today is known as the Catacomb of Callistus, where his epitaph appears in the Tomb of the Popes. He was also to be celebrated there with an epigram of Damasus.

[2]6 August.

the brotherhood everywhere can be strengthened by their exhortation, and made ready in advance for the spiritual arena. My prayer is that every one of us will not be concerned with their dying rather than their immortality, and that, in their commitment to the Lord, in full faith and with complete courage, they will be joyful rather than fearful in this confession of faith.

In their confession they know that as soldiers of God they are not perishing but receiving the victor's wreath. I pray, dearest brother, that you will always be well in the Lord.

Cyprian Awaits His Final Sentence

Cyprian writes shortly before his arrest on 13 September AD 258. He has avoided arrest in Utica, which in any case would have involved imprisonment in wait for the proconsul to arrive for his trial. He has therefore gone into hiding in Carthage, with the intention of presenting himself on the proconsul's arrival. Thus the bishop of Carthage was to witness to Christ in his own diocese, and in the process to confound his critics for going into hiding in the Decian Persecution.

Cyprian to the Presbyters and Deacons, and to the General Assembly of the Holy Laity

1.1 When the announcement was made to us, dearest brothers, that the agents from the police had been sent who were to take me to Utica, persuasion was brought to bear on me through the advice of my dearest brothers that I should withdraw into order to wait for them from my gardens. I agreed to this, assisted by a just consideration of their case. That case was that it is fitting for a bishop to confess his Lord in the place in which he presides in authority over the Lord's Church, and that the laity generally should feel as their own the fame of the confession in their midst of their presiding bishop.

2 For whatever the bishop as confessor says at the moment of his confession he speaks, under the inspiration of God, as the mouth of them all. On the other hand, the renown of our so glorious a Church would suffer damage if I should accept my moment to confess at Utica, and make my journey to the Lord as his martyr from there. I would be there as a bishop with the authority of presiding over another Church.

3 My obligation and my prayer is rather instead that I make my confession both for myself and for you in your presence, and suffer there. I pray that I might depart from there to the Lord accompanied by your continuous prayers and with your supplications.

We are therefore found here in a secret hide-away waiting in expectation for the arrival of the proconsul on his return to Carthage, hoping to hear what the emperors will have instructed on their authority concerning the Christian laity and bishops, and ready to say what the Lord will have us say in that hour. **4** Nevertheless, dearest brothers, continue to make no active resistance, and keep your inner peace in accordance with the spiritual discipline that you have always heard from me on the subject of the Lord's commandments.

You have so often been taught these with my explanation of them. Let no one influence any one of you to engage in public disorder against the interests of the brotherhood, nor to offer himself voluntarily to the pagans.[1] One is under an obligation rather to speak only when arrested and handed over, should God deign to speak through us in that hour. God has his place in our hearts, and his wish it is that we fulfill our confession of faith in him rather than fulfill our legal obligations.[2]

5 We shall settle in the interval before the proconsul shall pass sentence how else it befits me to conduct myself in my confession in God's name. The Lord will lead me at that time that is now close at hand. May the Lord Jesus cause you to continue to remain unharmed, dearest brothers, in his Church, and may he deign to keep you safe.

---

[1]Cyprian reaffirms the policy of passive resistance, whereby if summonsed by name, one is to appear, but otherwise not to deliberately and vaingloriously seek martyrdom.

[2]I.e., "Fulfill our confession . . . (*confiteri*)" and "fulfill our legal obligation (*profiteri*)." *Profiteri* means more than "profess" here, and is used of making a return in submission to the proper authority, or, indeed, of submitting one's name for inclusion in a register. Servilius is said to have forbidden a soldier's property to be seized whilst on military service. In consequence, debtors enlisted their names in the army, or, in the words of Livy 2.24.7: "they placed their names immediately on the legal list (*profiteri extemplo nomina*)."

Select Bibliography

Adolph, A., *Die Theologie der Einheit der Kirche bei Cyprian*, Europäische Hochschulstudien 33, 460 (Frankfurt am Main: Peter Lang, 1993).

Benko, S., "Pagan Criticisms of Christianity," in *Aufstieg und Niedergang der römischen Welt: Geschichte und Kultur Roms im Spiegel der neueren Forschung*, H. Temporini and W. Haase, eds. (Berlin and New York: De Gruyter Verlag, 1980), II.23.2, 1055–1118.

Benson, E. W., *Cyprian: His Life, His Times, His Work* (London: Macmillan, 1897).

Bévenot, M., *St Cyprian's De Unitate Chap. 4 in the Light of the MSS*, Analecta Gregoriana 11 (Rome, 1937).

———. "'*Primatus Petro datur*.' St Cyprian on the Papacy," *Journal of Theological Studies* 5 (1954): 19–35.

———. *The Tradition of Manuscripts: A Study in the Transmission of Cyprian's Treatises* (Oxford: Clarendon Press, 1961).

Bobertz, C. A., "The Historical Context of Cyprian's *De Unitate*," *Journal of Theological Studies* 42.1 (1990): 107–111.

———. "Patronal Letters of Commendation: Cyprian's *Epistulae* 38–40," *Studia Patristica* 24 (1991): 252–59.

———. "Patronage Networks and the Study of Ancient Christianity," *Studia Patristica* 24 (1991): 20–27.

———. "An Analysis of *Vita Cypriani* 3, 6–10 and the Attribution of *Ad Quirinum* to Cyprian of Carthage," *Vigiliae Christianae* 46 (1992): 112–28.

———. *Cyprian of Carthage as Patron: A Social and Historical Study of the Role of Bishop in the Ancient Christian Community of North Africa* (Ann Arbor: UMI, 1993).

Brent, A., *Cultural Episcopacy and Ecumenism: Representative Ministry in Church History from the Age of Ignatius of Antioch to the Reformation, with Special Reference to Contemporary Ecumenism*, Studies in Christian Mission 6 (Leiden: E. J. Brill, 1992).

————. "The Ignatian Epistles and the Threefold Ecclesiastical Order," *Journal of Religious History* 17.1 (1992): 18–32.

————. "Diogenes Laertius and the Apostolic Succession," *Journal of Ecclesiastical History* 44.3 (1993): 367–389.

————. *Hippolytus and the Roman Church in the Third Century: Communities in Tension before the Emergence of a Monarch-Bishop*, Supplements to *Vigiliae Christianae* 31 (Leiden: E.J. Brill, 1995).

————. *The Imperial Cult and the Development of Church Order: Concepts and Images of Authority in Paganism and Early Christianity before the Age of Cyprian*, Supplements to *Vigiliae Christianae* 45 (Leiden: E. J. Brill, 1999).

————. "Cyprian's Exegesis and Roman Political Rhetoric," in *L'Esegesi dei Padri Latini dale origini a Gregorio Magno*, in *Studia Ephemeridis Augustiniuanum* 68 (2000): 145–158.

————. "Cyprian and the Question of *ordinatio per confessionem*," *Studia Patristica* 36 (2001): 323–37.

————. "Cyprian's Reconstruction of the Martyr Tradition," *Journal of Ecclesiastical History* 53.2 (2002): 241–68.

Burns, J. Patout, "Social Context in the Controversy between Cyprian and Stephen," *Studia Patristica* 24 (1991): 38–44.

————. "On Rebaptism: Social Organization in the Third-Century Church," *Journal of Early Christian Studies* 1.4 (1993): 366–403.

————. "The Role of Social Structures in Cyprian's Response to the Decian Persecution," *Studia Patristica* 31 (1995): 260–67.

Clarke, G. W., "The Secular Profession of St Cyprian of Carthage," *Latomus* 24 (1965): 633–38.

————. "Some Observations on the Persecution of Decius," *Antichthon* 3 (1969): 63–76.

————. "The Epistles of Cyprian," in *Auckland Classical Essays Presented to E. M. Blaiklock*, ed. B. F. Harris, (Auckland: Auckland University Press; Wellington: Oxford University Press, 1970).

————. "Two Measures in the Persecution of Decius? Two Recent Views," *Bulletin of the Institute of Classical Studies* 20 (1973): 118–123.

————. "Double Trials in the Persecution of Decius," *Historia* 22 (1973): 650–63.

————. "Prosopographical Notes on the Epistles of Cyprian: III. Rome in August 258," *Latomus* 34.2 (1975): 437–48.

————. *The Letters of St Cyprian*, 4 vols, Ancient Christian Writers, 43, 44, 46 and 47 (New York: Newman Press 1984, 1986, and 1989).

De Ste. Croix, G. E. M., "Why were the Early Christians Persecuted?—A Rejoinder," *Past and Present* 27 (1964): 28–33.

Dunn, G., "Infected Sheep and Diseased Cattle, or the Pure and Holy Flock: Cyprian's Pastoral Care of Virgins," *Journal of Early Christian Studies* 11.1 (2003): 1–20.

Fahey, M. A., *Cyprian and the Bible: A Study in Third-Century Exegesis*, Beiträge zur Geschichte der Biblischen Hermeneutik 9 (Tübingen: Mohr-Siebeck, 1971). [Augustin. P323.2]

Fitzgerald, P. J., "A Model For Dialogue: Cyprian Of Carthage On Ecclesial Discernment," *Theological Studies* 59.2 (1998): 236–253.

Frend, W. C. H., *Martyrdom and Persecution in the Early Church* (Oxford: Blackwell, 1965).

Hein, K., *Eucharist and Excommunication: A Study in Early Christian Doctrine and Discipline* (Frankfurt: Herbert and Peter Lang, 1973).

Janssen, L. F., "'Superstitio' and the Persecution of the Christians," *Vigiliae Christianae* 33.2 (1979): 131–59.

Justinian, *Digest*, edited by T. Mommsen and P. Krueger, with an English Translation by A. Watson (Philadelphia: University of Pennsylvania Press, 1985).

Keresztes, P., "The Decian Libelli and Contemporary Literature," *Latomus* 34.3 (1975): 761–81.

————. "Two Edicts of the Emperor Valerian," *Vigiliae Christianae* 29 (1975): 81–95.

Knipfing, J. R., "The Libelli of the Decian Persecution," *Harvard Theological Review* 16 (1923): 345–390.

Lampe, G. W. H., *The Seal of the Spirit: A Study in the Doctrine of Baptism and Confirmation in the New Testament and the Fathers* (London: SPCK, 1967).

Laurance, J. D., *The Priest as Type of Christ: The Leader of the Eucharist in Salvation History according to Cyprian of Carthage*, American University Studies 7.5 (New York: Peter Lang, 1984).

————. "'There Is but One Baptism in the Holy Church': A Theological Appraisal of the Baptismal Controversy in the Work and Writings of Cyprian of Carthage," *Theological Studies* 59.4 (1998): 763–63.

Leppin, V., "Reinstating Episcopal Representation after Christian Persecution according to Cyprian of Carthage—Developing a Theology of Church Unity," *Zeitschrift für Antikes Christentum* 4.2 (2000): 255–69.

Moorhead, J., "Papa as 'Bishop of Rome,'" *Journal of Ecclesiastical History* 36.3 (1985): 337–50.

Musurillo, H., *Acts of the Christian Martyrs. Introduction. Texts and Translations* (Oxford: Clarendon Press, 1972).

Osborn, E. F., "Cyprian's Imagery," *Antichthon* 7 (1973): 65–79.

Rives, J. B., *Religion and Authority in Roman Carthage from Augustus to Constantine* (Oxford: Clarendon Press, 1995).

Sage, M. M., *Cyprian*, Patristics Monographs Series 1 (Philadelphia Patristic Foundation: Philadelphia, 1975).

Scott, J., "Saint Cyprian's Episcopal Letters," *Journal of Theological Studies* 52.1 (2001): 359–61.

Stewart–Sykes, A., "Ordination Rites and Patronage Systems in Third-Century North Africa," *Vigiliae Christianae* 56.2 (2002): 115–30.

Torrance, I., "They Speak to Us across the Centuries. 2. Cyprian," *Expository Times* 108.12 (1997): 356–59.

Walker, G. S. M., "The Churchmanship of St Cyprian," *Ecumenical Studies in History* 9 (London: Lutterworth, 1968).

Ward Perkins, J. B. and Goodchild, R. G., "The Christian Antiquities of Tripoli Tania," in *Archaeologia* 45 (1953): 1–84.

POPULAR PATRISTICS SERIES

ST VLADIMIR'S SEMINARY PRESS
1-800-204-2665 • www.svspress.com

We hope this book has been enjoyable and edifying for your spiritual journey toward our Lord and Savior Jesus Christ.

One hundred percent of the net proceeds of all SVS Press sales directly support the mission of St Vladimir's Orthodox Theological Seminary to train priests, lay leaders, and scholars to be active apologists of the Orthodox Christian Faith. However, the proceeds only partially cover the operational costs of St Vladimir's Seminary. To meet our annual budget, we rely on the generosity of donors who are passionate about providing theological education and spiritual formation to the next generation of ordained and lay servant leaders in the Orthodox Church.

 Donations are tax-deductible and can be made at www.svots.edu/donate. We greatly appreciate your generosity.

To engage more with St Vladimir's Orthodox Theological Seminary, please visit:

www.svots.edu
online.svots.edu
www.svspress.com
www.instituteofsacredarts.com